# Critical Issues in Victimology

## International Perspectives

**Emilio Viano** is Professor, Department of Justice, Law and Society, The American University, Washington, DC, and Editor, *Victimology: An International Journal*. He has been active in the field of victimology and victim/witness services since the early 1970s. He has conducted research and has organized and chaired several national and international congresses and meetings in the field; has directed several programs, including the National Victim and Witness Resource Center; and has served as a national and international expert on various projects. He has published various books and articles in victimology and in other fields of justice.

# Critical Issues in Victimology

## International Perspectives

Emilio C. Viano

Editor

SPRINGER PUBLISHING COMPANY
New York

Copyright © 1992 by Springer Publishing Company, Inc.

All rights reserved

No part of this publication may be reproduced, stored in a retrieval system, or transmitted in any form or by any means, electronic, mechanical, photocopying, recording, or otherwise, without the prior permission of Springer Publishing Company, Inc.

Springer Publishing Company, Inc.
536 Broadway
New York, NY 10012-3955

92 93 94 95 96 / 5 4 3 2 1

---

**Library of Congress Cataloging-in-Publication Data**
Critical issues in victimology : international perspectives / Emilio C. Viano, editor.
    p. cm.
  Includes bibliographical references and index.
  ISBN 0-8261-7250-4
  1. Victims of crimes.  I. Viano, Emilio.
HV6250.25.C75  1992
362.88—dc20                              91-30283
                                                                           CIP

---

Printed in the United States of America

Dedicated to the memory of the six Jesuit priests killed by government troops in El Salvador on November 17, 1989: Ignacio Ellacuria, Arnando López, Joaquín López y López, Ignacio Martín-Baro, Segundo Montes, Juan Ramón Moreno—and also of their aides, executed with them: Julia Elba Ramos and Cecilia Ramos.

# Contents

1 Introduction    1
  *Emilio C. Viano*

## I Victimization and Its Context
Introduction    13

2 Victims, Crime, and Social Context    17
  *Augusto Balloni*

3 The News Media and Crime Victims: The Right to Know versus the Right to Privacy    24
  *Emilio C. Viano*

## II The Trauma of Victimization
Introduction    35

4 Traumatized Populations: Roles and Responsibilities of Professionals    37
  *Lenore E. A. Walker*

5 An Empirical Investigation of the Coping Strategies Used by Victims of Crime: Victimization Redefined    46
  *Rosa Casarez-Levison*

6 Victims of Violent Crime and Their Coping Processes    58
  *Otmar Hagemann*

7 Victims of Violence in Everyday Life: Considerations about a Qualitative Research    68
  *Patrizia Faccioli and Simonetta Simoni*

8 Familial Violence in India: The Dynamics of Victimization    80
  *Ranjana S. Jain*

| | | |
|---|---|---|
| 9 | An Analysis of Cases Involving Elderly Homicide Victims and Offenders<br>*Peter C. Kratcoski* | 87 |

## III The Child Victim
Introduction    97

| | | |
|---|---|---|
| 10 | Analysis of Child Abuse and Neglect Court Cases in Three Cities in Turkey<br>*Esin Konanc, Sezen Zeytinoglu, and Seyda Kozcu* | 101 |
| 11 | Aftereffects of Childhood Abuse and Incest<br>*Irving Kaufman* | 110 |
| 12 | The Victimology of Children: A Transpersonal Conceptual Treatment Model<br>*Carol L. Bryant* | 118 |
| 13 | Mental Health Professionals' Treatment of Child Abuse: Why Professionals May Not Report<br>*Seth C. Kalichman, Mary E. Craig, and Diane R. Follingstad* | 130 |
| 14 | The Trauma of False Allegations of Sexual Abuse<br>*Michael Robin* | 140 |

## IV Sexual Harassment and Assault
Introduction    149

| | | |
|---|---|---|
| 15 | Sexual Harassment of Students: Victims of the College Experience<br>*Richard B. Barickman, Michele A. Paludi, and Vita Carulli Rabinowitz* | 153 |
| 16 | Sexual Assault in Canada: A Social and Legal Analysis<br>*Rita Gunn and Candice Minch* | 166 |
| 17 | Preventing Rape: How People Perceive the Options of Defending Oneself during an Assault<br>*Lita Furby, Baruch Fischhoff, and Marcia Morgan* | 174 |
| 18 | The Adolescent Sexual Offender: Victim and Perpetrator<br>*Carol B. DiCenso* | 190 |

## V Society's Reaction to Victimization
Introduction    201

| | | |
|---|---|---|
| 19 | Police Reactions to Victims of Burglary<br>*Joop van den Bogaard and Oene Wiegman* | 205 |

| | | |
|---|---|---|
| 20 | The Victim and the Failure to Report the Crime in Italy<br>*Paola Violante* | 217 |
| 21 | Implementation of Federal Legislation to Aid Victims of Crime in the United States<br>*Mario Thomas Gaboury* | 224 |
| 22 | Assessing Restitution's Impact on Recidivism: A Review of the Evaluative Research<br>*Thomas C. Castellano* | 233 |
| | Index | 249 |

# Contributors

**Augusto Balloni**, Department of Sociology, University of Bologna, Italy

**Richard B. Barickman**, Department of English, Hunter College, New York, New York, USA

**Joop W. van den Bogaard**, Department of Psychology, University of Twente, The Netherlands

**Carol L. Bryant**, Child Abuse Prevention Council of Contra Costa County, California, USA

**Rosa Casarez-Levison**, Casarez and Associates, Palo Alto, California, USA

**Thomas C. Castellano**, Center for the Study of Crime, Delinquency, and Corrections, Southern Illinois University, Carbondale, Illinois, USA

**Mary E. Craig**, Department of Psychology, University of South Carolina, Columbia, South Carolina, USA

**Carol B. DiCenso**, Clinical Services, Rhode Island Training School, Cranston, Rhode Island, USA

**Patrizia Faccioli**, Department of Sociology, University of Bologna, Italy

**Baruch Fischhoff**, Carnegie Mellon University, Pittsburgh, Pennsylvania, USA

**Diane R. Follingstad**, Department of Psychology, University of South Carolina, Columbia, South Carolina, USA

**Lita Furby**, Eugene Research Institute, Eugene, Oregon, USA

**Mario Thomas Gaboury**, (formerly) Office for Victims of Crime, U.S. Department of Justice, Washington, DC, USA

**Rita Gunn**, Prairie Research Associates, Winnipeg, Manitoba, Canada

**Otmar Hagemann**, Department of Law, University of Hamburg, Germany

**Ranjana S. Jain**, Department of Sociology, University of Rajasthan, India

**Seth C. Kalichman**, Department of Psychology, Loyola University, Chicago, Illinois, USA

**Irving Kaufman**, (emeritus) School of Social Work, Smith College, Northampton, Massachusetts, USA

**Esin Konanc**, Department of Educational Sciences, University of Ankara, Turkey

**Seyda Kozcu**, Department of Psychology, Aegean University, Izmir, Turkey

**Peter C. Kratcoski**, Department of Criminal Justice Studies, Kent State University, Kent, Ohio, USA

**Candice Minch**, Manitoba Attorney General's Office, Winnipeg, Manitoba, Canada

**Marcia Morgan**, Eugene Research Institute, Eugene, Oregon, USA

**Michele A. Paludi**, Department of Psychology, Hunter College, New York, New York, USA

**Vita Carulli Rabinowitz**, Department of Psychology, Hunter College, New York, New York, USA

**Michael Robin**, University of Minnesota, Minneapolis, Minnesota, USA

**Simonetta Simoni**, Department of Sociology, University of Bologna, Italy

**Emilio C. Viano**, School of Public Affairs, The American University, Washington, DC, USA

**Paola Violante**, Faculty of Law, University of Bari, Italy

**Lenore E. A. Walker**, Walker and Associates, Denver, Colorado, USA

**Oene Wiegman**, Department of Psychology, University of Twente, The Netherlands

**Sezen Zeytinoglu**, Psychology Department, Aegean University, Izmir, Turkey

# 1

# Introduction

*Emilio C. Viano*

---

### THE GROWTH OF VICTIMOLOGY IN THE UNITED STATES

The past two decades have seen the development of a victim movement in various countries as a separate political force. It is in the United States that the victim movement was begun in the 1970s. The women's movement, inspired by the civil rights movement, was its primary moving force. Also influential were the substantial efforts undertaken after the urban riots of the late 1960s to improve the operations of the criminal justice system, as well as the consumer movement, which demanded more accountability not only of producers of consumer goods but also of the state and of the justice system.

Feminists forcefully pointed out the problems faced by women victims of sexual assault when they came in contact with the police, hospitals, and courts. Practitioners and academics in the justice system realized that the system did not serve the victims of crime. Instead, it "used" them to obtain needed information, cooperation, and services (e.g., as witnesses) without giving them any active role, respect, or consideration in return. In essence, it was said, the system "revictimized" the victim.

Other groups founded in response to specific problems facing society also greatly contributed to the development of a general awareness of the concept of victim and of the plight of various victims, of the need for support services and, most of all, for appropriate legislative reforms. The best example of such a group is Mothers Against Drunk Drivers (MADD).

Child abuse and neglect, domestic violence, missing and exploited children, the elderly, the survivors of victims of homicide, date rape, sexual harassment, and patient abuse by therapists have been added to the focus of concern of victimology as it grew.

The success of these groups concerned with particular crimes and crime victims has served to highlight the general importance of "victims" as an effective political symbol and as a rallying point for a variety of grievances, dissatisfactions, and political agendas.

The early 1980s saw several expressions of this political awareness and recognition: the establishment of the Victims of Crime Task Force (1980), subsequently called the Presidential Commission on Victims of Crime, and of the Family Violence Task Force (1984), as well as the passage at the federal level of the Victims and Witness Protection Act of 1982, the Victims of Crime Act of 1984, and the Justice Assistance Act, also of 1984.

Several developments at the state level also demonstrated the growth and importance of the victim movement in the United States. In 1982 California voters approved the widely publicized Victim's Bill of Rights, or Proposition 8, amending the state constitution. Florida voters passed a similar constitutional amendment in 1988. Twenty-eight states have enacted similar bills of rights.

The enactment of compensation for victims of crimes by 40 states and the District of Columbia, the provision of funds to support domestic violence shelters by 49 states, and the funding of victim-witness programs in countless jurisdictions and localities are other positive developments engineered by organizations, professionals, academics, and volunteers concerned about the victim.

An important innovation in the criminal justice system has been the introduction and use of victim impact statements. These statements represent one of the major and most promising breakthroughs of the victims' rights movement. Mandated by law in some states, they inform the sentencing judge of the physical, financial, and emotional impact of the crime on the victim or on the victim's survivors so that these elements can be taken into account when reaching a sentencing decision. Thirty-five states presently allow for some form of victim participation at sentencing.

After initially banning the use of victim impact statements in death penalty cases [*Booth v. Maryland*, 1987 (482 U.S. 496); *South Carolina v. Gathers*, 1989 (490 U.S. 805)], the U.S. Supreme Court affirmed the legitimacy of using this important element in the sentencing process when it decided *Pervis Tyrone Payne v. Tennessee* (no. 90-5721; June 27, 1991). The Court held that:

> "The Eighth Amendment erects no *per se* bar prohibiting a capital sentencing jury from considering "victim impact" evidence relating to the victim's personal characteristics and the emotional impact of the murder on the victim's family, or precluding a prosecutor from arguing such evidence at a capital sentencing hearing. To the extent that they held to the contrary, *Booth* and *Gathers* are overruled" (59 LW 4814).

## INTERNATIONAL GROWTH OF VICTIMOLOGY

The field of victimology has also grown internationally. Serious interest in victims of crime began and grew considerably in the 1970s for some of the same reasons that had led to the earlier birth of the victims' movement in the United States: the increase in crime, the inefficiency and lack of care on the part of the criminal justice system, and the growing realization of the complicated and long-lasting negative effects of crime on its victims. The European victim movement, however, did not grow, as did the American one, from the struggle of women or others for their rights in society. The emphasis on the rights of the individual and the struggle for the recognition of the rights of groups discriminated against are historically rather unique to the United States and cannot be considered the roots of the victim movement in European countries.

In those nations a strong central government has traditionally played a major role in providing extensive social services from "cradle to grave." Thus, the needs of the victims of crime have been addressed by appealing to the already existing responsibility of the government for the social welfare of the citizenry. Victim services represent an extension of the role of provider and protector that European central governments have been fulfilling for decades. Consequently, the transition there was different, smoother, not as confrontational as in the United States.

For this reason, the victim movement in Europe has concentrated more on providing services than on pursuing victim rights and has done this in cooperation with governmental agencies. As a matter of fact, in all European countries victim services are funded by the government. Thus, the strong effort to enact legislation empowering victims and allowing them a larger and more active role in the justice system, which has consumed considerable energy and resources in the American victim movement, is basically unknown in Europe. Also, European victim services are not based in the criminal justice system and particularly in prosecutors' offices as they are in the United States. Rather, they are independent social agencies, often staffed by professionals. This again represents a significant difference from the American experience where services were founded and still function in many localities on a grass-roots basis because of the deep tradition of volunteerism existing in the country. Volunteer work is definitely not valued as much in Europe, with the notable exception of Great Britain.

In Europe, victim services were first established in Great Britain, Germany, and the Netherlands and then in France and some Scandinavian countries. Few services for victims exist in Southern and Eastern Europe. Canada and some states in Australia have also made impressive strides in providing assistance to victims. Community-based or volunteer organizations offer services to victims, particularly of sexual assault and domestic violence, in several countries in Europe and elsewhere. One of the difficulties faced by the victim movement in some countries is the complacent and convenient belief that the legal and social welfare systems of the country already provide more than adequately for the needs of the victim.

## THE UNITED NATIONS

The growth and importance of victimology were officially recognized at the international level in the fall of 1985 when the UN General Assembly adopted Resolution 40/34 and the accompanying Declaration of Basic Principles of Justice for Victims of Crime and Abuse of Power, the first major pronouncement of the United Nations on the question of victims.

The Eighth United Nations Congress on the Prevention of Crime and the Treatment of Offenders, held in Cuba in 1990, reaffirmed international support for the declaration and recommended that governments consider the availability of public and social support services for victims of crime and abuse of power and foster appropriate programs for victim assistance, information, and compensation (A/CONF.144/27). The congress also dedicated specific attention to the issue of domestic violence and adopted a related resolution (A/CONF.144/26).

Another international organization, the Council of Europe, prepared and adopted in 1983, at its Committee of Ministers level, a European Convention on Compensation of Victims of Crime; and in 1985, a Recommendation on Assistance to Victims and the Prevention of Victimization.

Although victims and witnesses of crime have received the most attention, victimology can and should also be concerned with other types of victims as well, for example, victims of earthquakes, natural disasters, occupational accidents and hazards, dislocation, and famine. In fact, the common denominator of victimological work is *crisis intervention* and the short- and long-term remedies that should be made available to victims.

## CURRENT AND FUTURE RESEARCH IN VICTIMOLOGY
### Theoretical Perspectives

It is said that victimology lacks a theoretical perspective and foundation. However, it is not necessarily improper or invalid for victimology to utilize and adapt to its needs and efforts the theoretical perspectives of social work, public administration, social policy, law, and justice. Victimology may simply represent a different focus of application of theoretical insights already developed by other disciplines that are germane because of their interest in people in crisis.

People who are *vulnerable* and/or *in crisis* may indeed constitute the common denominator linking victimology with other relevant disciplines and providing a focus of research and intervention. The uniqueness of victimology may stem from its focusing on populations and crises that have been neglected in the past by more established disciplines.

As we become increasingly aware of the complexities of life in society, a *new* discipline may be justified in existing not just because it is able to claim for itself a completely new area but also because it sees new relationships and dynamics and offers an integrated approach to research and intervention that transcend existing disciplines and utilize the best that each has to offer.

## Abuse of Power and Collective Victimization

Governments, police and military forces, multinational corporations, medical personnel, and parents have, in different degrees, power over the very existence, future, and destiny of other human beings. In many nations of the world, laws have been enacted to control and neutralize the use of these positions as weapons against those whose lives can easily be affected by the powerful. Unfortunately, laws are often disregarded or not enforced, and the resulting harm is similar to behavior that would definitely be considered criminal if engaged in by anyone other than those in control of the victims.

Examples of these victimizations are abundant: unlawful human experimentation, hostage taking, random seizure and detention, genocide, apartheid, slavery, torture, serfdom, and forced prostitution. Many are at times targeted for mistreatment and abuse because of their membership in a certain group, like the poor, women, children, minorities, the homeless, political dissenters, religious minorities, and the elderly.

Amnesty International states that governments in some 98 countries use *torture* to combat insurgencies or as an administrative tool. The most insidious aspect of this inhuman practice is that the torturers are not necessarily or always sadistic psychopaths but state employees carrying out a state policy. Particularly troublesome is the reported or alleged collusion and collaboration of health professionals in physical and psychological torture.

In some countries, because of the resurgence of religious fundamentalism, forms of torture like flogging, stoning, and amputation are again legal. The fact that large regions of the world are controlled by dictatorships clearly indicates that serious or wholesale disregard for human rights and dignity is widespread and affects millions of persons. The expanded powers of police and the military and their use of intimidation and detention outside of court supervision is increasing in almost all countries. Reasons given at times are that these measures are necessary to combat growing terrorism, insurgency, and drug trafficking, but the reality remains that state powers are greatly increased to the detriment of civil rights and civil liberties. The bloody repression of the student-led democracy movement in China offers dramatic evidence of how a "people's army" can be used against the people to support and maintain the entrenched power of the oligarchy. Moreover, even in democratic societies, delays and inequities in the administration of justice represent forms of effective victimization of defendants and victims alike and of their families.

It is also believed that *slavery* is still a flourishing trade in many areas of the world, especially in certain countries of the Middle East and Asia. In particular, women and children have been collectively victimized throughout the centuries and still are. Thousands are kidnapped and sold into prostitution and slavery and traded in remote areas of the world, at times for the pleasure and entertainment of visiting tourists from Europe, North America, the Middle East, and Japan.

In many countries, especially in the third world, *children* are still sold to work in factories, brothels, and massage parlors or for adoption in foreign countries. Child labor is a fact of life in many third world countries, from the dump pickers of Mexico City and the carpet weavers of the Middle East to migrant field hands in farming societies around the world. In India alone, the last official census counted 11 million children under the age of 14 in the labor force. Studies by nongovernmental groups put the figure at 40 million or higher. Ignorance, tradition, and—above all—a crushing poverty have forced these millions of children, some as young as 5 years, into the workplace. Some are virtual slaves, bonded to a farmer, a handicraft artisan, or a small shopkeeper by parents so desperate that, in effect, they sell their children so that the family can eat. The number of homeless and abandoned children living on the streets is estimated now at 50 million worldwide, with 25 million in Latin America alone. Many of them are trying to escape repeated abuse at home. It is reported that in some countries, notably in Brazil, these children are the targets of kidnapping, abuse, torture, and killing on the part of the police and other vigilante groups.

Unfortunately, children are not even safe in their own homes, as the statistics on child abuse and neglect and child sexual abuse indicate. In some developing countries, newborn babies are "dumped"—killed or left to die—when no one is willing or inclined to raise them. Strict government-enacted and -enforced practices to limit family size, especially in China, have led to charges of widespread infanticide, particularly of baby girls; forced abortion; and violations of human rights.

Even in countries like the United States, a report issued by the U.S. Congress estimates that, if current trends continue, the number of children living in foster homes, hospitals, and detention facilities could increase nearly 75%, from nearly half a million to more than 840,000 by the year 1995. Skyrocketing reports of child abuse, new conditions resulting from crack cocaine and alcohol abuse, and homelessness among families with children are driving an increasing number of children into costly out-of-home placements with inadequate services and accountability. The net results is that more children are harmed by the system that is designed to protect them, and more kids are separated from their families, whereas only minimal efforts are being made to support and strengthen their families. Conditions that contribute to these problems, such as racism, sexism, and inequality in educational and career opportunities, are not given the serious consideration and the concerted action that are necessary to correct the situation.

*Women* are another group often targeted for victimization. The murder, mostly by burning, of brides in India because of greed or dissatisfaction with the dowry paid to the husband's family appears to be a larger and more serious problem than anticipated or acknowledged by officials there.

In parts of Africa and the Middle East, young women suffer another form of violence, genital mutilation. This operation, often done in a crude, painful, and septic manner, removes all or part of the external female genitalia, including the clitoris. This practice has its roots in the male desire to control female sexuality but is sustained today by a host of other superstitions and wrong beliefs, including that it is required by the Koran. Others defend it as an "important African tradition." According to the World Health Organization, more than 80 million women have undergone sexual mutilation in Africa alone. In all of these instances and more, women are targets of violence and repression because of their sex. This is no random violence. The risk factor is easy to identify: it is being female.

The adverse impact that *multinational corporations* can have on the life and health of people around the globe has been amply demonstrated in recent examples. Multinationals can easily alter traditional nutritional habits through full-scale advertising and promotional campaigns to the detriment of the long-range needs of the populations involved. For example, the introduction of baby formula for infants in the third world as a more advanced means of raising them than utilizing the abundant supply of mother's milk led to widespread malnutrition, intestinal diseases, and death. It was only after a worldwide campaign and boycott that the offending companies agreed to stop their lucrative but deadly practices. Other examples of collective victimization perpetrated by multinationals in the third world are the dumping of toxic wastes, selling drugs that are banned in advanced countries, and promoting tobacco products and selling cigarettes manufactured with high-tar tobacco that cannot be sold in the United States and the European Community.

Collective victimization has generally been neglected as a field of study and research. More attention should be directed at the effects and impact of white-collar crimes, corporate misconduct, abuses of power on the part of the state, and illegal business practices. The gross and pervasive *violations of human rights* that are occurring in several areas of the world and are affecting many millions of people should become a focus of increased inquiry.

## Pervasive Cultural Values

Pervasive cultural values that create a climate that is permissive or conducive to victimization should be identified, examined, and targeted for change. *Violent acts reflect environments of violence*. It can be said that at the foundation of many patterns of abuse of the "weak"—children, women, the elderly, the mentally retarded—is the overwhelming acceptance of violence in our society as the legitimate and necessary means of solving problems at the personal, national, and international levels. This concept of dominance/submission, controller/controlled pervades parenting, relations between the sexes and the ages, and marital patterns.

While society at large and most of the research in the field focus on the more sensational, violent, or evident forms of victimization and on the more obviously distorted values, approaches, rationalizations, and beliefs that support them, there are in our society actually more insidious, pervasive, and widespread expressions of victimization, although they are less visible and objectionable.

The violent and victimizing behavior that is condemned and abhorred is often only the bolder, exaggerated expression of values and beliefs actually rooted and widespread in the larger culture. For example, the diffused pedophilia that transpires in advertisements that portray grown-up women as children, and vice versa, with an unmistakable sexual undertone; the pervasive exploitation of the female body as a commodity in commercials and advertisements, regardless of the item offered for sale; the violence and exploitation portrayed in detail in many television programs and films; and the climate of ageism and sexism that permeates much of what our society does all express and create a climate where victimizers express in a blunt, overt, and exaggerated manner what society at large believes and practices in a more subtle or carefully disguised fashion.

Research in the more obvious forms of exploitation and violence is easier to justify, obtain funds for, and even conduct, but it will be research and intervention in the arena of the diffuse and camouflaged that will effectively attack the root of the problem.

## Addiction and Compulsion

A better understanding of victimizing behavior, particularly in the area of sexual assault and exploitation, may be reached through the study of addictive, compulsive, and ultimately self-destructive behavior. Efforts should be undertaken to create a framework for understanding addictive behavior and to outline a model of the relationship among cultural, social, psychological, pharmacological, and other components of addictive motivation, based on the idea that addiction is a response to socially and individually conditioned needs for specific psychophysiological or experiential states.

This model should be designed to apply equally well to all areas of repetitive and compulsive behavior. Until now this approach has been used almost exclusively to study, analyze, and attempt to explain and treat various forms of drug addiction. It should be expanded to other types of compulsive behavior, including those that lead to the criminal victimization of others. It should also address the larger issue of how our society is actually designed to encourage addictive behavior, filled as it is with pervasive and intrusive messages advertising or portraying certain addictions in a positive light—for example, when the drug or behavior in question is "legal"—while sternly and hypocritically condemning others.

Even more important, ours is an addictive society because, in many ways, we are taught to depend on large institutions for our ideas, our morality, even our survival. Modern culture has made the media, the school, the government, the church, the military, and the corporations that produce and sell products appear to be absolutely necessary for life itself. This fosters and even justifies feelings of dependency, powerlessness, and helplessness, acceptance of substance use and abuse, and widespread habit reliance.

The linkages between this wider cultural context and compulsive behavior that victimizes and exploits others should be investigated and clarified. Thus, treatment and prevention efforts will focus not only on the individual offender but also on the cultural makeup that is equally to blame for its role in aiding and abetting the offending behavior and in creating a climate conducive to it. More obviously, many would agree that the abuse of alcohol and drugs runs like a very thick thread through the fabric of criminal violence.

The glorification of violence and the sexualization of everything in our society, from toothpaste to shoes to wines to automobiles to travel, also play a large part in creating an addictive and compulsive environment and should be taken into account for study and action.

Although some resist this approach to the study of the dynamics of sexual assault, domestic violence, and sexual abuse of children, in particular, and advocate the mandatory imposition of criminal sanctions, it is important to keep in mind that, in the long run, locking up sexual offenders and spouse abusers in the hope that they will just go away will not work. It is also important to realize that, whereas some offenders have no real moral conflict between their sexual or violent desires and their personal convictions, others are very tortured by the fact that they are, for example, sexually attracted to children. For them it is a constant struggle to fight off temptation. At the same time, every person in prison because of such offenses is an example of the failure of the fear of incarceration to deter.

It is essential that through research, discussion, and public education we look at these problems with a realistic and dispassionate attitude, stripping away the fear, prejudice, and loathing that often and quite understandably accompany their consideration and that we at least distinguish between political agendas fueled by predetermined objectives (and therefore uncompromising and narrowly focused) and a genuine and compassionate attempt at a fuller understanding of the dynamics at work. The stigma that is currently attached to the sexual abuse of children and that affects not only the offenders but, ironically, also the victims and their families makes it very difficult to engage in open and dispassionate research and discussion addressing victims *and* offenders. This also stands in the way of developing and experimenting with treatment models.

Finally, one more cogent reason why such an approach is crucial is found in the often mentioned fact that some of the offenders of today were victims yesterday and that some of today's victims will be tomorrow's offenders. If we truly believe and accept this fact, then we should be ready to follow it to its ultimate conclusions and therefore look at offenders in a different light because many of them are or were victims.

This approach—applicable to all types of victimization—would also be extremely useful in dispelling the perception that to be concerned about the victims entails an "offender be damned" attitude; that victimology is the antithesis of an enlightened and progressive movement in criminal justice, particularly corrections; and that victimologists want to dismantle reforms recently introduced in the administration of justice. It is true, of course, that some with a "right wing" political agenda have been exploiting victimological concerns for exactly those reasons. However, it does not have to be that way. Actually, it *cannot* be that way. Genuine victimology is perfectly compatible with and supports the efforts aimed at humanizing and improving the criminal justice system because it recognizes that the line distinguishing the victim from the offender is often blurred, that the scenarios of victimization are not starkly drawn in black-and-white, that offending behaviors are often the consequences of a normalization process steeped deep in an attempt to make sense of a nightmarish victimization experience.

In some cases more than others, of course, it is difficult to tell who is the victim and who is the offender. Certainly, the physical actions, the blows, the violence, the sexual assault, the improper fondling are carried out by one person while the other is at the receiving end, but to stop there in the analysis of the situation is to offer only a "first impression" and at times a self-serving view of what is truly occurring.

The appearances indeed confirm the black-and-white approach; but if we look more deeply, we may find a different reality. In this tragic ballet of fear, victimization, and exploitation both actors may be acting out parts they learned as victims while assuming different roles as dictated by wider cultural beliefs. To approach one as the all-evil offender who deserves only punishment and the other as the all-innocent victim who needs only vindication is just too easy. Victimology should have reached by now a sufficient level of sophistication and assuredness to be able to reveal the complexity of the situation and to point the way to a truly healing process that encompasses both the victim and the victimizer.

To say that the offender needs treatment based on understanding and compassion is not to be "soft on crime"; to say that the victim needs treatment as well—for example, to snap out of self-destructive patterns—is not "blaming the victim." Those who maintain that it is so may be more concerned about defending an ideological position than about truly serving the victim.

The black-and-white approach has been undeniably useful in the initial stages of the process of recognizing the reality and dynamics of victimization. At that point, it was important to "draw the line" so that society could be confronted with what had been overlooked and neglected for too long. The shock and outrage felt by those active in the field when they realized the depth and seriousness of the problem understandably contributed to this view. Political agendas also require that issues be simplified, that the right side be clearly distinguishable from the wrong side, and that battle lines be drawn. In the world of politics, there is no time or place for nuances, qualifiers, and niceties.

# Introduction

However, the scholarly search for understanding should take responsibility for approaching the problem as a complex reality that defies easy description and solutions.

## Victims' Wants and Needs

Another area needing more attention and effort is research directed at what victims want and need. Some feel that the field in certain instances may be working under a set of assumptions and beliefs influenced by differing political and value orientations that do not necessarily reflect the actual desires and needs of victims.

The question raised here is that what victims really want or need may not necessarily be what people in the field assume it is, however disappointing this realization may be. Class, cultural, educational, and racial differences may play a part in creating different understandings and expectations. For example, the *most common needs mentioned by victims* are improving the security of their homes and emergency financial assistance. Yet relatively few programs offer this type of support. Their effectiveness has also been questioned in light of the fact that they reach only a small number of those who need them. Most victims simply do not know that such services exist and are available to them. It appears that victim programs need to be much more active in reaching out to the community.

Unrealistic expectations of the needs and wants of victims may also lead to the possible rejection of the needy victim who does not meet the preconceived notions of what she should feel, believe, and want. The concept of "deserving" victim has generally been attributed to the society that creates or supports victimization and then sits in judgment on the victim, but those coming to the rescue of the victim may also have a preconceived notion of who deserves help and assistance: the victim would lose again but this time at the hand of those who are ostensibly there to help.

## OVERVIEW OF THE CONTENTS

The main purpose of this book is to bring together under one cover and to present coherently current and representative contributions in research, prevention, treatment, and public policy. The contributions for this volume were specially chosen because their authors were able to present their ideas, research, or practical knowledge in a cogent and interesting way and also able to address some of the most urgent and representative issues facing the field today.

The book has been divided in five parts:

1. Victimization and Its Context
2. The Trauma of Victimization

3. The Child Victim
4. Sexual Harassment and Assault
5. Society's Reaction to Victimization

It has been designed to provide a balance between practical and theoretical issues and concerns and to offer a sample of international perspectives and approaches, in the hope that it will constitute a positive contribution to the development of the field.

The ultimate goal of all work in criminology, victimology, and related sciences is the establishment of a caring, fair, and just society. A society without violence, oppression, and suffering should be the ultimate objective of the process of social change generated by our concern for victims of crime.

The various facets of victimization addressed by different groups are but variations on the same theme: a fundamental lack of appreciation and understanding of the commonality of our humanity, of what truly makes us human, of the bonds that support and nourish us.

The victim movement holds great promise as a force of genuine change in society's attitudes and patterns of caring for its members. The publication of this volume is intended to be a useful contribution to help it gain momentum, reach its full potential, and become an integral part of the values, beliefs, and policies of our contemporary society.

This book would not have been possible without the generous cooperation and dedication of its contributors. They have earned the gratitude of the editor and of the readers for their willingness to share their work and to contribute significantly to the development of victimology through the publication of this volume.

# PART I
# Victimization and Its Context

---

Violence and aggressive behavior have been present throughout human history and have been recorded prominently from the Scriptures to today's tabloids. Aggression is found in the simplest and the most complex forms of life. All of the approaches to the understanding and explanation of human personality underline the aggressive component.

Similarly, the concept of victim appears among the most ancient ones of humanity. Inextricably connected with the idea and practice of sacrifice, the notion of victim belongs to all cultures. Most religions, for example, are fundamentally sacrificial.

Today, notwithstanding all of the various efforts toward reform, violence, killings, and aggression are still poorly controlled, not very well understood, and on the increase. Fantasy and defense mechanisms lead most people to associate crime and violence with the lower-class, uneducated, and unsocialized segments of the population. Stereotypes dominate the beliefs that many have about violence and those practicing it. That many acts of violence take place, for example, in the households of respected and professional citizens escapes or is vehemently denied by most people.

The historical fluctuations associated with defining what is violent behavior and who are the legitimate victims show that the definition of an act as violent, its evaluation as socially tolerable or not—indeed its very surfacing in the consciousness of the population—depend on a complex interplay of several factors. Whether or not an act is violent and whether or not that violence is appropriate or inappropriate depend, for example, on who the actor is, the reasons and circumstances prompting the act, who the recipient of the violence is, and the degree of harm inflicted.

When it comes to the agent, if he or she is regarded as legitimate, then the violent act will also be regarded as such. It is accepted that certain individuals in society have the right to use force to make others act in a certain way. Parents, police, and teachers may be included in the category of legitimate agents of violence.

Who the victim is, is also crucial in determining whether or not violence is appropriate. Generally, throughout the ages and cross-culturally, the higher the status of the victim, the less tolerated has been any violence against him or her.

The situation in which violence takes place also colors society's perception of its legitimacy. Self-defense is a clear case in point. The degree of harm inflicted on the victim is another variable taken into consideration in evaluating violence. One variable that may increase the probability of the violence being perceived as inappropriate is its visibility—a factor at times taken well into account by perpetrators—and its coming to the attention of others like doctors, teachers, and neighbors.

Thus, ultimately personal and social values shape our concept of the victim. The victim is actually a social construct used as a means of social control by those in power.

Part I of this volume contains two chapters that address the social and political processes that influence and control the definition, depiction, and societal reaction to the victim.

Augusto Balloni in his "Victims, Crime and Social Context" examines the influence that victims have had after World War II on the general human consciousness and particularly on our awareness of human rights. In the past, he says, the victim was reached and considered through the itinerary followed by the criminal. Thus, the victim assumed a very marginal role in criminal dynamics.

According to Balloni, current victimological perspectives require a new orientation in developing and coordinating studies on victims because becoming a victim is a behavior (B) that is a function of the person (P) in relation to a particular environment (E) at a given moment, as expressed by Kurt Lewin's formula: $B = f(P,E)$. Professor Balloni focuses in particular on victims of violence and terrorism considered within the overall context of the event surrounding their victimization.

The main objective of the chapter contributed by Emilio Viano is to review the portrayal and treatment of crime victims in the American print and electronic media within the framework of the constitutional, legal, and ethical tensions created by the *media's right to know versus the victim's right to privacy*. Within the past decade, both crime victims and some journalists have begun to ask whether crime reporting is victimizing the victims again. The issue is not what newspapers and electronic media have the right to do legally but what they ought to do ethically.

The records of crimes are public records. The public has a right to know. But, for example, where does the right to know end and the privacy rights of private citizens begin? Even when the media are well within their rights, how are these rights and duties exercised? How can we reconcile responsible and accurate journalism with the victims' needs for privacy, compassion, and concern?

Viano's chapter discusses the major variables affecting the media performance against the background of the social, cultural, and political forces influencing it. It is expected to generate a dialogue on the media performance in this area, lead to a better understanding of the dynamics and tensions existing between the media's and victim's interests, and contribute to the development and strengthening of public policy and of a code of ethics.

# 2

# Victims, Crime, and Social Context

*Augusto Balloni*

---

Soon after World War II, following the Nuremberg trials, the images of a multitude of victims poured into history: these trials had, in fact, to take a stand regarding the enormous crimes committed against prisoners, and not only them. All of the victims of World War II brought home the tremendous need to reestablish ethical frontiers as well as lines of conduct that would be valid for everyone and in all circumstances. In the international field the phenomenon of the codification of human rights was generated from those victims, beginning with the *Universal Declaration of Human Rights*, published by the United Nations in 1948, which was followed by the *Convention to Protect Man's Rights and the Basic Freedoms* (Treaty of Rome, 1950). There followed, almost year by year, declarations, conventions, charters and codes, both worldwide and regional in character. In this way many juridico-philosophical cases get their background from victims of the most varied nature who, directly or otherwise, lead back to investigating human values and needs in every sphere of human life by facilitating philosophical and ethical reflection. So, when considering the victim theme one must reflect on human rights in a historical context.

As a result of scientific progress and the great technological advances, the role of victim presents new possibilities for study and, at the same time, new operative urgency in the prevention and repression of all of those situations that may lead to victimization. Despite increasingly efficient technology the fact remains that social ills are very serious, thus generating victims. There are, in fact, problems connected with having a low level of education due to interrupted schooling, of unskilled labor, of organization and social responsibility that generate tension and conflict, and those between criminals and their victims—the businessmen who act dishonestly (e.g., damaging the consumer or, for the sake of profit, spoiling the countryside). There are problems of attitude and prejudice, such as those of the enemies of blacks' civil rights, or those who believe it is necessary, in order to solve the problems of drug addiction, to deprive drug consumers or the mentally ill of their personal freedom, thus obtaining a mandate without any control. Finally, there are the problems of the victims of every type of ill-treatment or abuse.

All of these problems, linked as they are to the victim's role, weigh heavily at the individual level. However, for many of them no specific legislation is possible. The means to prevent the risk of victimization must be sought in human behavior and in those ethics of conduct whose principles must in any case be clear: life is precious and belongs only to the individual; people have the right to do what they want insofar as they do no harm to others.

## THE PROCESS OF BECOMING A VICTIM

Becoming a victim is not a rare situation for some people, even though it is never a comfortable situation as regards the consequences of the role. Thus, it is most important to know the *forces* that promote the risk of becoming a victim. To find an answer one has to consider the nature of social action and of social relations even though one is accustomed to view planning and social action not from the victim's viewpoint but from the opposite side.

In the criminal sphere a crime may, in fact, be examined meticulously, keeping in mind the means or the instruments available so that a more detailed investigation of the situation is necessary in order to achieve one's object; at other times the protagonist appears to act impulsively without having prepared an elaborate, overall plan.

Clearly, it is easier to arrive at the victim through the itinerary followed by the author of the crime. This is the traditional perspective of the great majority of researchers in criminology.

Cheating and circumventing an incapable person, for example, consists of successive moments, which include the execution and planning of the act. On the other hand, theft and robbery frequently appear to lack planning of any kind, being characterized by an apparently rapid and violent performance. Kidnapping for a ransom or extortion usually seems to develop through a spiral of measures consisting of planning, execution, and evaluation of the results. This course of action may be characteristic of premeditated murder but certainly not of a crime of passion, in which the objective is struck in an apparently sudden and rapid manner.

These two positions still appear to be exercised in the spheres of terrorism and political violence. In fact, the victims are symbolically very representative. This is valid whether we are thinking of Kennedy or Palme or, in Italy, of Moro and others. In these cases planning and social action are macroscopically evident. In the case of the symbolic victim, the objective is chosen after evaluation of other possibilities and after consideration of the most suitable ways and means.

In the cases being examined, the action was launched in a specific place at a given moment. Later, a close examination of the resulting situation was made by different parties, politically and operatively different, with different evaluations, in which the role of symbol-victim was interpreted differently.

From another viewpoint, apparently the opposite, the victims of massacres would appear to be placed randomly. Here, I shall recall two bloody massacres in Bologna: the Italicus train attack on August 4, 1974, at San Benedetto Val di Sambro, near Bologna, that left 12 dead and 105 injured; and the Bologna Railway Station disaster of August 2, 1980, in which 85 died and 200 were injured.

During the preparation of this chapter, I read over again the names and the demographic and socio-personal data of the victims. They were people of the most varied characteristics, from a 14-year-old student to a 60-year-old housewife and from workers to pensioners and even foreigners. Every category of person is found in this list of victims so that one comes to the conclusion that the perpetrators wanted to strike at random but with premeditated, reasoned impulsiveness.

It is precisely the complexity of political violence or terrorism that forces us not to rely on an oversimplified, interpretive dichotomy but to examine, in general, the process of becoming a victim as an interaction of humans with fellow humans. Thus, one must examine the relationship existing between the behavior of the victim and that of the aggressors. In fact, every individual comes to develop his or her own model of adaptive tendencies, a model that becomes, to a greater or lesser extent, part of one's character, appearing at a relatively early stage in life. It is also manifested when one becomes a victim.

When the individual who has suffered the role of victim is subjected to a serious or prolonged frustration, there may arise feelings of personal failure or anxiety, which will be followed by behavior aimed at defending one's image against the threat to one's self-esteem. In the course of this defensive behavior the victim may develop or reinforce gestures of interpersonal response, such as unsociableness, aggressiveness, and rejection of others. Thus, the victim must be studied in a very different perspective.

## THE AFTERMATH OF VICTIMIZATION

The Stockholm syndrome has for some years become an interpretive pattern of kidnapping. It is the so-called paradoxical behavior of affective attachment that is set up between hostage and keeper. This syndrome (like all situations of dependence or negative adjustment) is a condition that requires careful study in order to avoid victimization phenomena and to help the victim after liberation.

This is not an absolutely new interpretation, because two well-known psychotherapists who went through the experience of Nazi concentration camps, Bruno Bettelheim and Victor E. Frankl, have provided studies still valid today, but forgotten by many, in which one can find aspects of the above-mentioned syndrome.

Bettelheim (1976), with lucid analysis, sets out the shock of imprisonment. Speaking of the middle-class prisoners, he states that after losing the typical positive qualities of their class, like correct behavior and dignity, they went so far as to adopt criminal methods or subject themselves unconditionally to those in command. They even took on the role of spy despite the contempt in which they were held by their jailors.

Frankl (1987), also reinforced by his own terrible experience, is able to declare: "The internee in a concentration camp is pushed back to a primitive level, not only outwardly but also in his intimate life; however, this does not prevent the symptoms, though sporadic, of an intolerable tendency to interiorization from coming to the surface" (p. 72).

Thus, along with Frankl (1987), we can say that in concentration camps, as in the case of hostages held for a long time, one can decline to primitive, infantile levels, but it is also possible to "behave differently," not only heroically but in a dignified manner.

The prisoner in a concentration camp, like a hostage held over a long period, is subjected to a series of experiences that always leave their mark on the personality and therefore on the victim's future, regardless of their differences.

One must, in the light of this, reconsider the experiences of some kidnap victims. At the outset the victim understands his position: there is no way out, all hope of freedom is firmly in the hands of his captor, who controls the entire environment or living space. Later the victim is seized by panic so that all hope of salvation lies precisely in his captor. Finally, the victim begins to feel himself completely isolated, a situation in which a prolonged contact with the criminal captor is established. The victim sets up an exclusive personal relationship with his captor and, as in any extreme situation (prisons, concentration camps, isolation of any kind), regressive behavior develops. This is especially true when circumstances force the individual, in the victim context, to maintain a role of dependence on others for all satisfaction, even life itself. One depends on the goodwill of people who elude all control. This, then, is the well-known regressive behavior that replaces the more mature one the victim had previously managed to develop. At this point the mechanisms that constrain the victim to cling to the very person who holds his life in his hands are set in motion, and the victim becomes submissive and condescending, thus displaying the so-called Stockholm syndrome (Ochberg, 1983).

Clearly, these are a victim's most conspicuous positions, but there exists a whole range of possibilities that have to be taken into consideration in a perspective completely free of hypocrisies.

Besides the direct victims of political violence, terrorism, and organized crime, it is well to remember that there are also less romantic victims, who experience different contacts with the author of a crime and manifest particular reactions.

There are situations in which there is no contact with the criminal as, for example, in larceny (burglary), or the contact is fleeting as during street assault when the crime is committed adroitly or by snatching something from the hand or from one's person, or when violence is used, as in robbery. There are also the victims of massacres, who do not know and may never know the author of the crime that has caused them damage.

Those who have had the opportunity to work professionally with crime victims have achieved surprising results independently of the type of crime. In fact, according to M. Symonds (1983), the victim's answers follow an almost stable model characterized by four clearly distinct phases. The sequence of these phases is the same, with variations as to the duration and intensity of each, and is related to the type of contact established between criminal and victim. The first two phases are violent: the first is a negation phase, characterized by shock and disbelief; the second arrives when the denial is overcome by reality and responses like fear and impulsive talking are observed in the victim's behavior.

Then, with variations from one victim to another, the third phase is entered, characterized by traumatic depression and self-accusation. The characteristics of the victim's personality emerge at this stage, in a very "personal" way when experiencing depression or other psychic problems. The personality characteristics influence, above all, the fourth phase described by Symonds (1983), when defense mechanisms develop in order to minimize or prevent the risk of future victimization. Some people, however, are unable to accept and overcome the experience of victimization, bearing it as a personal affront. Such people's sentiments are shaped so as to see society as indifferent to their situation; therefore, they will be conditioned by a feeling of injustice and anger, and later by feelings of desire for revenge and vindication.

These stages, following the experience of having been victims, may point the way to deeper study of this subject. They could also lead to positivistic or mechanistic-aggregative typologies. Thus, the victimization experience would be characterized by well-defined personality structures and stereotyped existential courses of behavior, whereas the typical romantic image deserving of study and biographical investigation is reserved for the criminal and the terrorist.

I previously mentioned Bettelheim and Frankl, eminent people who drew outstanding lessons from their terrible experiences of participant observation. However, at the beginning of the 1970s I was able to verify that some concentration camp survivors had not succeeded in settling down in their own environment. They ended up as alcoholics, completely dependent on a total institution, having become inmates of a psychiatric hospital.

Considering all of the motives presented, the experience of victims, in the broadest possible sense of the term, calls for developing and coordinating research and studies on victims. To become one is a behavior (B) that, like all behavior, is a function of the person (P) with respect to that particular environment (E) at a given moment, according to K. Lewin's expressive formula: $B = f(P,E.)$ (Balloni, 1983, 1984; Lewin, 1961, 1965, 1972).

## CONCLUSIONS

Victims must no longer be unknown, neglected persons but human beings who, in their experience as victims, have to be examined in the overall context of the act in relation to their personality and the environment. For the victim, analysis of every problem must be carried out within the limits of a precise situation, defined with respect to factors of both objective and subjective order that are found in the victim's history and cover the period prior to victimization—that in which the role of victim was assumed and afterward.

In an analysis of this type one always finds factors connected with the personal world of perceptions, representations, knowledge, emotions, and plans by means of which the "life space" is constituted, that is, the space in which the person and the psychological representation of the environment are placed.

In victimology, too, one is obliged to determine the characteristics of the situation at a given moment. This is entrusted to analysis and empirical research and can constitute an appreciable stage in the future of victimology.

These hypotheses of work and research tend to place both the author of the crime or of the damage and the victim and his or her reaction on the same level, thus overcoming the limited dialectics between the damaging event (the crime) and the social reaction (punishment).

Answering the question of what the law is, Durkheim says that it is the living symbol of social solidarity; crime is the breakup of social solidarity, and punishment is social vengeance for the violence suffered by solidarity. Thus, the reasoning is homogeneous and always leads to solidarity—consequently, to the collective conscience and then to the entire morality (Toscano, 1975).

It is clear that the victim must be inserted in this context, whose function is to maintain social cohesion intact, saving all of its vitality for common knowledge. In fact, in the breakup of solidarity caused by the crime, one has to take into account not only the social vendetta and the consequent indemnity to the victim but all of those interventions that may favor his or her not becoming a victim again or not suffering from the fact of having been one. This calls for interventions that hold and develop a multiplicity of aspects, from the individual to the social, the psychological to the juridical, the economic to the cultural. All of these, however, have the human being as leading actor and receiver.

In this perspective victimology must not be limited to describing a situation but must distinguish itself by proposing standard values too.

In other words, the duty of victimology must not be limited to describing what is done first against, then for the individual who has been the victim of some wrong, offense, or crime. It has to state what must actually be done for the victim. This presumes the acceptance also on the victim's part that objective, universal, and unchangeable values based on reality exist.

The victim, who at times must feel ashamed at having been such, must no longer be subjected to interpretations that depend on the subject's sentiments, the position taken by the majority, changing culture, and therefore odious exploitation or unilateral evaluations—in brief, to subjectivism and relativism in the most varied versions. In this sense, the study of the victim or victimology fits in with criminology and human sciences in general but also embraces a very broad field ranging from pedagogy to the interest shown by the judicial system. Consequently, there is an urgent need to propose and define problems concerning method and research in this sector.

The research panorama is wide, and the debate on the subject of victimology grows ever deeper. The commitment to create centers of study, research, and documentation, both interuniversity and interdepartmental, must remain so that the victim of any form of injustice or crime will be treated with the dignity due to every human being and understood.

## REFERENCES

Balloni, A. (1983). *Criminologia in prospettiva*. Bologna, Italy: Clueb.
Balloni, A. (1984). La criminologia di fronte alla nuova criminalità. In A. Balloni & P. Bellasi (Eds.), *La nuova criminalità* (pp. 63-80). Bologna, Italy: Clueb.
Bettelheim, B. (1976). *Il prezzo della vita*. Milan: Bompiani.
Frankl, V. E. (1987). *Uno psicologo nei lager*. Milan: Ares.
Lewin, K. (1961). *Principi di psicologia topologica*. Florence: O.S.
Lewin, K. (1965). *Teoria dinamica della personalità*. Florence: Universitaria.
Lewin, K. (1972). *Teoria e sperimentazione in psicologia sociale*. Bologna, Italy: Il Mulino.
Ochberg, F. (1983). Hostage victims. In B. Eichelman, D. Soskis, W. Reid (Eds.), *Terrorism* (pp. 83-88). Washington, DC: American Psychiatric Association.
Symonds, M. (1983). Victimization and rehabilitative treatment. In B. Eichelman, D. Soskis, W. Reid (Eds.), *Terrorism* (pp. 69-81). Washington, DC: American Psychiatric Association.
Toscano, M. A. (1975). *Evoluzione e crisi del mondo normativo: Durkheim e Weber*. Bari, Italy: Laterza.

# 3

# The News Media and Crime Victims: The Right to Know versus the Right to Privacy

*Emilio C. Viano*

---

The main objective of this chapter is to review, analyze, and evaluate the portrayal and treatment of crime victims in the American print and electronic media within the framework of the constitutional, legal, and ethical tensions created by the media's right to know versus the victim's right to privacy.

Within the last decade both crime victims and some journalists have begun to ask whether crime reporting is victimizing the victims again. The issue is not what newspapers and electronic media have a right to do legally. It is what they ought to do ethically.

The records of crimes are public records. The public has a right to know, but where does that right to know end, and where do the privacy rights of private citizens begin? Even when the media are well within their rights, how are these rights and duties exercised? Are there areas needing attention and improvement? How can we reconcile responsible and accurate journalism with the victim's need for privacy, compassion, and concern?

This chapter discusses the major variables affecting media performance against the background of the social, cultural, and political forces influencing it. It is expected to generate a dialogue on the media performance in this area, lead to a better understanding of the dynamics and tensions existing between the media's and victims' interests, and contribute to the development and strengthening of public policy and of a code of ethics.

## MEDIA AND VICTIMS: PROBLEMS AND CONFLICTS

There is no doubt that the media must be counted among the forces that help define, measure, and interpret victimization and limit our perceptions of its nature and extent. As a mediator between government and the public, how have the media, for example, translated official statistics and statements into public perceptions? Some maintain that sensationalized, misleading, and at times inaccurate cover stories that have appeared in the recent past typify this type of coverage.

The problems most often mentioned in connection with the media coverage of crime vicitimization are listed and examined below.

### Newsworthiness

Newsworkers view their work in terms of selecting the most important events and portraying those in an interesting and informative way. Talk about newsworthiness is a commonplace newsroom activity. Seemingly, such talk merely reports or reflects social reality. However, when the talk-world dichotomy is analytically suspended, an alternative perspective emerges. Accounts of newsworthiness do not present reality; rather, they forge it. They are one crucial set of practices for managing newswork routines.

When it comes to newsworthiness, there are some marked differences between television and print news. Since most cities have more television stations than newspapers competing against each other, the pressures on television news organizations are more intense than are those on newspaper organizations. The concern with "marketable" news leads to speculation that television crime news departs more widely from objective reality than does newspaper crime news. Certainly, time is a far more important variable in television news reporting (Gelles & Faulkner, 1978; Schlesinger, 1977). "Good" news for television means immediate news, and immediate news does not necessarily imply accuracy. Television is less concerned with newsworthiness than with the presentation of an appealing product (Epstein, 1973; Sheley & Ashkins, 1981).

There is considerable controversy between the media and victims and their advocates about the genuine newsworthiness of certain instances of crime reporting, particularly as it affects the manner, content, and frequency of the news broadcast.

## Sensationalism

The media are often accused of sensationalizing crime, pandering more to prurient and voyeuristic angles than to reality. When it comes to victims, many believe that, to accomplish this, the media do not hesitate to violate the privacy rights of victims and of their relatives or survivors. The graphic depiction of grief and anguish; of victims in embarrassing (e.g., nudity), gruesome, and bloody situations; of bloodstains and body bags, as well as seeking out and publishing unnecessary details and the selective emphasis of headlines, are examples of the mutually reinforcing process of pandering to the violence and bloodthirstiness of the readers while also feeding them; of providing models, examples, even challenges to potential or would-be criminals and encouraging them to translate their sick dreams into action; of reminding certain segments of society (e.g., women, the elderly, children, the poor) of their vulnerability and thus quite likely inducing fear, apathy, and helplessness in them.

## Superficiality

The media have been accused of almost always viewing crime superficially, not only closely reproducing official explanations but virtually ignoring the underlying sources of crime and victimization, such as social values and conditions, and promoting a superficial view of the appropriate responses.

When it comes to the victims, the media are accused of being superficial, for example, by ignoring the victim while focusing on the offender, thus perpetuating that "victorology" approach to crime that shows a greater interest in the winners than in the losers of criminal activity; by describing victims selectively and negatively, utilizing stereotypes that lead to blaming the victim while overlooking other, positive attributes of the victim; or by presuming to know what a victim thinks or feels.

According to some, the media impose or reinforce simplistic notions through superficial psychological appeals. They may mystify instead of clarify, especially in a society generally adverse to critical thought. They may influence and shape people's views and yet claim to be merely responsive (Scheingold, 1984).

## Entertainment Stereotypes

The media are also seen as conveying distorted images of crime, criminals, victims, and police work that constantly reiterated, profoundly affect public perceptions, values, and even behavior. Some describe television in particular as propaganda for the status quo. About law enforcers, the media are accused of promoting a "Dick Tracy mentality" that separates police and criminals or law-abiding citizens and lawbreakers into "good" guys and "bad" guys; of incorrectly portraying businesses and middle and upper, instead of lower, classes as bearing most victimization; and of overstating the violent crime levels.

The media also mislead when they portray certain groups (e.g., blacks or Hispanics in the United States; Turks and other immigrants in Europe) as naturally violent, lower classes and minorities as naturally criminal, men as heroes when they dispense lethal violence, women and minorities as deserving their fate, offenders as isolated individuals separated from social forces, privileged victims as innocent, and underprivileged victims as culpable.

Media present the exotic and peculiar as commonplace and propose a worldview featuring an abnormally high proportion of sexy women, violent acts, and extralegal solutions to legal problems. The media also exploit victims with splashy headlines and riveting dramas, either exaggerating the victimization experienced or underestimating the victim's reaction (Cumberbatch & Beardsworth, 1976; Gilsinan, 1982; Saltzman, 1978).

## Violence

Quantitatively, the media present a considerable amount of violence, both as entertainment and as part of the news. The impression gained by some researchers (Goldstein, 1986) reading a good selection of articles on violence, aggression, and crime in leading American newspapers (*Los Angeles Times, New York Times, Washington Post*) and newsmagazines (*Newsweek, Time, U.S. News & World Report*) is that journalistic accounts present a "mechanistic" view of violent behavior. This view postulates the following:

1. The causes of human violence exist within the individual.
2. If only psychiatrists, psychologists, and biologists were clever enough, they could identify the genetic or personality factors that give rise to violent behavior.
3. Given the "fact" that the causes of violence reside within the individual, it is at least theoretically possible to identify potential offenders before they ever commit an offense (Rosnow, 1981).

The implications of such a reductionist perspective for society's understanding, approach, and intervention to violence and victimization are substantial.

The large amount of violence in the media artificially reinforces an aura of crime, while it may well desensitize us to its effects. Moreover, it generates fear, anxiety, and an identification with the unconstrained and violent forces of the law (Gerbner & Gross, 1973). On the other hand, it raises false hopes and expectations that violence could be easily prevented if only we were willing to institute Draconian measures directed at the lower, criminal classes.

## Fear of Crime

Public opinion about crime and punishment, including the death penalty, exhibits considerable volatility, unrelated to changes in official crime rates or to actual crimes, suggesting the media's possible influence. Many people believe that the common crime rate exceeds what the media portray (Gaquin, 1978). This indicates that it is the media that set a base perception level, which the public believes actually does not reveal enough.

In particular, the media affect our fear of crime. It has been stated that whereas the public fairly accurately estimates neighborhood victimization, it is induced by the media to vastly exaggerate national levels (Mawby & Brown, 1984; McPherson, 1978). Research shows that those reading newspapers with the greatest crime coverage show the highest levels of fear and that those watching television the most (e.g., the elderly) have the most distorted view about crime and its victims (Lewis, 1981).

## Social Control

One concept that is receiving some attention in the United States and Europe is that of media hegemony. As initially articulated by Antonio Gramsci (1971), media hegemony refers to the dominance of a certain way of life and thought and to the way in which that dominant concept of reality is diffused throughout public as well as private dimensions of social life.

Television news departments have indeed been seen by some researchers as further extensions of a capitalistic economic order. Stuart Hall (1979), for example, has argued that media products are messages in code about the nature of society, the nature of productive relations within the media themselves, and institutional domains and social processes (Altheide, 1984).

According to this view, one of the consequences of media domination is that journalists tend to cover topics and present new reports that are conservative and supportive of the status quo.

## Official Perspective

It is said that the media convey information about specific crimes and about crime trends almost entirely through official law enforcement statements and perceptions—not necessarily an unbiased source. They routinely portray crimes of violence and crimes against property committed by individuals against individuals (the FBI "index" crimes) as society's most serious threats and forms of victimization. They do not question how society defines crime, ranks its seriousness, and subsequently measures it, thus conveying a highly selective version of the problem and view of its perpetrators.

## Media Collusion

Conventionally and particularly after Watergate, many believe that the media vigorously scrutinize state activities. However, debates about media-government collusion have also been ongoing. Some feel that we cannot discount the relationship of the media with government and the symbiotic interactions that they pursue for mutual purposes. Others suggest that, intentional or not, we can hardly discount the "social production" of the news and the orchestrating of public opinion through official statements and media acquiescence. Some believe that the media readily allow officials to manipulate the news through symbolic appeals, often lacking in substance yet free of critical media review. Given the structure of media control and ownership, the media may have as much at stake in preserving the current social order as do officials and other elites (Cronin, 1981; Hall, 1978; Scheingold, 1984).

In this vein, one of the most articulate critics of British television, the Glasgow University Media Group (1976, 1980) states: "Contrary to the claims, conventions, and culture of television journalism, the news is not a neutral product. For television news is a cultural artifact; it is a sequence of socially manufactured messages, which carry many of the culturally dominant assumptions of our society."

One need not accept the most extreme views nor assume any sort of conscious and overt conspiracy between the media and government to wonder whether a certain ideology of crime and victimization may nevertheless not pervade public opinion. Taken together, for example, one could say that the way we selectively define, measure, and convey conceptions of victimization suggests that crime victims represent victims officially recognized as legitimate through a highly political process. Victims who challenge society's tenets, mores, and stereotypes are excluded from consideration, sympathy, and support or are included only grudgingly after a prolonged struggle for recognition. Those who suffer victimization by the state generally receive no recognition at all (Viano, 1983).

## Racism and Classism

A question often raised is whether or not the race of the victims and of the perpetrators in crime stories is a factor with editors who decide the scope, nature, and slant of their crime coverage. There are those who believe that the media continue to deal with minority crime victims with inconsistency and insensitivity, often displaying prejudices that must be overcome before the news treatment can become fair and equitable. Often the result, they say, is coverage with racial overtones.

There is evidence suggesting that American media—especially big-city newspapers—routinely downplay news of minority crime. Investigations in Chicago,

New York, and Washington, DC, have found newspapers to be less likely to publish stories about homicides with minority suspects and victims than about homicides with white suspects and victims (Blake, 1974; Cox, 1976; Stephens, 1981).

But the reasons for unequal treatment go beyond race. Probably even more relevant is the victim's socioeconomic status. The poor, transient homeless person who is clobbered with a bottle or shot and dumped under a bridge is likely to get the same treatment whether the person is black, white, or brown, male or female. Those cases have historically drawn little attention in the courts. The media have been seen as reflecting the same attitude. Where the crime occurred is said to control very much what the reaction and coverage of the media and of the establishment will be.

## Media-Police Coziness

Research has found that routine coverage of crime carries a strong pro-police and pro-prosecution bias (Cohen, 1975; Drechsel, Netteburg, & Aborisade, 1980; Sherizen, 1978). This area of investigation offers instructive insights into the relationship, symbiosis, and mutual influence between the media and the justice system. For example, some people maintain that, through the relationship of working side by side for many years, police and the media have developed similar approaches to crime stories, with the police officer knowing that certain crimes would draw little attention and the reporter in turn showing little interest.

Conversely, detectives are much more likely to pass on to reporters a tip about a crime story in a rich neighborhood or involving rich, powerful people. The close working relation between police and other justice officials and the media has been highlighted in the United States in some celebrated court cases like, for example, *Andren v. Knight Ridder Newspapers*, a Michigan case; *Hyde v. City of Columbia*, a Missouri case; and, in the most important crime victim case of all, *Cox Broadcasting v. Cohn*.

The fact that, ironically, the major source of crime news for reporters is the police wire service, which signals reporters only about certain sensational offenses, crimes in which the police have an interest, or types of crimes about which reporters have expressed an interest, seems to indicate that the work of the media is more reactive than proactive and that the images of crime that reach the public through the media are filtered through the eyes of the establishment (Sheley & Ashkins, 1981).

Thus, there are four major possible prejudices affecting crime coverage and the determination of what is news: geographic bias, socioeconomic bias, racial bias, and lack of cultural understanding.

On the other hand, there are those who argue that the media have at times performed an excellent public service by helping draw much-needed attention to a crime; that the media today are reporting on crime more thoroughly than ever before and not just on criminal acts but on related issues as well: public safety policy, crime watches, prevention measures, and the like; and that we see more and more profiles of crime victims, not just as names and statistics but as people who had brothers and sisters, sons and daughters, fathers and mothers.

## Disregard for Victim's Rights and Concerns

Media coverage of violent crime and victimization ranges, as can be expected, from good to bad, sensitive to callous, humane to incredibly inhumane. Although the cases of bad, callous, and inhumane reporting may be few, they represent a larger, direct challenge to both news media and victim advocates. The ideal would be to find a common ground that encourages accurate, complete coverage of crime and its aftermath without violating the rights and interests of crime victims.

The development in recent years of a strong concern for victims of crime and of a remarkable network of programs serving the victims has generated a challenging tension between victims' interests and advocates and the media. The major problem facing these two camps, leading at time to friction and disagreement, is how to secure thorough coverage of crime victims' stories without further adding to the subjects' personal trauma and grief.

Some examples of media behavior considered offensive and intrusive by victims and their advocates follow:

- Publicizing a victimization prior to notification of the victim's family.
- Printing a victim's name and address, particularly when the offender is still at large.
- Graphically describing women victims and survivors.
- Interviewing victims and/or survivors at inappropriate times.
- Chasing victims and survivors into hospital rooms, police stations, etc.
- Choosing unflattering, inaccurate terms to describe victims, often to sensationalize the event.
- Glamorizing the offender.
- Inappropriately delving into the victim's past.
- Behaving aggressively toward victims, survivors, and their advocates.
- Ignoring the victims' and survivors' wishes regarding how and when they wish to deal with the media.
- Filming, photographing, and prominently broadcasting and printing scenes with bodies and body bags.
- Reporting unconfirmed innuendos.
- Searching for and stressing the "negative" about the victim.
- Interviewing and photographing child victims or child relatives of victims.
- Interfering with police investigations.
- Publishing reports on the progress of investigations and negotiations that

may reveal critical information and endanger the safety of the victims of kidnapping and terrorism over the objections of authorities or of the families of the victims.
- Intimidating or misleading victims by claiming to have rights that the media actually do not have (e.g., to be on private property, to interview them, etc.).
- Improperly using police "cover" and support to gain access to victims and survivors and to confidential information about them (e.g., diaries, letters).

Balancing the public's right to know and the victim's right to privacy and respect is at times a difficult undertaking. The media are often accused of abusing their First Amendment rights and of arrogantly taking cover under them to defend inappropriate and unsavory behavior in reality not protected by the Amendment. Besides the legal and constitutional aspects, a deeper question is one of ethics, morality, concern, and compassion. Even if what the media intend to do is legal, is it really necessary and does it truly serve a "vital public interest"?

## CONCLUSIONS AND RECOMMENDATIONS

Several recommendations can be offered to defuse the tensions existing between the media's and the victims' interests and to improve the media's coverage of victims:

1. The development and adoption of a code of conduct and ethics that will result in a more sensitive and appropriate coverage of victims.
2. Undertaking a concerted effort on the part of the appropriate government agencies, professional associations, unions, victim organizations, and universities to improve the media's understanding of what it means to be a victim of crime and/or a survivor; to develop approaches and techniques that will allow for sensitive and compassionate reporting that is also objective, accurate, and complete; and to help reporters deal with the stress of working in traumatic situations.
3. Developing and revising the content of related courses taught in schools of journalism and communication and possibly developing a specialized course on crime reporting to specifically address the problems mentioned above.
4. Raising people's consciousness about their right to privacy, to be treated respectfully, to be left alone if they do not wish to talk, and to objective and sensitive reporting.

Because the mass media are businesses, responsive like any other to market pressures, victims and victim organizations should not hesitate, if needed, to organize boycotts of offending publications and radio and television stations and to put pressure on their sponsors and advertisers.

TV news is consumed differently from print news. It is presented to an audience that may not want to have anything to do with the subject matter. This has important implications when anticipating the likely reactions of viewers and also when considering the impact television has on educating and shaping the opinions of the public. A concerted effort should be made to articulate and develop broadcasting standards that take into account the public's values, sensitivity, and diversity (e.g., by age) and to affirm the rights of the audience to respectful treatment.

The role that the media play in democratic societies is of utmost importance to ensure the free flow of ideas and news, maintain the vitality of debate and discourse, provide an appropriate outlet for dissent and disagreement, and furnish the citizens with versions of events that are relatively truthful.

The victim movement does not want to curtail any rights of the media, deprive them of any of their protections and privileges, or interfere with the accomplishment of their mission. What the victim movement wants is more responsibility, sensitivity, restraint, and compassion on the part of the media whose image and reputation is often tarnished by sensationalism, exploitation, and callousness toward grieving and suffering people.

The accurate, sensitive, and compassionate media coverage of crime victims is an important objective for all those working in the field of crime and justice. It will be achieved only through the joint efforts of and cooperation between criminologists, victimologists, victims' advocates, and journalists and reporters. The examination of the portrayal and treatment of victims of crime in the printed and electronic media provided by this chapter should contribute to reaching this goal by generating a better understanding of the dynamics and tensions existing between the media's and victims' interests, by leading to suggestions and recommendations that will be instrumental in improving the media's understanding of what it means to be a victim of crime and/or a survivor, and by contributing to the development and strengthening of a code of ethics that will result in a more sensitive and understanding coverage of victims of violent crime.

# REFERENCES

Altheide, D. L. (1984). Media hegemony: A failure of perspective. *Public Opinion Quarterly, 48*, 476-490.

Blake, P. (1974, December 7). Race, homicide, and the news. *The Nation*, p. 592.

Cohen, S. (1975). A comparison of crime coverage in Detroit and Atlanta newspapers. *Journalism Quarterly, 52*, 726-730.

Cox, C. (1976, April). Meanwhile in Bedford-Suyvesant . . . : Why whites die on page one. *MORE*, pp. 18-21.

Cronin, L. (1981). *U.S. against crime in the street*. Bloomington: Indiana University Press.

Cumberbatch, G., & Beardsworth, A. (1976). Criminals, victims, and mass communications. In E. Viano (Ed.), *Victims and Society*. Washington, DC: Visage.
Drechsel, R., Netteburg, K., & Aborisade, B. (1980). Community size and newspaper reporting of local courts. *Journalism Quarterly, 57*, 71-78.
Epstein, E. J. (1973). *News for nowhere*. New York: Random House.
Gaquin, D. (1978). Measuring fear of crime: The National Crime Survey's attitude data. *Victimology, 3*, 314-318.
Garofalo, J. (1977). *Public opinion about crime: The attitudes of victims and nonvictims in selected American cities*. Washington, DC: U.S. Department of Justice.
Gelles, R., & Faulkner, R. (1978). Time and television news work. *Sociological Quarterly, 19*, 89-102.
Gerbner, G., Gross, L. P., & Melody, W. (1973). *Communications technology and social policy: Understanding the new cultural revolution*. New York: Wiley.
Gerbner, G., Gross, L., Signorielli, N., Morgan, M., & Jackson-Beeck, M. (1979). The demonstration of power: Violence profile no. 10. *Journal of Communication, 29*(3), 177-196.
Gilsinan, J. (1982). *Doing justice*. Englewood Cliffs, NJ: Prentice-Hall.
Glasgow University Media Group. (1976). *Bad news*. London: Routledge.
Glasgow University Media Group. (1980). *More bad news*. London: Routledge.
Goldstein, J. (1986). *Aggression and crimes of violence*. New York: Oxford University Press.
Gramsci, A. (1971). *Prison notebooks*. New York: International Publishers.
Hall, S. M. (1978). *Policing the crisis: Mugging, the state and law and order*. New York: Holmes and Meier.
Hall, S. (1979). Culture, the media and the "ideological" effect. In J. Curran, M. Gurevitch, and J. Woollacott (Eds.), *Mass communication and society* (pp. 315-345). Beverly Hills, CA: Sage.
Lewis, D. A. (Ed.). (1981). *Reactions to crime*. Beverly Hills, CA: Sage.
Mawby, R., & Brown, J. (1984). Newspaper images of the victim: A British study. *Victimology, 9*, 82-94.
McPherson, M. (1978). Realities and perceptions of crime at the neighborhood level. *Victimology, 3*, 319-328.
Rosnow, R. L. (1981). *Paradigms in transition*. New York: Oxford University Press.
Saltzman, K. (1978). Women and victimization: The aftermath. In J. R. Chapman & M. Gates (Eds.), *The victimization of women*. Beverly Hills, CA: Sage.
Scheingold, S. A. (1984). *The politics of law and order: Street crime and public policy*. New York: Longman.
Schlesinger, P. (1977). Newsmen and their time-machine. *British Journal of Sociology, 28*, 336-349.
Sheley, J. F., & Ashkins, C. D. (1981). Crime, crime news, and crime views. *Public Opinion Quarterly, 45*, 492-506.
Sherizen, S. (1978). Social creation of crime news: All the news fitted to print. In C. Winick (Ed.), *Deviance and mass media*. Beverly Hills, CA: Sage.
Stephens, M. (1981, December). Crime doesn't pay (except on the newsstands). *Washington Journalism Review*, pp. 39-43.
Viano, E. (1983). Violence, victimization and social change: A socio-cultural and public policy analysis. *Victimology, 8*, 3-4, 54-79.

# PART II
# The Trauma of Victimization

Common sense and research show that being a victim of crime generates strong, often unexpected feelings. Negative feelings common to all victims include *fear, anger, guilt, and helplessness.* Emotions differ in individuals only in degree and in length of endurance.

Victims have suffered a loss that leaves deep scars, most of all because of its unexpected nature. They no longer possess a very basic sense of safety, predictability, and control over their lives. Whereas illness, death, and interpersonal conflict are somewhat expected, few of us prepare ourselves or anticipate being a victim of crime. And so there is an immediate, unexpected wrenching away of things we thought we could count on: safety, security, and in many cases the inviolability of our bodies. When physical and sexual assault are experienced, there is an additional traumatic loss of our concept of having control over what we do and what is done to our bodies.

On the other hand, the victim's experience is not unlike that of the surviving spouse when death occurs, the victim of a tragic accident, or the members of a household divided by divorce. These events are ones to which we have become more and more responsive, and they have prepared us to care for victims of crime more effectively than we might first suspect.

According to Lenore Walker (chapter 4), the idea that victims of traumatic events have special needs and can develop an emotional reaction from exposure to the trauma and also that they may respond to a particular set of treatment interventions is a relatively new one, compared to the knowledge that we have about other causes of mental distress, even those directly relating to other social issues, such as poverty.

Dr. Walker states that it is possible to define the study of victimology by looking at the impact of behaviors on the victim rather than by trying to define the negative behaviors themselves. She then proposes such a classification scheme from a psychological perspective, feeling that it can be particularly useful in planning interventions. She believes that we know enough to form the type of classification system she is proposing, ranging from minor impact and mild trauma reaction to posttraumatic stress disorder (PTSD), dissociative states, and more serious forms of mental disorders such as psychotic states and personality disorders. Finally, she addresses appropriate intervention models and techniques.

Rosa Casarez-Levison discusses in chapter 5 a study conducted at Stanford university on coping strategies used by victims of crime, including various models that are directly related to victimization. The author also presents a comprehensive victim-coping model that she formulated along with a characterization of the "adaptive" crime victim.

In chapter 6, Otmar Hagemann presents results of a research project on the impact of crime on victims. A sample group of 26 victims was interviewed three times within a year, using qualitative research techniques. The research findings indicate that victimization, regardless of degree, is a significant life event that leads to changes in life-style and attitudes. Psychological harm is seen as being more severe than physical injury or material loss. The reactions of significant others and of officials are also extremely important.

Patrizia Faccioli and Simonetta Simoni, in chapter 7, focus on Italian women's perception of violence and show that such perception can be phenomenologically interpreted within a topology subdivided into three classes of experiences: self-denial, violence as love, and the latent victim.

The results of a study of family violence in India are presented by Ranjana Jain in chapter 8. Her study was based on male and female respondents representing different sociocultural characteristics. Various cases are presented to show how the victim provoked the offender. This chapter displays an approach to family violence that is somewhat different from the one prevalent in Western literature. For this reason it is noteworthy and sure to elicit some readers' reactions.

The study presented in chapter 9 by Peter Kratcoski focuses on elderly victims and is based on a large number of homicide cases recorded in Illinois and Ohio. The majority of the incidents were found to be domestic in nature. Information on the victim-offender relationship, location of the offense, type of weapon used, use of alcohol prior to the incident by the victim and/or the offender, and the circumstances surrounding the act is analyzed.

# 4

# Traumatized Populations: Role and Responsibilities of Professionals

*Lenore E. A. Walker*

---

The idea that victims of traumatic events can develop an emotional reaction from exposure to the trauma and have special needs that may respond to a particular set of treatment interventions is a relatively new one in understanding the etiology of mental distress, even when acknowledging situational factors directly relating to other social issues, such as poverty. Although Freud, in his papers written in the late 1890s, at first appears to have understood that incest could be the cause of some of his women patients' psychological distress, a series of events, including the threat of professional ostracism, changed his mind; he developed his theory of psychoanalysis based on fantasy and wish fulfillment rather than on the actual sexual abuse of little girls by their fathers (Lerman, 1986; Masson, 1984). More recent work in the area of sexually abused children, such as is documented in the review of the literature by Finkelhor and Browne (1988), in the empirical studies by Conte and Berliner (1988), and in the studies of men and women abuse survivors in mental hospitals by Carmen, Rieker, and Mills (1984), indicates the extent of psychological damage that can be caused by child sexual abuse as well as by other forms of victimization.

## WHO IS THE VICTIM?

European countries and other members of the international community have recognized responsibility for victims of crime and violence earlier than did the United States despite the better-developed American psychotherapy industry. However, this societal concern for victims is not new. Viano (1976) has traced such concern for victims back to the beginnings of recorded history, when victims were created by sacrifice and by war, with its violence, rape, spoiling, and stealing of property. As societies became more civilized, governments took on more responsibility for protecting their citizens. The violation of the state's implied or stated promise to protect people from violence can create personal harm and secondary victimization responses. Interest in studying the impact of this harm on individual victims' lives, as well as helping to define what actually is a proper societal response to its victims, constitutes the field of victimology—originally a branch of criminology but now legitimately defined as its own field of study, using an interdisciplinary perspective to answer its questions.

Defining who is a legitimate victim has always preoccupied conferences on victimology. Broad, inclusive definitions frequently include those individuals and groups who have been victimized at the hands of institutions such as corporations and political states, whereas more narrow definitions focus on individuals harming other individuals such as in prosecutable crimes. Some have argued that policies that impact on the quality of everyone's life are just as oppressive and can be as emotionally harmful as are those that choose to target only certain parts of the population.

The relatively recent criminalization of family violence, such as battered women, child abuse, marital rape, and parent abuse, has placed a whole new group of victims into the victimology community. In fact, the first article I published on my work with battered women appeared in the 1977-1978 *Victimology* journal (Walker, 1978). Because so many family violence victims are women and female children, the addition of family violence has added a decidedly feminist view to the victimology field. It has taught us that it is essential that gender and power issues must be analyzed in addition to looking at other specific variables known to cause harm. In fact, the systematic study of such power issues has become a recognized part of scientific methodology. In my work, I label this new methodology *feminist political gender analysis* (Walker, 1989a).

## PSYCHOLOGICAL PERSPECTIVES ON VICTIMS

It is also possible to define the study of victimology by looking at the impact of behaviors on the victim rather than by trying to define the negative behaviors themselves. I propose here such a classification system from a psychological perspective. It can be particularly useful in planning interventions. Obviously, not all traumas impact on people in the same way. Many victims exhibit a hardiness that minimizes the damage from the experience. We know that there are certain vulnerabilities an individual brings into the situation that in combination with the traumatic act itself can produce a negative impact. Although some have argued that crises can produce healthy psychological growth, I believe that the positive effects come from an effective resolution of the trauma, not from the trauma itself, and thus it is misleading to describe the victimizing event itself as having positive characteristics that eventually have a positive influence on an individual's life. Although logically it would seem that the development of good coping skills may make an individual less vulnerable, should further tragedy befall her or him, studies have shown that this does not usually happen. Even if it did, wouldn't it be more positive not to have to experience any trauma at all? Most victims do develop serious psychological symptoms, including the seemingly permanent loss of some of their resilience to stress, making the experience of another trauma likely to cause even greater psychological damage over time.

## Issues of Vulnerability

The question of vulnerability to becoming a victim is one that has fascinated those who work in the field. To suggest that the victim does something to attract her or his victimizer or has a particular personality pattern that causes tragedy to befall comforts those who are afraid of becoming victimized themselves. Such a cognitive framework, often referred to in the literature as "blaming the victim," suggests that one can make oneself "victim-proof"; that is, protect oneself from becoming a victim by not having the personality or not behaving in a particular way that is thought to cause a specific event.

So, for example, for some it is comforting to believe that if you do not go out alone late at night wearing sexy clothes, then you will not be raped. This belief pattern is so strong that it often continues in the face of contradictory evidence such as research that shows that women are more likely to be raped indoors by a man they know than in the street by a stranger. Other similar myths about victims also exist. Battered women are likely to be beaten whether or not they fix dinner on time or say nasty things to their husbands. Burglaries happen whether or not you forget to lock the doors and windows, and so on.

The unreasonable guilt that victims themselves accept, such as believing they did something they shouldn't have done that caused their trauma, may actually be a step toward helping themselves to heal. If a victim can figure out what he or she did wrong and change such behavior so that it is never done again, then a sense of safety in the world may be regained. However, to the extent that it is at all helpful, this faulty belief is only a temporary step on the path to healing by integrating the trauma into the rest of the victim's life. Professionals who emphasize a person's vulnerability or try to change the person's personality may actually be preventing the complete healing process, which must include an acceptance of the randomness of victimizing events. Traditional psychotherapy that focuses on the person's internal response to stimuli simply cannot help victims heal and become survivors.

## Psychological Harm to Victims

Psychological damage resulting from events usually impacts on the three major domains measured by psychology: what we think (cognition), how we feel (affect), and what we do (behavior). The experience of becoming a victim impacts on these three areas, too. Although most victims recognize a traumatic event as a negative experience, for a few it has less of a negative psychological impact than for others who share the same or similar experience. I believe that these fortunate individuals are able to immediately restructure or reframe the event cognitively so that the way they think about it does not have a serious effect on their feelings or behavior. *Cognitive restructuring* is one of the tasks of later intervention, too. Perhaps, these individuals are particularly strong-willed, perhaps it is some unconscious process, or maybe they have had practice in redefining reality so that it is less distressing to their total mental state. We really do not know because this is a group of victims/survivors who have not been studied very much. Whatever their own personal process, they short-circuit the typical response process and do not perceive themselves as having been victimized by events causing others more serious problems.

Sometimes, however, these individuals are able to suppress only temporarily the psychological response, which then just delays the traumatic experience and subsequent healing. In any case, they set one end-point of the continuum upon which the psychological impact of victimization is measured. On the other anchor-end is death from the extreme amount of physical and psychological devastation and the total and permanent lack of joy in one's life that sometimes causes later death by suicide or slower forms of self-mutilation and self-destruction. In between these two end-points are various responses that result in a readjustment of one's life-style. Limitations caused by physical, sexual, or psychological debility are frequently observed. Sometimes they clear up spontaneously, but more often they need some form of intervention. The impact can last anywhere from weeks to years, often compounded by various secondary victimizing experiences (Walker, 1987).

## POSTTRAUMATIC STRESS DISORDERS

Recognizing the psychological symptoms that result from victimizations and differentiating them from other mental disorders has been the recent focus of study for mental health professionals (Brown, 1988; Douglas & Colantuono, 1987; Figley, 1988; Rosewater, 1987). There is a large enough data base to form a classification system that takes into account the range of distress from minor impact through to posttraumatic stress disorder (PTSD) and on to dissociative states, abuse disorders, and more serious forms of mental disorders such as psychotic states and personality disorders. In some cases, physical head injury causes organic brain syndromes that also affect behavior.

The 1980 edition of the *Diagnostic and Statistical Manual of Mental Disorders* (DSM-III) (APA, 1980) for the first time included a diagnostic category for PTSD, which is the most commonly seen psychological reaction to trauma. Although PTSD was originally included primarily at the urging of Vietnam war veterans, many of whom were experiencing stress reactions related to combat that sometimes were delayed as long as 10 years, it soon became obvious that the criteria applied as well to rape, assault, battery, and other trauma and disaster victims. The PTSD criteria were further refined in the newly revised DSM-III-R (APA, 1987).

## Criteria for PTSD

The common features exhibited in a PTSD include cognitive disorders such as reexperiencing the traumatic event(s) through flashbacks, nightmares, and conditioned thoughts; heightened arousal responses such as exaggerated startle response and hypervigilance to cues of further danger; and numbing or depression with disturbances in interpersonal relationships. The DSM-III-R fell short of delineating by name the various subcategories such as battered woman syndrome, rape trauma syndrome, battered child syndrome, child abuse accommodation syndrome, postsexual exploitation syndrome, postwar syndrome, toxic shock syndrome, employment disaster syndrome, and so on. Although the criteria can be found to some degree in most victims who come for an evaluation, each subcategory has a separate constellation of additional symptoms. For example, rape victims usually exhibit some disruption of their sexual patterns, whereas battered women often exhibit higher levels of denial, minimization, and repression. Battered women who have also been sexually abused exhibit the symptoms for both syndromes.

## Dissociative Disorders

Dissociative disorders, which include various forms of memory loss, depersonalization, and splitting of mind and body, frequently occur along with PTSD, especially in situations where there is repeated abuse. The more serious the abuse and the longer it has gone on, the more likely the abuse victim has learned how to dissociate as a psychological protection. In young children, particularly those under the age of 5 years who are severely sexually and physically abused, multiple personalities may form from the dissociation. In later years, fragmented personalities develop, which are recognized by the minimal amount of integration between the various parts of the personality.

## Other Mental Health Conditions

Some victims, particularly those who have been repeatedly victimized early in life by people who betray their trust, develop more serious mental health problems. Common is the development of boundary problems, with difficulties in recognizing limits to relationships. These victims may become crazy or chemically depenent to numb the pain; they themselves may become victims or abusers, or both at times; and in the case of family violence victims, they may pass on the violence to their children. Research tells of the gender differences here: men are more likely to become active abusers and women more likely to become their victims (Walker, 1984). In fact, the well known Straus, Gelles, and Steinmetz (1980) study suggests that boys who witness their fathers batter their mothers are 700 times more likely to grow up and batter their own wives.

## RESEARCH FINDINGS

In my research study of 400 battered women, about two-thirds said that they had witnessed or experienced violence in their childhood homes, and about 80% said their batterers had witnessed or experienced abuse in their homes, too. Of our sample of battered women, about 50% had been sexually abused or molested as children. Analogue studies of young children in the developmental psychology laboratories (Cummings, Dannotti, & Zahn-Wexler, 1985) as well as those of children in battered women's shelters (Geraldine Stahley, personal communication, 1988) suggest that "empathy," or the ability to put oneself in another's shoes—to feel what the other person feels—fails to develop when children are exposed to frightening anger and violence. Witnessing and/or experiencing abuse is the single most important risk marker found in predicting violence in the family.

Studies of 9- and 10-year-old aggressive boys by Patterson (1982), Reid et al. (1983), and their colleagues found that more negative than positive acts are observed in the dysfunctional homes; but in abusive dysfunctional families those negative acts occur in blasts, chaining one after another, along with blasts of positive acts, all of which occur cross-gender—that is, from males to females in the abusive dysfunctional homes they observed. Thus, violence against women specifically, as well as violence in general, is learned in abusive homes.

## CRIMINAL JUSTICE SYSTEM

Most of those arrested and prosecuted for criminal acts have witnessed or experienced violence in their family homes. In my work as a forensic psychologist, I hear similar childhood stories from men who steal from, rape, and murder other men as well as women. All were victims of violence as children, and many were also victimized by poverty, racism, and other forms of institutionalized abuse. Most had their school learning interrupted, losing whatever chance they had at raising their self-esteem through other avenues of competency.

Prison and the criminal justice system itself can be a victimizing experience for victims as well as offenders. The use of more humane ways of treating less serious crimes, such as restitution and community service, has been attributed to the greater knowledge we now have about victims. Much of the newer work in the area of battered women in the United States has been focusing on women in prison (Walker, 1989b). Estimates suggest that as many as 80% of this fast-growing population have been battered. Perhaps as many as one-half committed their crimes because of a relationship with a batterer. More battered women are being allowed to introduce expert witness testimony at their criminal trials, sometimes to justify killing their abusers in self-defense and sometimes to explain the duress they were under when they did whatever got them into trouble with the law. Self-help groups are being formed in prisons to help these women learn how to avoid or remove themselves from victimizing relationships when they get out of prison (Bauschard, 1988).

## INTERVENTIONS

Interventions for working with victims have also been developing rapidly. Self-help groups for most crime victims have proved effective in Western Europe, particularly in Great Britain and the Netherlands. An inexpensive network of trained volunteers provides support and educational information. Battered women and rape victims need more specialized intervention, but for many other victims, these cost-effective self-help groups are quite successful.

Many battered women need the protection of the battered woman shelter to escape the violence and feel safe enough to start the healing process. Women who are hurt by men frequently need other women, not men, to help them heal. This is especially true for sexual assault victims. Shelters work closely with the criminal justice system and other psychotherapists. In the United States, the Victim Compensation Act, passed by Congress in 1986, authorizes funds that the victim/witness programs in prosecutor's offices can offer to victims to pay for brief, crisis-focused psychotherapy, along with other compensation. Of course, access to these funds is an encouragement to cooperate with the justice system to obtain a conviction against the batterer.

For some crime and violence victims, good, fast intervention often does speed the recovery process. Perhaps it is most useful in that it builds a cognitive grid from which the victim can understand all that has happened. Actually, society's recognition that it was not their fault and that they didn't cause the trauma they were forced to experience may be the single most significant message necessary for victims to regain their sense of power.

## CONCLUSION

In conclusion, the goal of all intervention is to reempower the victim. This means changing some of what professionals learn in school about the need for the therapist to keep the power and control within a therapy session. Victims heal faster when they observe the abuser receiving some punishment: there is a need to right the wrong that has been done to them. This is not a typical wish for revenge but rather a demand for justice. Victims do not understand neutrality; they need a professional who is also an advocate on their side. Issues such as confidentiality, transference, and countertransference need to be rethought using the victim's perspective. But most of all, victims need contact with good, decent, and compassionate professionals.

## REFERENCES

American Psychiatric Association. (1980). *Diagnostic and statistical manual of mental disorders* (3rd ed.). Washington, DC: Author.

American Psychiatric Association. (1987). *Diagnostic and statistical manual of mental disorders* (3rd ed. rev.). Washington, DC: Author.

Bauschard, L. (1988). *Battered Women and Justice Conference*. St. Louis: Women's Self Help Center.

Brown, L. (1988, December). Feminist therapy perspectives on psychodiagnosis: Beyond the DSM and ICD. Paper presented at the International Congress on Mental Health Care for Women, Amsterdam.

Carmen, E., Rieker, P., & Mills, T. (1984). Victims of violence and psychiatric illness. *American Journal of Psychiatry, 141*, 378-383.

Conte, J., & Berliner, L. (1988). The impact of child sexual abuse: Empirical findings. In L. E. A. Walker (Ed.), *Handbook on sexual abuse of children*. New York: Springer Publishing Co.

Cummings, E. M., Dannotti, R. J., & Zahn-Wexler, C. (1985). Influence of conflict between adults on the emotions and aggression of young children. *Developmental Psychology, 21*(3), 495-507.

Douglas, (Dutton) M. A., & Colantuono, A. (1987). *Cluster analysis of MMPI scores among battered women.* Paper presented at the Third National Conference for Family Violence Researchers, Durham, NH.

Figley, C. R. (1988). Toward a field of traumatic stress. *Journal of Traumatic Stress, 1*(1), 3-16

Finkelhor, D., & Browne, A. (1988). The traumatogenic effects of child sexual abuse. In L. E. A. Walker (Ed.), *Handbook on sexual abuse of children*. New York: Springer Publishing Co.

Lerman, H. (1986). *A mote in Freud's eye*. New York: Springer Publishing Co.

Masson, J. (1984). *Assault on truth: Freud's seduction theory*. New York: Farrar, Straus, Giroux.

Patterson, G. (1982). *Coercive family processes*. Eugene, OR: Castaglia Press.

Reid, J., Taplin, P., & Lorber, R. (1983). A social interactional approach to the treatment of abusive families. In R. B. Stuart (Ed.), *Violent behavior: Social learning approaches to prediction, management, and treatment.* New York: Brunner/Mazel.

Rosewater, L. B. (1987). A critical analysis of the proposed self-defeating personality disorder. *Journal of Personality Disorders, 1*(2), 190-195.

Rosewater, L. B., & Walker, L. E. A. (Eds.). (1985). *Handbook on feminist therapy: Women's issues in psychotherapy.* New York: Springer Publishing Co.

Straus, M. A., Gelles, R. A., & Steinmetz, S. (1980). *Behind closed doors: Violence in America.* Garden City, NY: Anchor/Doubleday.

Viano, E. (1976). *Victims and society.* Washington, DC: Visage Press.

Walker, L. E. (1978). Battered women and learned helplessness. *Victimology, 2*(3-4), 525-534.

Walker, L. E. (1979). *The battered woman.* New York: Harper & Row.

Walker, L. E. (1984). *The battered woman syndrome.* New York: Springer Publishing Co.

Walker, L. E. (1987). Intervention with victims. In I. Weiner & A. Hess (Eds.), *Handbook on forensic psychology* (pp. 630-649). New York: Wiley.

Walker, L. E. (1988, July). *Post traumatic stress disorder and DSM-III-R.* Paper presented at the Victimology Congress, Il Ciocco, Italy.

Walker, L. E. (1989a). Psychology and violence against women. *American Psychologist, 44,* 695-702.

Walker, L. E. (1989b). *Terrifying love: Why battered women kill and how society responds.* New York: Harper & Row.

# 5

# An Empirical Investigation of the Coping Strategies Used by Victims of Crime: Victimization Redefined

*Rosa Casarez-Levison*

---

## INTRODUCTION

In all criminal and violent interactions, members of society become victims. As a result, individuals are permanently changed or affected. Victimization is a "break in the human lifeline. . . . someone is assaulted, damaged, and affected for a lifetime" (Salasin, 1981). The victims of crime and violence may be men or women, adults or children. They may be murdered, battered, kidnapped, raped, or burglarized. They may undergo physical, sexual, or mental abuse; or they may be the parent, friend, or spouse of a victim—a secondary or co-victim (Bard & Sangrey, 1986). In today's world they may also be survivors of war, victims of terrorism, or victims of AIDS (Dave, 1985; McCann, Sakheim & Abrahamson, 1988; Ochberg & Soskis, 1982; Schneider, 1982).

# Coping Strategies Used by Victims of Crime

As the direct result of activist pressure by private and public victim-support groups within the past 15 years, the needs of the victims of crime and violence have finally been recognized in the United States (Kahn, 1985; U.S. Department of Justice, 1984). During this period the three branches of government have initiated actions that address (a) the legal and social ramifications affecting crime victims, (b) the victim's legal rights, (c) criminal procedure and law, (d) compensation and witness assistance, (e) protecting and assisting the victim, (f) the role of the legal system as helper rather than as perpetrator of further victimization, and (g) societal awareness and suppport.

An important area of research that addresses the crime victim's welfare is the study of the victim as a "whole" person—in all human and personal dimensions—whose physical and psychological self has been injured (Bard & Sangrey, 1986; Moos, 1976; Ochberg, 1988). Current areas of research in the United States (APA, 1984) have focused on the following:

1. Describing the victim's reactions.
2. Identifying the causes of these reactions.
3. The process of coping with victimization.
4. Crisis intervention and psychological help.
5. Evaluation and accountability in services to the victim.
6. The merging of service and research to help the victim.

## PURPOSE

Consistent with these trends, this chapter has a twofold purpose:

1. To present a new model formulated by the author for understanding coping in victimization. This model consolidates several models of coping stages and redefines the victimization process.
2. To discuss a study currently in progress that views the crime victim as a "whole" person: a complete living system. This investigative perspective will afford an understanding of the impact of victimization and of the coping efforts of these individuals in all of their "complexly organized humanness" (Ford & Ford, 1987b).

## THE STUDY

The investigation mentioned above, now in its final phase, is being conducted in the United States. The study is an empirical, descriptive, time-series correlational investigation using a structured interview and standard measures.

The following questions have been proposed in this study:

1. How do crime victims (CVs) cope immediately and in the short and medium term (0–11 months) following the crime?
2. What do they do, think, and feel?
3. How do they approach the task of organizing their lives after this disorganizing event?
4. What characteristics are associated with pattern maintainers (PMs), individuals who persist in employing coping patterns that are identical to behaviors displayed prior to the victimization, and pattern reorganizers (PRs), persons who reorganize their coping strategies after victimization? How do PM individuals differ from PR types?
5. What previctimization factors contribute to or detract from adaptive coping?

Some of these questions have been partially addressed by recent studies of victims of crime. Most of these issues, however, have only begun to be investigated. The current research will attempt to extend the present understanding of coping and adaptation in crime victims. This will be accomplished by examining the range of human experience involved in the victimizing episode and its sequelae.

## THE VICTIM

### Definitions

The crime victim is defined as one who has "directly or indirectly suffered as the result of a specific illegal or violent act considered to be a crime" (Barkas, 1978). Another definition notes that the crime victim is a "person who has been threatened (whether the threat has been to life, bodily integrity, security, or self-image) and who has measurable stress reactions with psychological manifestations" (Fields, 1977). In addition, one can distinguish between two types of victim: primary and secondary (or co-victims). The primary victim experiences the criminal act or violence directly, as in case of assault, rape, or murder. In contrast, secondary victims are injured psychologically and in many instances materially as a result of their social and emotional ties to the primary victim (Bard & Sangrey, 1986; National Organization for Victim Assistance, 1984).

An act of crime or violence, whether severe or less virulent, is considered a stressful and traumatic event (APA, 1984; Bard & Sangrey, 1986; Moos & Schaefer, 1986). Individuals may experience various kinds of reactions to such an act. For example, they may feel fear of being alone or abandoned, humiliation, embarrassment, revenge, self-blame, feelings of loss, rejection by others, insomnia, or restlessness (Burgess & Holmstrom, 1974, 1979; McCann et al., 1988). More recently, victims have been characterized as undergoing posttraumatic stress disorder (PTSD) (Figley, 1986; Piquet & Best, 1986). The APA *Final Report*

(1984) on victims of crime and violence states: "A number of explanations for these communally experienced reactions have been proposed, and all of the proposed explanations are based on the premise that being criminally victimized is a stressful experience" (p. 29).

## Conceptual Framework

The overall conceptual framework guiding both the theoretical and empirical aspects of this research is the Living Systems Framework (LSF) (Ford, 1987). This framework is particularly useful for addressing the problem of crime victimization because it is designed to represent all aspects of humanness, not just a particular facet of behavior or personality. The LSF incorporates descriptions of how various "pieces" of the person—the goals, emotions, thoughts, actions and biological processes—function, both semiautomatically and as a part of a larger unit (i.e., the person) in coherent "chunks" of context-specific, goal-directed activity (behavior episodes) (Ford & Ford, 1987b).

Moreover, virtually every leader in the field of counseling psychology asserts that his or her expanding task requires a multidisciplinary theory of "the whole person" understood as an "integrated human system" living in variable environments (Thoresen & Eagleston, 1985). Thus, by definition the LSF is consistent with the direction of this research, which emphasizes the study of the crime victim as a whole person, whose entire self, both physical and the psychological, is affected by the victimizing experience (see Figure 5.1).

## The Need For Protection

A traumatic victimizing event is "one that provokes stress beyond the resources of the individual to cope and is thus experienced as overwhelming" (Nadelson & Notman, 1982). The individual has experienced a severe disruption of daily routine, losing internal and external equilibrium (Ford, 1987).

The stress induced by this event is not accommodated quickly, as are normal, everyday stressors; the event "sends the victim into an emotional tailspin. The victim, therefore, requires time, energy, and support in order to overcome this traumatic event" (Bard & Sangrey, 1986; see also Ochberg, 1988).

Crime victims are in a state of personal danger after their experience but also in one of potential growth. If they receive the proper protection during the disorganization phase following their victimization, growth is more likely to occur. The judicial and legal systems have just recently begun to deal with the critical problem of protecting the victim. Similarly, the psychological profession is only now addressing this serious concern (APA, 1984).

Crime victims have traditionally been left to protect themselves and heal alone during an acute crisis period that, in fact, dictates that they be carefully protected from the atrocities that have occurred to their whole person. The difficulty

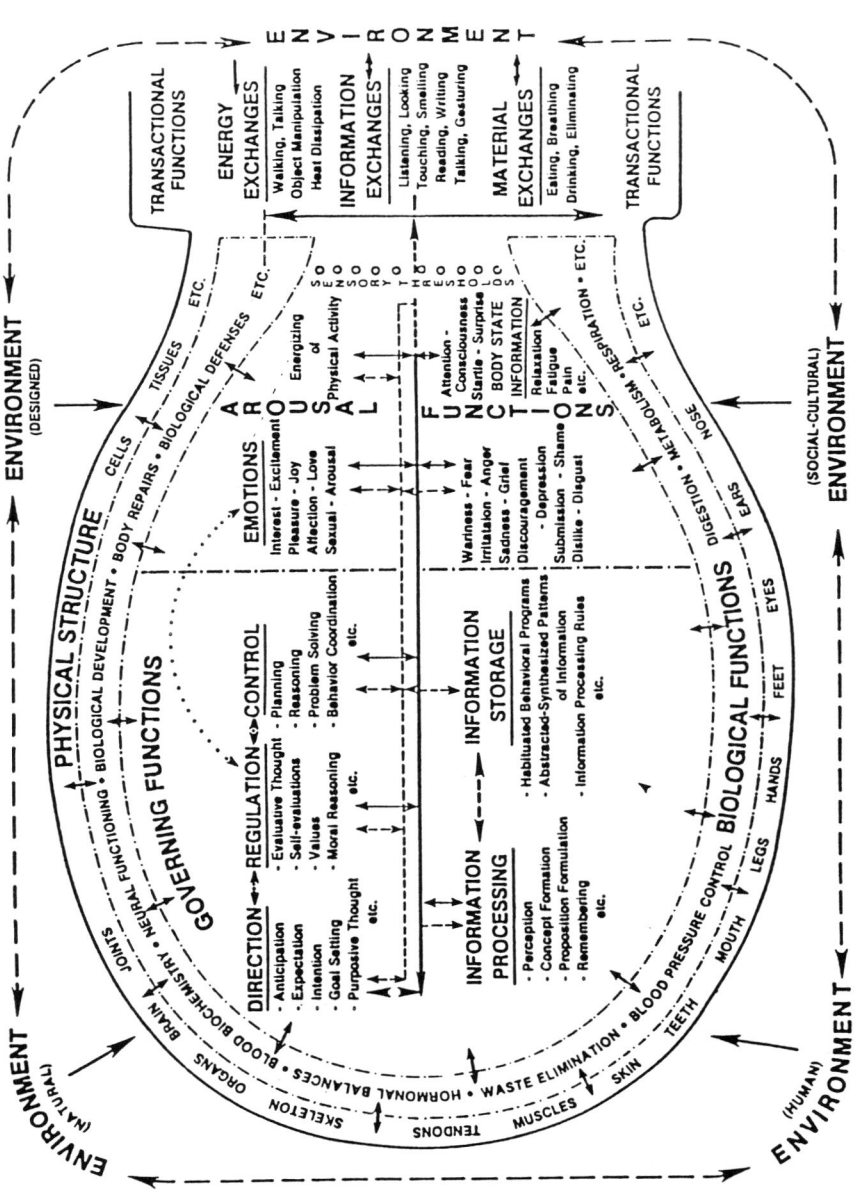

FIGURE 5.1 Living Systems Framework (LSF), illustrating the components that constitute a person: the goals, emotions, thoughts, actions, and biological processes. This figure shows the complexity and thoroughness of the LSF system. The LSF is key to understanding the victim as a whole. From Ford and Ford (1987a). Reprinted by permission.

encountered by many Vietnam veterans is an example of what can happen to individuals who face acute stress and trauma without transition protection; 15 to 20 years later, the aftermath of this war haunts the individual and society (Kelly, 1985; Wilson, Harel, & Kahana, 1988).

## MODELS OF STAGES OF COPING

Various types of coping models describe the process that victims experience (see below). The length of time required to contend with victimization is what D. H. Ford (1987) calls "the transition protection period." This varies, depending on such factors as the intensity of the victimization, the victim's coping capabilities and bodily condition, and the effectiveness of the victim's social support network and larger environment. A consolidation of the models presented below and their synthesis into a new model are shown in Figure 5.2. Below is a brief description of the following models: (a) Victims of Crime Model (Bard & Sangrey, 1986), (b) the Disaster Victim's Model (Cohen & Ahearn, 1980), (c) Death and Dying Model (Kubler-Ross, 1969), (d) the Living Systems Framework Model (Ford & Ford, 1987a), and (e) the General Adaptation Syndrome (Selye, 1982).

### Victims of Crime Model

*Stage 1.* Impact and disorganization: immediate hours and days after the crime. The victim experiences intense emotions including numbness, denial, disorientation, and helplessness.

*Stage 2.* Recoil: from 3 to 8 months after the event. The victim responds with defenses and contradictory emotions such as guilt, acceptance, and desire for revenge. These are accompanied by physiological reactions.

*Stage 3.* Reorganization: from 6 months to 1 year. Victims begin to restructure and balance their lives. This phase if maladaptive may last up to 6 years or more (Bard & Sangrey, 1986; Burgess & Holmstrom, 1979; Horowitz, 1976; Krupnick & Horowitz, 1981).

### The Disaster Victim's Model

Cohen and Ahearn (1980) describe the following stages to explain how disaster victims experience the trauma of disaster. Phase 1, preimpact—the previctimization coping experience of the victim; Phase 2, impact—actual disaster occurs and impacts on victim; Phase 3, postimpact—the degree and duration of the victim's social and emotional disorganization and the presence of a social network; Phase 4, behavioral outcome—the victim adapts or maladapts.

| | Stage 1<br>Previctimization/<br>Organization | Stage 2<br>Victimization/<br>Disorganization | Stage 3<br>Transition/<br>Protection | Stage 4<br>Reorganization/<br>Resolution |
|---|---|---|---|---|
| Time | Preimpact:<br>Pre-event | Impact:<br>Hours, days | Recoil & Post-impact:<br>Weeks to 6–8 months | Outcome:<br>"Normally" 6–12 months<br>Up to 6+ years in "difficult" cases or more severe victimization. Reintegration into stable functioning pattern begins. |
| Framework | Course of the individual's life:<br>Previctimization adaptation level. | Alarm response:<br>Body adapts to stressor. | Individual begins to reintegrate. Requires protection/assistance. If stressors continue, individual reaches stage of exhaustion. | |
| Personal Reactions | The individual brings:<br><br>• Personal attributes<br>• Self-esteem<br>• Strength/weakness of defenses<br>• Ability to appraise and interpret<br>  - coping mechanisms<br>  - metacognitive perceptions<br>  - problem-solving capabilities<br>  - emotion-focused coping<br>• Personal history<br>  - home life/support<br>  - mental health<br>  - environment<br>  - previous negative life history<br>  - proclivity to illness & depression<br>  - use of chemical substances<br>  - intimacy capability<br>• Goals, aspirations, values, altruism<br>• Sex differences<br>• Sex preferences<br>• Physical health, stamina<br>• Proneness to violence | The individual becomes a victim and experiences:<br>• Threat and danger<br>• Disruption, acute disorganization<br>• Injury—physical, mental, emotional<br>• Loss—material, physical,<br>• Traumatic stress—lack of stability<br><br>Universal Reactions<br>• Helplessness, vulnerability, anger<br>• Denial, displacement, numbness<br>• Shock, disorientation, disbelief<br>• Loneliness, depression, fear<br>• Grief, loss, intrusive thoughts<br><br>Individual Reactions<br>• Previctimization influences determine these reactions:<br>• Physiological/visceral reactions: nausea, diarrhea, vomiting, headaches, sexual dysfunction. Arousal functions disrupted.<br>• Psychological reactions:<br>  - coping capabilities function/ do not<br>  - attributions appropriate/not<br>  - self-esteem intact/threatened<br>  - transactional behaviors: seeks help/avoids it | The individual victim continues to experience:<br>In some cases, repeated violations during this phase. Symptoms will continue.<br><br>Universal Reactions<br>• Helplessness, vulnerability, anger<br>• Denial, displacement, numbness<br>• Shock, disorientation, disbelief<br>• Loneliness, depression, fear<br>• Grief, loss, intrusive thoughts<br>• Bargaining<br><br>Individual Reactions<br>• Physiological/visceral reactions: headaches, sexual dysfunction, sleeplessness, etc. Body may begin to break down.<br>• Psychological reactions:<br>  - confidence/lack of confidence<br>  - feeling well/not feeling well<br>  - thoughts of suicide<br>  - agitation, crying<br>  - desire for revenge<br>  - feeling of numbness | The individual develops effective, vigilant behaviors:<br>Return to activity and responsiveness<br><br>Universal Reactions<br>• Denial<br>• Acceptance<br><br>These must be further determined by research:<br>What is a successfully adaptive crime victim?<br><br>Individual Reactions<br>• Experience of meaning or life devoid of meaning (cynicism)<br>• Successful coping or maladaptive coping<br>• Psychogenic amnesia<br>• Multiple personality disorder<br>• Proneness to violence<br>• Chemical/substance abuse<br>These must be further determined by research. This stage may continue 20 years after the event, e.g., PTSD in the Vietnam veteran. |

52

|  | | | | |
|---|---|---|---|---|
| **Personal Resources** | Income, socioeconomic status, education<br>Health<br>General state of well being, adjustment | - problem-solving capability:<br>• reality- or fantasy based<br>• identifies alternatives/does not<br>• seeks information/does not<br>- regulation of feelings/attitudes<br>• discharges emotions/does not<br>• dissociates<br>• experiences suicidal ideation<br>- trust/withdrawal<br>- projection, displacement<br>- blame of self, society or perpetrator<br>• Second injuries occur | Medical attention: financial assistance/none<br>Psychological:<br>- access to help<br>- mental well being<br>- coping capabilities<br>Social: friends, family, support networks<br>Income, education, socioeconomic status | - self-regulation of feeling<br>- self-blame<br>- low self-esteem/self-love<br>- deterioration of relationships/increase of support<br>- addictive behaviors:<br>increased use of drugs, medication, food, relationships or other compulsive behaviors (e.g., gambling)<br>- functions cognitively/does not<br>- outward appearance of adjustment<br>- withdrawal<br>• Second injuries may continue | To present these accurately, further research is needed.<br><br>For example, exactly what resources assist the victim in healing more effectively?<br><br>Income, education, functional home, strong self-esteem, love |
| **Sociocultural Resources** | Teaching and learning of coping responses<br>Home-life support<br>Medical, psychological sources<br>Support networks, e.g., church groups, etc.<br>Daily-task and life activities | Intervention is critical.<br>Victim needs support, understanding from:<br>• police/criminal justice system<br>• mental health groups, agencies<br>• Individuals with close kinship/ties to the victim<br>• work environment<br>• society as a whole | Medical attention: financial assistance continues/none<br>Psychological:<br>- access to help<br>- mental well being<br>- coping capabilities<br>Social: friends, family, support networks<br>Income, education, socioeconomic status | Protection is critical.<br>Need for intervention continues:<br>• improvements of maladaptive chronic stress may begin to show<br>Factors affecting recovery:<br>• behavioral norms of the victim's culture<br>• support: societal/support networks<br>• mental health groups<br>• friends/family | Society, support networks, police and the criminal justice system, social attitudes, mores, and values: all of these will either help the victim or further impede healing. |

FIGURE 5.2 Victimization, the stages redefined: the stages shown here represent a synthesis of four of the more comprehensive models of victimization.

## The Model for Death and Dying

This well-known model by Elizabeth Kubler-Ross (1969) describes a five-part coping process experienced by those victims facing imminent death and loss: denial—a buffering of feelings; anger—the displacing of rage; bargaining—the negotiation for time; depression—the experiencing of intense emotions and loss; and acceptance—a surrendering to the imminent loss.

## The Living Systems Framework

The LSF model shares common features with the three previously cited models. Of particular importance is the process characterized as Organization—Disorganization—Reorganization. "Transition protection" is critical for adaptive healing during the period between disorganization and reorganization (Ford, 1987). All LSF process are affected during these stages:

1. Biological functions: physical and viscerogenic functions.
2. Arousal functions: emotions, attentional arousal, activity.
3. Transactional functions: relationships, sexual behavior, oriented behavior.
4. Governing functions: information processing, goal setting, evaluative behavior, problem solving.
5. Context: social support, individuals and groups.

## General Adaptation Syndrome

A related psychological construct, the General Adaptation Syndrome (GAS), further corroborates the commonality and similarity of responses to stress and can serve as a basis for understanding the other models. Ochberg (1988) refers to this syndrome as an explanation for the physiological impact of stress. This construct posits that an organism continuing to experience noxious stress agents will undergo a series of indentifiable stages, as follows: alarm reaction—the organism is alerted; stage of resistance—the body adapts to the stressor; and stage of exhaustion—with continued stress, adaptation is lost, and parts of the body begin to weaken.

## Integration of Models of Stages of Coping: Victimization Redefined

These different models, distilled for commonalities, represent what appears to be potentially "universal, human responses" in individuals who experience victimization in different forms, who face imminent death and the loss of things of value (Janoff-Bulman & Frieze, 1983). Individuals victimized across groups and situations experience extreme stress reactions similarly (e.g., posttraumatic stress disorder in crime victims, victims of disasters, victims of child abuse, concentration camp survivors, Vietnam veterans, rape victims, and multiple personality disorder (Horowitz, 1982; Piquet & Best, 1986; Spiegal, 1984).

Figure 5.2 consolidates the information from these models of human reactions to victimization and traumatic life events. From this model it is possible to conceptualize the psychological impact of the crime victim's experience (as well as that of any other type of victim) from the onset of the trauma through adaptation to it.

## Study Design

The study is a descriptive, time-series correlational investigation that employs a structured interview, four standard measures, and a demographic questionnaire. The categorical variables—PM and PR behaviors—are examined in relation to eight outcome variables addressing the victim as a *whole* person. The results from this study should provide a substantial amount of descriptive data on the coping strategies of crime victims, information that is critical to the field and is presently lacking. It should also shed additional light on the behaviors described in the reorganization stage outlined in Figure 5.2.

## CONCLUSION

The goals of this chapter were (a) to provide the reader with a brief overview of current judicial and investigative trends in crime victimization in the United States, (b) to convey some background information on the study the author is conducting based on the conceptual framework outlined in this chapter, (c) to present various models of coping pertinent to victimization, (d) to synthesize these coping models into a more comprehensive model of victimization, and (e) to offer a possible definition of what an "adaptive" victim might be.

It is hoped that these goals have been realized.

## ACKNOWLEDGMENTS

The author wishes to thank Dr. Martin E. Ford for the profound influence he has had on the course of this work. His ready encouragement has been invaluable in sustaining motivation. A grateful acknowledgment is also due the School of Education for providing a grant for travel to the World Congress session in Italy, where this work was first presented. Finally, heartfelt gratitude is extended to the victims who have so generously shared of their time and experience.

# REFERENCES

American Psychological Association. (1984). *Final Report: APA Task Force on the Victims of Crime and Violence.* Washington, DC: Author.

Bard, M., & Sangrey, D. (1986). *The crime victim's book* (2nd ed.). New York: Brunner/Mazel.

Barkas, J. K. (1978). *Victims.* New York: Charles Scribner.

Burgess, A. W., & Holmstrom, L. L. (1974). Rape trauma syndrome. *American Journal of Psychiatry, 131,* 981-985.

Burgess, A. W., & Holmstrom, L. L. (1979). Rape: Sexual disruption and recovery. *American Journal of Psychiatry, 136,* 1278-1282.

Cohen, R. E., & Ahearn, F. L. (1980). *Handbook for mental health care of disaster victims.* Baltimore: Johns Hopkins University Press.

Dave, L. F. (1985). *The Iran hostage wives: Long term crisis and coping.* Doctoral dissertation, Florida Institute of Technology, Melbourne.

Fields, R. (1977). *Society under siege.* Philadelphia: Temple University Press.

Figley, C. R. (1986). *Trauma and its wake.* New York: Brunner/Mazel.

Ford, D. H. (1987). *Humans as Self-Constructing Living Systems: Developmental Perspective on Personality and Behavior.* Hillsdale, NJ: Lawrence Erlbaum & Associates.

Ford, D. H., & Ford, M. E. (1987a). "Humans as Self-Constructing Living Systems: An overview." In D. H. Ford (Ed.), *Humans as Self-Constructing Living Systems: Developmental Perspective on Personality and Behavior.* Hillsdale, NJ: Lawrence Erlbaum & Associates.

Ford, M. E., & Ford, D. H. (1987b). *Humans as Self-Constructing Living Systems: Putting the Framework to Work.* Hillsdale, NJ: Lawrence Erlbaum & Associates.

Horowitz, M. (1976). *Stress response syndromes.* New York: Aronson.

Horowitz, M. (1982). Stress response syndromes and their treatment. In L. Goldberger & S. Breznitz (Eds.), *Handbook of stress: Theoretical and clinical aspects.* New York: The Free Press.

Janoff-Bulman, R., & Frieze, H. I. (1983). A theoretical perspective for understanding reactions to victimization. *Journal of Social Issues, 39*(2), 1-17.

Kahn, A. (1985). Crime victims: The role of psychologists. *American Psychologist, 40*(1), 97-99.

Kelly, W. E. (1985). *Post-traumatic stress disorder and the war veteran patient.* New York: Brunner/Mazel.

Krupnick, J., & Horowitz, M. (1981). Stress response syndromes: Recurrent themes. *Archives of General Psychiatry, 38,* 428-435.

Kubler-Ross, E. (1969). *On death and dying.* New York: Macmillan.

McCann, L. I., Sakheim, D. K., & Abrahamson, D. J. (1988). Trauma and victimization: A model of psychological adaptation. *Counseling Psychologist, 16,* 531-594.

Moos, R. (Ed.). (1976). *Human adaptation.* Lexington, MA: D. C. Heath.

Moos, R., & Schaefer, J. (1986). Life transitions and crises: A conceptual overview. In R. Moos (Ed.), *Coping with life crises: An integrated approach.* New York: Plenum Press.

Nadelson, C. C., & Notman, M. T. (1982). *Aggression, adaptations, and psychotherapy.* New York: Plenum Press.

National Organization for Victim Assistance. (1984). *The victim service guide in action.* Washington, DC: NOVA.

Ochberg, F. M. (Ed.). (1988). *Post-traumatic therapy and victims of violence*. New York: Brunner/Mazel.

Ochberg, F. M., & Soskis, D. A. (Eds.). (1982). *Victims of terrorism*. Boulder, CO: Westview Press.

Piquet, D. C., & Best, R. A. (1986). *Post-traumatic stress disorder, rape trauma, delayed stress and related conditions*. Jefferson, NC: McFarland.

Rich, R., & Cohn, D. (1984). Victims of crime: Public policy perspectives and models for service. In A. S. Kahn (Ed.), *Final report of the APA Task Force on the Victims of Crime and Violence*. Washington, DC: APA.

Salasin, S. (Ed.). (1981). *Evaluating victim services* (Vol. 7). Beverly Hills, CA: Sage Publications.

Saldana, T. (1986). *Beyond survival*. New York: Bantam Books.

Schneider, H. J. (1982). Victims of terrorism. In H. J. Schneider (Ed.), *The victim in international perspective* (pp. 398-404). Berlin: Walter De Gruyter.

Selye, H. (1982). History and present status of the concept of stress. In L. Goldberger & S. Breznitz (Eds.), *Handbook of stress: Theoretical and clinical aspects*. New York: The Free Press.

Spates, R. (1982). *Research on victims of crime: Accomplishments, issues and new directions*. Rockville, MD: National Institute of Mental Health.

Spiegal, D. (1984). Multiple personality as a post traumatic stress disorder. *Psychiatric Clinics of North America*, 7(1), 101-110.

Symonds, M. (1980). The "second injury" to victims. In L. Kivens (Ed.), *Evaluation and change: Services to survivors*. Minneapolis, MN: Minneapolis Medical Research Foundation.

Thoresen, C. E., & Eagleston, J. R. (1985). Counseling for Health. *The Counseling Psychologist*, 13, 15-87.

U.S. Department of Justice, Law Enforcement Administration. (1984). *Crime victim compensation*. Washington, DC: U.S. Government Printing Office.

Wilson, J. P., Harel, Z., & Kahana, B. (1988). *Human adaptation to extreme stress: From the Holocaust to Vietnam*. New York: Plenum Press.

# Victims of Violent Crime and Their Coping Processes

*Otmar Hagemann*

Although many crime surveys have been conducted all over the world, some very important questions in this field remain unanswered. There are three main reasons for carrying out this research project:

1. Again and again I have come across the so-called paradox in others' findings (e.g., Skogan & Maxfield, 1981) "that people who are least likely to be victimized are among the most likely to report being fearful" (p. 11) and vice versa.
2. A previous research project at the University of Hamburg showed that crime victims are significantly less preoccupied with what happened as more time passes since their experience—32% within 3 months but only around 10% within 1 to 3 years after the event (Sessar, 1990), irrespective of the severity of the experienced incidents. But does time heal?
3. Although people in Hamburg, a city of about 1.5 million inhabitants,

The author expresses gratitude to Rachel McNicholl for her help in the translation.

are victimized daily in criminal incidents, only very few ask for help and advice. This means that the local victim support schemes have great difficulty in justifying their existence.

These quite different motives all lead to the same question: How do people cope with their own or with indirect victimizations?[1] It will be shown that this is the central problem in the context of victimization from the point of view of the individual victim. Personal crime is seen here from the perspective of the victim, as intentional and destructive violation of the self (as Bard & Sangrey [1986] also pointed out). Because, under certain conditions (mainly elapsed time span), a victim can become a nonvictim again and because self-healing plays a dominant role, these conditions need to be specified.

This chapter deals first with some specifications of crimes against people. Then it takes up how Lazarus's coping theory explains these phenomena. The next section provides information about the interview methodology used and the sampling procedure. Finally, the first findings of my investigation are presented, including two case descriptions.

## SPECIFICATION OF CRIMES AGAINST PEOPLE

What is the real harm to the individual victim of crime? When is it appropriate to speak of a victim, indicating that solutions to severe problems have to be found? It seems to make no sense in this context to use the undifferentiated term "crime victim" as it is used in penal law because all types of offenses, ranging from minor theft (not related to things of sentimental value) or fraud to rape or homicide, cannot be subsumed in the same category. There will always be a coping problem to some degree, providing that the victimization is realized; but in minor incidents it will last only a short time without leaving traces. Bard & Sangrey (1986) have ranged several types of offenses on a continuum of personal crimes; their criterion was the degree of threat or violation of the self of the attacked person. This project concentrates on coping processes of the more serious section of that continuum.

Previous research on crime victims has estimated material losses and physical injuries. But the loss of the material basis for one's existence or serious, long-term injuries as a result of victimization are exceptions in the reality of crime. The role of these types of harm is very clear in the cases of raped women (Weis, 1982) or hostages (Bastiaans, Jaspers, Van der Ploeg, Van den Berg-Schaap, & Van den Berg, 1979), where the fact that there may not be material or long-term physical harm does not diminish the impact (in the eyes of the victims). And as Maguire (1982) concluded concerning the emotional impact of burglary, it is also true that it "is more important to victims than financial loss" (p. 129). This is confirmed by the interviews of this study.

## THE COPING PROCESS

Before the concept of stress and coping is applied to this context, we shall have a look at psychological well-being: the status before a stressor (i.e., victimization) occurs. Therefore, we need to emphasize some important assumptions. Every individual has his or her own equilibrium of life. It is a dynamic equilibrium, mainly of psychological well-being, meaning a permanent alteration process within individual limits. Bard & Sangrey (1986) define two essential components: the development of trust (see Erikson's [1963] concept of basic trust) and the sense of autonomy (see Rotter's [1966] locus of control). This equilibrium is part of the self or identity of a person. The self is constituted in the process of socialization from biologically determined needs and impulses, which are in the individual itself ("I") and social expectations of others and social roles ("Me") (Mead, 1934). The two aspects combined constitute an identity.

The process of building an identity[2] implies an increase in individual options and possibilities of action and leads to increased psychological stability (Tatschmurat, 1983). But securing this growing status becomes more and more difficult. If a direct attack from someone (e.g., in the form of an assault) occurs, this present basis of existence is endangered. The conflict and the resulting fear can be overcome (1) by mastering the conflict (i.e., realistically appraising one's own situation and options); vague anxiety is reduced to real anxiety, which can be removed by removing the cause of that fear or by flight from that situation; and (2) by defense with the help of several techniques: a reduction of fear is achieved by loss of a sense of reality. Fear increases to neurotic fear, which can only be avoided through a constant reduction of reference to reality.

Long-term victimizations, as in cases of concentration camp prisoners or hostages, can result in total destruction of the self; but short-term victimization, like rape in most cases, leads to psychological imbalance, too. As Janoff-Bulman (1985) has pointed out,

> The tremendous disequilibrium following victimization can be understood in terms of a breakdown in people's conceptual system. People's basic assumptions . . . (the belief in personal invulnerability, the perception of the world as meaningful, and the perception of oneself as positive) . . . about themselves and their world are seriously challenged and/or shattered by the experience of victimization, and psychological instability results. (p. 499)

Whenever people are involved in this kind of trouble, stress arises.[3] The intensity of stress can vary. Steinmetz (1983) proposes a model of four hierarchic thresholds (activation, frustration, stress, and exhaustion), and the more thresholds crossed, the greater the coping problems.

Following Lazarus and Folkman (1984), coping can be related to primary appraisal or to secondary appraisal. If stress arises relatively slowly in an interaction, primary appraisal defines the process in which the meaning of this transaction with the environment is appraised for one's own well-being. This transaction can be seen as irrelevant, positive, or stressful and thus leads to different continuations of the interaction.

Secondary appraisal, on the other hand, presumes that the incident has already led to a negative outcome. Stress is caused by stressors. A stressor is a stimulus of great intensity. Because of the duration, lack of predictability, and loss of control, it is a burden for someone confronted with it and leads to psychological and physiological disequilibrium.

## COPING FUNCTIONS AND STRATEGIES

Coping is determined by cognitive appraisal. The central function is the reduction of tension and the restoration of equilibrium. We have to distinguish between coping that is directed at managing or altering the problem causing the distress (problem-focused) and coping that is directed at regulating emotional response to the problem (emotion-focused).

> However, if we were to look at a longer period, as in recovery from traumas, we might see a clearer pattern of sequence of strategies . . . in which a period of denial or minimization (emotion-focused coping) occurs immediately after the event, to be gradually replaced by problem-focused concerns having to do with treatment programs, accommodating to the limitations imposed by the trauma, etc. . . . in general getting on with one's life. (Lazarus & Folkman, 1984, p. 155)

Problem- and emotion-focused coping can both facilitate and impede each other throughout a stressful encounter.

Coping behavior can also be analyzed as an applied strategy—as an individual constellation of acting—to meet or challenge a problem. We assume that there is no such thing as a "right" or "wrong" strategy because of individual resources and specific situational constraints. Contrary to the trait approach, Lazarus points out that there will be an alternation of coping forms both between different stressful incidents as well as in different phases. Coping processes do not develop linearly. The first period after the incident brings about the most changes in coping behavior.

## METHODOLOGY

Process-oriented research that investigates coping behavior from social as well as from psychological and physical perspectives, as required by Lazarus (1981), has first of all to be designed as a longitudinal study. For this reason each person has been interviewed three times within a year. Assault has been defined as a crime in which the victim suffers a physical attack (see Steinmetz & Straus, 1974). The offender may or may not have used a weapon.

All interviewees had become victims in the immediate past, in general about 2 months prior to the initial interview. For getting in contact with them, the help of victim-assistance employees and other intermediaries was used.[4] For reasons of confidentiality, there was no referral without the victims' permission. No one received any compensation for participation.

The first interview was conducted, when possible, in the victim's home. It was narrative, mainly in the form of a free conversation, took about 90 minutes, and was recorded on tape. This conversation included how the victims experienced the attack, what the consequences were, what support they got, what needs they still had in this respect, and their attitudes toward victim assistance and police.

The second interview was, in a way, a continuation of the previous encounter between victim and investigator (Fuchs, 1984). However, this interview was structured and was conducted by telephone[5] except in one case. It took place 2 months after the first interview and focused on the development of and changes in coping. A question usually asked was, of course, whether there had been a further victimization or whether there were other stressors to cope with in the meantime.

The third and final interview was also conducted by telephone, 1 year after the victimization incident. Young (1987) calls this "anniversary" of the event a trigger event in long-term crisis reactions. So this key date was used as an indicator as to whether the coping process had reached completion. The only serious danger in using this indicator is related to the severity and duration of the incident. Burgard (1985), for example, reports a case of a battered woman for whom the first symptoms (sleeplessness and nightmares) appeared 4 years after the last beating. However, this is seen to be limited to long-term victimizations, as in war, concentration camps, hostage situations, or living with a violent partner, or to very serious short-term victimizations like rape.

The final sample covers a maximum structural variety of assault victims (Kleining, 1982) as indicated by their occupations (architect, scientist, teacher, owner of a small business, clerk, social worker, secretary, stonemason, workingmen, retired prison guard, housewives, and students), ages (5 under 30; 7 between 30 and 55, and 5 over 55), and other characteristics. This would imply that victimization is an everyday experience restricted neither to outsiders or minorities nor to the typical victim, who is described as male and young with a life-style prone to dangerous behavior.

## FINDINGS

In this section I will present a more general description, which will be followed by two short exemplary cases. This report refers to 17 first interviews and 25 follow-up interviews. All of the victims, 8 men and 9 women, live and/or work in Hamburg; 15 of the 17 victimizations took place there. Only in four cases was there any previous victim-offender relationship; (three were neighbors but had no contact; one was a kind of client to the victim).

Victimization was seen as a significant life event in at least 14 cases. This means that it was the central problem for the victim at least for some days. Victimization marked a changing point in life, which in one case involved moving to another residence; in other cases new locks were installed. But mostly the change was only in terms of attitudes (more suspicious, more cautious, fearful, more sensitive) or in preventive behavior, including arming in five cases.

Most assaults occurred in public (four on a public transport system, eight on a street, one in a park, and one in a store); two took place in an apartment house. In one case there was no actual victimization but the threat of a pimp prisoner that he would order free members of his gang to beat up two social workers who had been instrumental in his being denied privileges. In this context, victimization was related to a dangerous profession; in another case it was related to a dangerous environment: an unaccompanied woman walked in the dark to her hotel outside the city in India.

Assault was usually beating with fists (in one case with a stick); two others were cases of strangling. In six cases weapons were used to threaten the victim (four cases involved a knife; one, a pistol; and one, a knuckle-duster). One victim avoided a stab only at the last moment.

Two attacks without arms led to very serious though not life-threatening bodily injuries. In fact, the elderly women in question suffered as much 1 year after the incident as at the time and can now be considered handicapped because both have only very limited use of their hands. (One was pushed away by two fleeing shoplifters; the other fell off her bike when stopped abruptly by hooligans.) Two injured men had overcome their injuries some months after the incident.

The police were informed in 15 cases. Two cases were taken to court, and the offenders were sentenced, which was seen as positive ("gave me back faith in justice"). Some of the proceedings were discontinued because of lack of public interest (e.g., the stabbing case), which the victims could not understand at all.

The cases of two women under 30 years of age who were assaulted by pairs of young men in daytime after school and work have been examined in detail. Whereas Carol had had several experiences of victimization, perhaps due to her lower social status, it was the first such experience, other than verbal abuse, for Anne (names changed by the author). Other differences are that Carol was victimized together with a female friend; also there were witnesses present during the whole incident, and Carol did not live alone.

## DISCUSSION

In both cases—and in all of the others, too—victimization constituted a kind of crisis, characterized by the following five elements: unpredictability, violation of social norms, imbalance of power, harm for the victims, and stress.

The imbalance of power emerged from the presence of weapons, the numerical superiority of offenders, or a power relationship between a male/young offender and a female/old victim. The victims were not vulnerable per se except in the specific contexts. Furthermore, 13 incidents involved no previous interaction and took the victims totally by surprise, giving them neither time to prepare for the attack nor a chance to escape.

The worst aspects of assault were the helplessness experienced ("I could do nothing"; "they could do what they wanted") and humiliation (to hear as a parting shot, "Heil Hitler"; to be called names; to be beaten in front of others; to be hit in the face; to be forced to say things one would never say). Phobias, fear, and distrust were also reported as further psychological harm. In two cases there was longlasting physical harm. The loss of property was not considered so important.

The victims' identities were damaged to a certain extent as can be seen from the reported impact. Victims used a variety of coping activities to restore their identities. Because of the limited space, it is impossible to discuss all of the more than 40 different coping activities reported in the study, so I will refer only to the coping activities in the exemplary cases and briefly to some other striking forms of coping. For Carol and Anne, coping means talking to others in order to express emotions, to seek information, and to be recognized as victims. Informing the police may also serve this purpose. To strengthen one's own forces by doing something concrete and tangible (i.e., karate or other direct action) reduces future vulnerability and thus fights fear. Intrapsychological processes like taking things from a personal to a social level, as implicated in interpreting the event as either political or gender conflict, can be done without external efforts and means. Carol's ability to see positive aspects within the negative experience belongs to this category; thereby the assault lost its only destroying power. Whereas Carol took action, Anne hid in her own flat ruminating about fighting the evil in the world while not even controlling her own life. Others accepted their fate or compared it with an even worse outcome. This leads to an inhibition of action and does not change anything about the problem. Some of the interviewees did not like being called victims because it implies weakness, being a loser. In this context there were attempts to "undo" the incident or a refusal to see what had happened (denial and self-deception). This strategy impedes victim assistance but may be helpful to overcome the initial distress. One victim, for example, reported that she took some pills and a weekend off to recover and gather strength to face the problem some days later. There was no one who did nothing at all, hoping that time alone would do the healing. Further activities, like praying or meditating, helped to reappraise the meaning of the event for one's future life.

Because all victims felt the need to communicate, the reactions of significant others played a crucial role for the development of coping processes. Victims attributed inadequate reactions leading to secondary victimizations, like guilt by implication, mostly to officials (policeman: "Who ventures into danger will perish there"; a train stationmaster who treated a victim almost as aggressively as the offender, who was still beating him, and threw both of them out of a train, regardless of the consequences). Obvious lack of concern and responsibility and treating victims as statistics led to negative views of police work. One victim whose call for help was rejected unless he gave his full name and address also felt that he was not taken seriously by the police. Another injured victim was given first aid at the police station, but nobody asked if he would be able to get home alone. These reactions were neutralized by more appropriate or explicitly helpful reactions from private persons. Exceptions in this respect were the people at a bus station who looked in the other direction as someone hit a woman and people who only wanted to hear an exciting story or else refused to listen when a victim needed to express emotions. In general victims looked very carefully for persons who could be trusted.

After one year the reestablishment of the personal integrity of the victims was successful except in two cases, meaning that the victimization had lost its central role in life and the emotional involvement had decreased, even though it still slightly influenced behavior. The new identity may differ largely from the old one, as in the case of a gay victim who "came out" and no longer hid his homosexuality. Where it was impossible to rebuild the previous self or resume previous activities, the main problem lay in the lack of acceptance of the new condition and the continual regret of the loss. Effective assistance would try to rechannel energy focused on hoping for a health miracle and try to find adequate alternatives by emphasizing what options are still open.

## CONCLUSION

This project has shown that the concept of coping can be applied successfully to phenomena emerging from victimizations. Throughout this process most victims become whole again. Although this study is not in a position to estimate the risks of being victimized, we find it necessary, however, to look more specifically at vulnerability, because even though one of the victims was an experienced karate fighter, he did not use this to his advantage as he was in a depressive phase and not able to utilize his resources. It also makes a difference whether a victim, although male and young, is also handicapped or only 1.55 meters in height. In each case of our sample the offenders did not just act spontaneously but checked the power relationship first. This indicates that there is actually a higher risk for women, unaccompanied persons, or others who seem highly vulnerable.

However, it is necessary to accept the victim's way of coping, never to blame him or her, and always to treat him or her seriously. Although it seems that most victims of assault recover without help from victim assistance organizations,[6] social aid and support can advance and accelerate this process. This support can prevent the victim from developing feelings of guilt, blame, and shame while brooding on the problems and is particularly needed by more isolated people with fewer coping resources of their own.

## NOTES

1. A person not directly involved in a criminal encounter, a co-victim (Waller, 1984), can feel and act like a victim.
2. Petzold and Mathias (1982) identified five sources of support: the body, the social context, work, material security, and values.
3. Cofer and Appley (1964) defined stress as a "state of an organism where he perceives that his well-being (or integrity) is endangered and that he must devote all of his energies to its protection" (p. 453). "Stress is indicated by four main classes of reaction: reports of disturbed affects, motor-behavioral reactions, changes in the adequacy of cognitive functioning, and physiological changes, both biochemical and autonomic" (Lazarus, 1966, p. 29).
4. See Hagemann and Sessar (1988) for further methodological details.
5. The change from personal to telephone interviews was unavoidable for pragmatic reasons. It was accepted by the victims, especially because there had been previous contact with the same interviewer and the victims could view their victimization more dispassionately. Others have also reported positive experiences with respect to this method (Holmstrom & Burgess, 1978; Licht, 1989; Weis, 1982).
6. In Germany the victim must take the initiative for this contact because there is no referral of addresses from police or hospitals to victim support schemes.

## REFERENCES

Bard, M., & Sangrey, D. (1986). *The crime victim's book* (2nd ed.). Secaucus, NJ: Citadel Press.
Bastiaans, J., Jaspers, J. P. C., Van der Ploeg, H. M., Van den Berg-Schaap, T. E., & Van den Berg, J. F. (1979). *Rapport: Psychologisch onderzoek naar de gevolgen van gijzelingen in Nederland*. s'Gravenhage: Staatsuitgeverij.
Burgard, R. (1985). *Mißhandelte Frauen: Verstrickung und Befreiung*. Weinheim: Beltz.
Cofer, C. N., & Appley, M. H. (1964). *Motivation: Theory and research*. New York: Wiley.
Erikson, E. H. (1963). *Childhood and society* (2nd ed.). New York: Norton.
Fuchs, W. (1984). *Biographische Forschung*. Opladen: Westdeutscher Verlag.

Hagemann, O., & Sessar, K. (1988). Copingprozesse bei Opfern schwerer Straftaten. In G. Kaiser, H. Kury, & H.-J. Albrecht (Eds.), *Kriminologische Forschung in den 80er Jahren* (pp. 983-1011). Freiburg: Eigenverlag Max-Planck-Institut.

Holmstrom, L. L., & Burgess, A. W. (1978). *The victim of rape*. New York: Wiley.

Janoff-Bulman, R. (1985). Criminal vs. non-criminal victimization: Victims' reactions. *Victimology, 10,* 498-511.

Kleining, G. (1982). Umriss zu einer Methodologie qualitativer Sozialforschung. *Kölner Zeitschrift für Soziologie und Sozialpsychologie, 34,* 224-253.

Lazarus, R. S. (1966). *Psychological stress and the coping process*. New York: McGraw-Hill.

Lazarus, R. S. (1981). Streß and Streßbewältigung—ein Paradigma. In S.-H. Filipp (Ed), *Kritische Lebensereignisse* (pp. 198-232). Urban & Schwarzenberg.

Lazarus, R. S., & Folkman, S. (1984). *Stress, appraisal, and coping*. New York: Springer Publishing Co.

Licht, M. (1989). *Vergewaltigungsopfer: Psychosoziale Folgen und Verarbeitungsprozesse*. Pfaffenweiler: Centaurus.

Maguire, M., with Bennet, T. (1982). *Burglary in a dwelling: The offense, the offender and the victim*. London: Heinemann.

Mead, G. H. (1934). *Mind, self and society*. Chicago: University of Chicago Press.

Petzold, H., & Mathias, U. (1982). *Rollenentwicklung und Identität*. Paderborn: Junfermann.

Rotter, J. B. (1966). Generalized expectancies for internal versus external control of reinforcement. *Psychological Monographs,* General and Applied, 80, whole number 609.

Sessar, K. (1990). The forgotten nonvictim. *The International Revue of Victimology, 1*(1), 113-132.

Skogan, W. G., & Maxfield, M. G. (1981). *Coping with crime*. Beverly Hills, CA: Sage.

Steinmetz, C. H. D. (1983). Het verwerken van een ernstig misdrijf: Zelfhulp en hulp van anderen. *WODC Justitielle Verkenningen, 6,* 36-68.

Steinmetz, S. K., & Straus, M. A. (Eds.). (1974). *Violence in the family*. New York: Dodd, Mead.

Tatschmurat, C. (1983). Der Einfluß der Arbeitswelt auf die Identität der Frau. In H. Petzold & H. Heinl (Eds), *Psychotherapie und Arbeitswelt* (pp. 234-249). Paderborn: Junfermann.

Waller, I. (1984). Assistance to victims of burglary. In R. Clarke & T. Hope (Eds.), *Coping with burglary* (pp. 223-348). Boston: Kluwer/Nijhoff.

Weis, K. (1982). *Die Vergewaltigung und ihre Opfer*. Stuttgart: Enke.

Young, M. A. (1987). *Crisis and stress: A training handout*. Washington DC: National Organization for Victim Assistance.

# 7

# Victims of Violence in Everyday Life: Considerations about a Qualitative Research

*Patrizia Faccioli and Simonetta Simoni*

## CONCEPTUAL AND METHODOLOGICAL PERSPECTIVES

In this work, we outline some considerations arising from a research project on the general topic of violence against women within the family circle. The initial incentive to perform this research originated from the public most directly concerned, in view of the increase in episodes of violence against women. A subsequent phase of reflection brought us to a definition of our theme and to the choice of the conceptual and methodological approach we shall attempt to describe.

Our consideration of acts of violence led us to place such acts *within a cultural and organizational context* of which *they are only one manifestation*. To limit research to acts alone would be similar to circumscribing violence to acts, that is,

Simonetta Simoni wrote the sections "Conceptual and Methodological Perspectives" and "The Results"; Patrizia Faccioli wrote the section "The Perception of Violence."

*considering the exceptional and manifestly pathological aspect of a complex phenomenon* while failing to observe the historical-structural and cultural factors from which it arises. The following observations are intended to clarify this point.

1. The observations of the sequence of attitudes and behaviors normally accompanying and following such events hint at a situation of *psychological pressure*, which is not limited to the act alone. It is worth remembering here the considerable overlapping among the stories recounted by the women and the interpretations accorded to them, the tendency to seek motivations in the behavior of the woman and the haste in resolving the "case" by means of largely unsatisfactory mediations. It is also true that many cases of sexual abuse are committed against women who, due to presumptions regarding their life-style or past history, are considered as more "willing." This culture of prejudice is transmitted to the woman and hinders the formation of a clear and accurate awareness of the fact. The answers given by the women are not always very clear, at times unsure, reticent, and contradictory, seeming to conceal fear or complicity.

2. With regard to acts of *violence committed within friendships*, which appear to be frequent (Ventimiglia, 1987), or *within couples*, there seems to be no doubt that the only possible explanation lies in the different ways in which men and women interpret and confront everyday life. They have different needs, which give rise to different expectations—a play of projections that transforms the other person into the instrument of one's own pleasure.

3. In the same way, acts of violence performed *within the family unit* can only be attributed to the *organizational system existing within the family*, with its role divisions and the expectations that are associated, above all, with the role of the woman.

On the basis of these considerations, it was decided to assume a very wide concept of violence as the conceptual theoretic reference point of our research. Thus, the literal definition of violence as the "overpowering of the will of others" is confined to acts—whether they be acts of sexual violence or others "involving lesions, damage or involuntary and painful changes in the psychological structure and contents of the conscious mind." The concept of violence adopted for this research refers to the overall organization of the social system. Violence is at the very origin of social interrelationships, in the *ambivalence* that constitutes the social order (Freud, 1921, 1927, 1930). With specific reference to women, violence is inherent in the distribution of roles and functions, a power based on sexual and biological diversity and the correlated value system accompanying this organization. Here we refer to the entire system of opinions, evaluations, and judgments that either positively or negatively sanction any form of female behavior.

In order to apply the concept of violence to the subject—women—we have used the category of *perception*. Perception, taken to be the process of interpreting stimuli originating from the external environment, is the indicator that permits us to (a) identify *what women have experienced as violence in situations, events, relationships that are not openly manifest as violent*; and (b) identify *the way* in which the woman *perceives and experiences, events, acts, and relationships that clearly qualify as being violent.*

Perception, as an operation that relates the subject with external reality, is a process of interpreting reality. As such, it must be considered in relation to the system of standards, values, and conditions that are assimilated by the subject, becoming an integral part of the personality and providing motivation for action (König, 1958).

Therefore, in interpreting the interviews, we have tried (a) to *identify the mechanisms making up the assimilation process*, permitting adaptation (Bartoli, 1976; Merton, 1957) by attenuating the perception of a constriction or act of violence, and (b) *to examine how*, due to a critical process that largely escapes the subject's conscious awareness, at a certain point in life *the adaptation mechanisms break down*, giving rise to a crisis.

This research was conducted by the authors in 1988 among a group of women living in a town not far from the city of Bologna. The participants were selected randomly but also in a manner that would ensure that major age groups between 20 and 55 years of age and different professional and status characteristics would be represented. However, given the qualitative nature of the research, this was not a rigorous random sample. Participants were interviewed following a semi-structured interview schedule. Conversations were tape-recorded.

## RESULTS

The results of the research show the relationship between biography and the perception of coercive and violent acts and behaviors, throwing light on different ways of living and interpreting the woman's role—between imposition and adaptation to a role that limits freedom of behavior, opinion, and the possibilities of emancipation and free personal choice. A tendency emerging from our group of interviewees, which can be generalized in some ways, is that of seeking to reconcile one's identity and daily working life with one's sentiments and family, a difficult mediation requiring the presence of a network of parental support and services (Balbo, 1978; Bimbi & Castellano, 1990). The private sphere is given a positive revaluation and is no longer seen as an obstruction to the woman's realization at work: "I think women are far luckier than men because they have the possibility of playing with many opportunities. The woman has a relationship with her home and family which is different from the man's and different from that of the past."

## The Family of Origin

In order to reconstruct the changes in the way of living femininity, which provide the framework in which to analyze the perception of violence, we considered life histories, starting from the relationship with the family of origin. The aim was to establish (a) the messages and values transmitted within the family of origin with specific regard to femininity, (b) the channels through which they are communicated, and (c) the responses formulated by the woman in relation to the type of message and channel.

From our interviews, three types of family situations emerge. For each type, we identify the following different behavioral tendencies on the part of the interviewees.

*Family situations strongly characterized by the female figure.* These are situations where the mother has exclusive responsibility for the family. While essentially living as a function of the husband and offspring, the woman transforms her dependency into power, succeeding in producing a value that goes beyond the specific functions she performs. In these cases, the mother is internalized as a female referent and is accorded all of the positive attributes of femininity, including the capacity to mediate and support the overburdening of family life: "I couldn't understand how my mother managed to put up with so much . . . while she was everything to the family. Anything she managed to save up was only for the children."

In this situation the woman-mother model is passed to the daughter almost automatically. Awareness of sex is also, nearly always, the awareness of role. In fact, at least initially the daughter will give a rigorous interpretation of the female role. In the family of origin, she has undergone a process of anticipatory socialization (Smelser, 1963) with this role, often assimilating the idea of the man through the father: "I wanted to marry a man who was different from my father . . . instead, he's a perfect copy of my father."

However, it is also true that the interiorization of the mother's model can lead to a rejection of this type of life and to a laborious formulation of a different way of living one's femininity.

*Family situations characterized by environmental factors.* These are perceived by the interviewees as restraints and frustrations affecting the process of maturation and as conditions limiting the planning of their lives: highly traditional family models, difficult economic situations, conflict between parents, authoritarianism and violence suffered at home. The contrast between the conditions of life imposed by the family and the perception of one's own way of being is the common denominator of these interviews. The conflict, the way of living and relating to the situation, can lead to a crisis resulting in a choice of independence—leaving home—or in a slow examination of the facts, a form of personal quest. Here too, the relationship with the family involves ambivalent mechanisms between a critical dismantling effort and the need for reconstruction through the personal relationships and in one's interior experience.

Moreover, in all cases, higher education has been viewed as a vehicle of emancipation and fundamental personal growth that can be used in different ways to activate processes of change and independence.

*Socialization taking place outside the family.* The third type of situation is one in which the relationship with the family appears not to condition strongly the formation of the interviewee. Elements of conflict with the family are perceived but accepted with a sense of passive resignation.

## The Body

The moment and the way in which the girl begins to be aware of the specificity of her body is particularly important in the process of socialization to femininity. In one group of interviewees, the instruction in beauty management is one of the elements, perhaps the most important, to integrate this process. Being beautiful, feeling beautiful, probably means being able to generate pleasure and therefore love. Thus, beauty is internalized almost as a duty inherent in the nature of woman, an essential value at the basis of a woman's destiny (Deutsch, 1962).

A different relationship with one's body is noted in another group of interviewees, who reveal a socialization founded basically on the values of work and study. In such cases the value of physical appearance is linked to one's way of being, in the attempt to integrate the perception of the body into the overall perception of personality.

## The Partner

In relation to the models internalized in family life and in the perception of the transformation of the girl's body into that of a woman, two main attitudes emerge vis-à-vis the encounter with the partner, who will then become husband or cohabitant:

1. The encounter can be experienced as a prelude to cohabitation or marriage, marking the passage from the family of origin to a new family nucleus and therefore entrance into adult life, with a consequent change of social status (Saraceno, 1988). Here all of the elements imply "waiting" for the encounter, a psychological preparation corresponding to a series of specific behaviors and attitudes, in short, almost a ritual (the dance, the choice of dress, the attention paid to physical appearance). The moment of the meeting is experienced as a sort of "gift" that the woman makes to the man. The attitude toward the man is not that of looking for another and for oneself through the other person; rather, the other person signifies conquest, possession, something to keep.

2. The encounter can also be experienced as an event that does not imply either a change of social status or a mode of behavior conforming to predetermined roles. The event assumes a place within normality, in life's continuity, and is not connected with a previous process of preparation, nor with specific future prospects. It is assumed that it may last indefinitely or be concluded in the short term. There emerges here a clear effort to attain equality with man, a tendency that often arises from an equal sexual liberty where needs and wishes coincide. To consent to sexual relations, to respond to the invitation is taken as a proof of love.

Although the attitudes are found to differ, we do not perceive a great difference in the way in which the woman internalizes the man and herself in relation to him. In the first case, the woman assumes a subordinate role to the man as regards rights-duties-expectations; in the second, by assuming a forced equality with the man, the woman becomes involved in a game governed by the man's wishes.

On a biographical level, another instance revealing the experience and perception of the woman's role in relation to the man is that of a crisis in the couple or in the matrimony. There are situations that appear, in objective terms, as violent, coercive, or intolerable to the external observer, but often the subjective awareness of those involved is not matched by acts aimed at modification or resolution.

Let us look at some of the main symptoms of the matrimonial crisis. First of all, *dialogue* and *communication* are fundamental elements of the relationship: these break down more frequently in couples who have a clear role division and who see matrimony as a passage from one social condition to another. This reciprocal distancing might occur because the marital condition fails to comply with initial expectations: the burden of daily life is borne by the woman alone, and she will process this overburdening within the system of rights and duties inherent in her role as wife.

The processing of this *overburdening*, accentuated by the *spirit of sacrifice*, may be interpreted as a form of control over the situation: "He wouldn't know what to do without me." The feeling of being indispensable to the other is a perception that reemerges at the moment of separation, when the man does not believe that the wife "will manage on her own" and vice versa.

There are various mechanisms leading to an awareness of the crisis. The crisis of couples and roles and the revision of the family model do not necessarily lead to change. In fact, we find different results:

1. The crisis ends with separation.
2. The crisis is brought under control by the accentuation of the self-sacrificing role of the woman—the crisis of the couple corresponds to an identity crisis.

3. The solution of the crisis is a good level of reciprocal independence and a loosely controlled communal life.
4. The crisis is resolved by negotiation and explicit discussion of the conflict.
5. The solution of the crisis in the maintenance of a "double life."
6. The solution to the crisis is adaptation and dismissal, even with elements of explicit conflict.

In this type of situation, given the extreme rigidity of the partner, the woman adapts, trying to understand and forgive, even to the extent of accepting forms of relating—including sexually—that she perceives as violent, justifying them in the name of love.

The crisis is overcome by various means involving a revision of the way of perceiving and *living* the female role within a couple or that of wife in a marital relationship (Saraceno, 1987), most often in two of the ways mentioned above. The first stresses the value of the female role of self-sacrificing mother and wife; the second, acceptance of a "doubling of the personality," a division in the woman's emotional life with, on the one hand, family, security, and affection and, on the other, fantasy, sex play, and eroticism.

## THE PERCEPTION OF VIOLENCE

Within this framework, perception of violence can be phenomenologically interpreted within a topology subdivided into three classes of experiences or attitudes:

1. Self-denial (interiorization of role).
2. Violence as love (justification).
3. The latent victim (self-blame).

We will now examine each of these three types of attitudes, exemplifying their logic with some material derived from our interviews.

### Self-denial

The woman perceives and assumes a series of functions and tasks as being inherent in her role. In the majority of cases, the internalization of role behavior is very rigorous. During the early years of cohabitation, the woman conforms to this internalized role, which is nearly always based on the maternal model. The interviews shed light on a form of self-inflicted violence derived from the woman's conviction that she must do what others expect her to do and center her life around her man. Role internalization may go as far as the total negation of oneself and one's own needs in favor of the needs of the partner, as the following examples show.

> Yes, I didn't mind, I didn't mind. . . . I mean I always . . . I always tried to protect him from any troubles, all those little, silly things. You know, he's such a victimistic person: "Oh, I'm tired, the telephone never stopped today!" Well, you know, when he got home, poor thing, I tried to protect him from silly problems.

> I lived for him, I mean to me he was . . . like, he used to go away Saturday and Sunday, so I'd go to see a film with my friend. But I never went out if he was at home.

> After all, I always kept everything so clean, everything. . . . He never found anything out of place. Even if I was out working from 8 in the morning to 9 at night, he never lacked anything—his nice crunchy sandwich for breakfast, his pajamas ready and slippers in place, served and revered from morning to night.

In some cases the role internalization and self-denial are so intense that women accepted sexual abuse without even perceiving it as such:

> It's not as if I went to bed with him right away, because we had been going out for a while. . . . You know, I felt obliged, I mean . . . I felt it wasn't natural and so I obviously didn't feel any pleasure in it.

> After my son was born all the burden fell on my shoulders—the family, the children, the house, and work I did at home so that I didn't have to leave the children: so, a continual stress. . . . And then having always to be ready at the right moment, to go out when he wanted to go out . . . walk for hours and hours because he liked walking, wake up at 5 in the morning because he had to do 200 press-ups on the bed . . . make love when he ate more because all in all he was always on a diet, if he ate more and didn't do any exercise, he had to consume more and I had taken all this in.

In the ultimate analysis, we witness the triumph of the model of feminine subordination and passivity, to dedicate herself entirely to the man and perhaps to be told:

> I'm a man and there are certain things I don't do. You do them because you're a woman. You knew, before getting married, what type of life you'd have; so you can't complain now that you're tired. You should have known that these are your duties as a mother, wife, housewife, worker and everything else.

In our opinion, the self-denial stemming from the internalization of the feminine role provides the key for interpreting the "normal" everyday violence that regulates male/female relationships. The most disturbing and exceptional manifestation, physical abuse, is no more than the natural consequence of the imbalance of such relationships, played out against stereotypical notions—active/passive, conqueror/conquered, strong/weak—or in other words, within the masculine myth according to which "all women want to be raped" (Brownmiller, 1976).

Thus, the acceptance of everyday violence, or rather its nonperception by women, is a natural consequence of a socialization process in which the role differences mentioned above are thoroughly internalized. When confronted with a situation of more explicit violence, the tendency we have observed is that of providing an excuse or justification for it, thus making it more tolerable to some extent.

## Violence as Love

We begin with the account given by one of our interviewees:

> My daughter was physically abused by her father when she was small, but I only found out about it when she was 13. That's why I left my husband. . . . I mean, my husband was a drunkard, used to drink a lot—even now, he's in and out of the hospital—and, well, we didn't get along. He was a truck driver, and when he was at home he was always drunk and hitting everyone; and after the usual bout I said to my husband, "I want a separation." "But I'll never give you my consent!" So the girl says, "No, you've got to give your consent; otherwise I'll report you." So I said, "Report what?" She says, "You know what." "No, you've got to tell me." So she says: "Because when I was little I thought it was a game that all fathers played with their daughters." . . . But I *believed you and didn't believe the girl*—she might have dreamt it—well, I wasn't really convinced.

Thus, sexual abuse of the daughter seems to be the last straw in a life already full of everyday physical violence. It marks the transition from a bearable to an unbearable situation. However, the interviewee still gives the presumed culprit the benefit of the doubt. Later, when the doubt is transformed to certainty, the mechanism of justification comes into play:

> We had her operated on when she was 6, with no money. So my husband would get up when it was still night to go collecting cardboard boxes. . . . My husband was crazy about his daughter. Since she was tiny, he would have done anything for her. He loved her with all his heart and would beat her for any little thing. . . . They still love each other even now.

Here we see how violence is interpreted and justified as an attempt to communicate love and is thus accepted in a certain sense. (It is worth mentioning that the interviewee has separated from her husband but has never filed an official complaint against him.)

We now turn to another account:

> I've never talked to him about it; I don't even know what it means. He only wants to laugh and joke about life. . . . Afterwards, in bed, worse than ever! Because after all he was in love . . . so anything I said or did, I was in a very vulnerable situation. . . . I had never had any sexual relations, I had never found myself in that type of situation, I mean I had never imagined that a man just does what he wants without even noticing the person underneath, I mean he . . . I don't know how to explain it. . . . He just has sex, a woman is just a sex object, he doesn't make love; yes, that's the difference, and so I didn't really understand him very much. . . . After, though, I tried to understand, also because I realized he loved me a lot at that time, and so I couldn't really believe he was just using me for sex, so I tried to understand.

Here we are confronted with a young engaged couple from a high socioeconomic class, both university-educated. The type of abuse takes a different form and is also perceived in a different way, but ultimately, it is accepted and—as in the previous case—justified. The change that takes place affects only the woman, who, according to her internalized model, must adopt to the behavior of her partner: "After, it was me who changed. I understood what he wanted. Little by little, I started to make myself like it, and now everything is going really well."

The mechanism of justification can go even further; there are those women who lay upon themselves the guilt for the violence they have undergone, as in the cases presented below.

## The Latent Victim

We borrow from Von Hentig the concept of the latent victim, used to describe "persons who hold a particular attraction for the criminal, facilitating the action" (Balloni, 1983, p. 240). With reference to women (while not even considering the hypothesis that feminine behavior is in itself provocative to the male), we believe that, in certain cases, the internalization of the role of a passive, weak, and vulnerable person may—in its most extreme form—become one with the role of victim, vis-à-vis the male/female relationship. This is the case, for example, of a girl who describes her relationship with her father in the following terms:

> I often thought about going to the *carabinieri* because I was in bed for days with bruises and didn't go to school anymore. One day they had to call in the doctor because I was bleeding. It was really bad. "No, she fell down the stairs." And the doctor . . . no worry; anyway, he let it be, you see? I mean, these situations made me realize that maybe it wasn't a good idea to go and tell because a father can always beat his daughter. He's justified in hitting her because he's responsible for everything she does.

The victim manages to escape from this situation and, far from home, tries to build a new life. Let's see in what way:

> It was such a violent relationship that . . . It was awful, really. Thank goodness it ended the way it did because we beat each other continuously. With him too it was torture—he had so many problems, even more than me. . . . He changed mood from one moment to another; he became violent. Whenever I tried to assert myself, he pushed me, beat me, hurt me. I stayed with him too much even because . . . maybe there was . . . a masochistic need, I don't know. Anyway, I sort of enjoyed being beaten, maybe because I never spoke to other women. . . . I wanted someone so much that I accepted anything.

The mention of masochism by the interviewee suggests an attempt to diminish the responsibility of the partner through self-blame. Evidently, what the model internalized when she was with her original family is a heavy load, difficult to shake off: subordination to the father/master and then to an identical partner seems to be the only possible reality for a woman.

In the second story, the mechanism of self-blame is even more evident. Here too we are confronted with an early family environment that was founded on violence:

> I had a terrible relationship with my father who represented the authority I always detested. . . . God only knows how many times he beat me, nearly every evening. . . . I had my first disturbing sexual experience when I was 6 . . . with a relative. . . . It added to the environment into which I was born, which was . . . you know, incredibly full of lust. I remember, when I was a tiny child, they took me in their arms and rubbed themselves up against me . . . and I felt the shape of the penis, but obviously I couldn't understand what it was, because . . . but I can remember it.

This is the setting of the interviewee's first sexual relationship:

> My first sexual relationship with a boy . . . I think I was about 13-14, and it was a highly traumatic experience. I invited to my house a boy who had been chatting with me; he was 3 or 5 years older than I. . . . Well, I was taken by force . . . thrown down and . . . raped. And I remember the fear of that bloodstain.

From that time on, this episode of sexual violence becomes a mark of shame, permitting anyone to take advantage of the situation:

> After, because I didn't have this thing anymore—what is it, hymen? So I didn't have a hymen, and anyone felt entitled because, after all, I mean, you're not a virgin anymore, what can you expect? . . . I resisted at the time with all my might, but after a while I would tell myself: all right, one more time. . . . You know, when you say: it's useless in any case, this situation has to go on, right? I went through this type of situation 3 or 4 times.

Our interviewee seems to have entirely appropriated the masculine myth of "she asked for it," just like the many rape victims who "after the assault, torture themselves in an attempt to discover what it was in their behavior, attitude or dress which triggered off the terrible aggression undergone" (Brownmiller, 1976, p. 395).

In the last case presented, the internalization of the passive female role seems to reach its most extreme limit: the woman thinks of herself as a male conquest and continues to punish herself for the sin of having lost her virginity. This, another cultural stereotype, is absorbed into the individual experience: in cases of rape, the only heroine is the woman who resists and pays with her life; the woman who survives an episode of rape is only a whore. After all, another male myth has it that "no woman can be raped against her will."

## REFERENCES

Balbo, L. (1978). La doppia presenza. *Inchiesta*, 32, 3-6.
Balloni, A. (1983). *Criminologia in prospettiva*. Bologna: Cueb.
Bartoli, G. (1976). Adattamento. In F. De Marchi & A. Ellena (Eds.), *Dizionario di sociologia* (pp. 23-34). Milan: Edizioni Paoline.
Bimbi, F., & Castellano, G. (1990). *Madri e padri: Transizioni dal patriarcato e cultura dei servizi*. Milan: Angeli.
Brownmiller, S. (1976). *Contro la nostra volontà*. Milan: Bompiani.
Deutsch, H. (1962). *La psychologie des femmes*. Paris: Presse Universitaire de France.
Freud, S. (1921). *Massenpsychologic und ich-Analyse*. Vienna: Internationaler Psychoanalitischer Verlag.
Freud, S. (1927). *Die Zukunft einer Illusion*. Vienna: Internationaler Psychoanalitischer Verlag.
Freud, S. (1930). *Das Unbehagen in der Kultur*. Vienna: Internationaler Psychoanalitischer Verlag.
König, R. (1958). *Soziologie*. Frankfurt am Mein: Fischerei Bucherei K.G.
Merton, R. K. (1957). *Social theory and social structure*. Glencoe, IL: Free Press.
Saraceno, C. (1987). *Pluralità e mutamento: Riflessioni sull'identità al femminile*. Milan: Angeli.
Saraceno, C. (1988). *Sociologia della famiglia*. Bologna: Il Mulino.
Smelser, N. J. (1963). *Theory of collective behavior*. New York: Macmillan.
Ventimiglia, C. (1987). *La differenza negata*. Milan: Angeli.

# 8

# Familial Violence in India: The Dynamics of Victimization

*Ranjana S. Jain*

---

Violence as a social phenomenon has a unique universality in all human societies. The expression of violence has certain similarities and variations in the situations that are personal, familial, and social. The nature of the relationship itself significantly determines the form and type of violence. This chapter deals with the victims of familial violence. Since familial situations provide a heightened and intense affective relationship, violent reactions tend to derive from questions of sexual fidelity and temperamental compatibility. Possessiveness between spouses is socially conditioned because of the normative framework ordained by the society. Any deviance from the institutionalized normative order leads to an intense reaction, which may include a potentially violent outburst. Domestic quarrels are also the result of temperamental incompatibilities or inability of couples to effectively perform their roles. On the other hand, the family is an instrument for the transmission of social customs, laws and roles. It also tends to create intense unhappiness from soured interpersonal relations, which result when the individual does not fulfill his expected roles in the family.

Wives at times fail to make a viable adjustment with their husbands and in-laws. The husband who fails as the family breadwinner also faces problems in all

# Familial Violence in India

of his social roles. Any deviation from the institutional normative pattern leads to conflicts, tensions, abuse, beating, torture, and murder in the family. The family, an institution meant to foster the most intimate relationships, can also become a caldron for the most intense mutual dislike. Since family ties cannot be willfully broken, the pressure to live together intensifies the hostility.

The present study has been undertaken in Indian society, which has a certain typical structural and cultural background. The typicality and the specificity of any society are important factors in helping one to comprehend the extent and nature of violence. It is in this context that cases have been examined in detail. Despite its high pluralism, Indian society reveals considerable uniformity at both the structural and cultural levels, providing a generalized framework to relate violence to the social structure.

Over the past few years there has been a sharp increase in the incidence of violence in the family. Glaring among these is the murder of young married women for nonfulfillment or insufficient fulfillment of dowry demands. We also hear and read about cases where the family members got involved in murder for such reasons as marital maladjustment, infidelity of spouse, property disputes, domestic quarrels on various issues, and so on. Ram Ahuja's (1969) study of female offenders in India indicated that of the total 136 female family murders, 81.5% had killed one of their own family members. Ranjana Kumari's (1989) study of dowry victims shows that one in every four were murdered or driven to commit suicide, and more than half (61.3%) were thrown out of their husband's house after a long-drawn-out period of harassment and torture. According to the anti-dowry cell set up by the police commissioner of New Delhi in 1983, 690 young women died in Delhi alone, of whom 23 were burned alive. Police records also reveal that, between 1969 and 1983, deaths of this nature increased.

Violence as used in the present study refers to those crimes of violence legally forbidden, intentionally or unintentionally committed, and punishable by the courts: murder or overt physical assault by one individual on another. Such an act may be undertaken for a variety of motives, ranging from fear and panic to sadistic pleasure, but the end result is harm to and total destruction of another human being. Both the victim and the offender have a role in family violence.

## THE STUDY

The study reported in this chapter used data from a population of 50 male and 50 female family offenders in the Central Jail, Jaipur, Rajasthan, India. Almost all of the respondents belonged to the lower socioeconomic classes and ranged in age from 16 to 55 years, with individuals between 16 and 30 years of age in the majority. The male respondents were engaged in diverse traditional occupations, like agriculture and pottery making, they were shepherds, or they worked as casual laborers. A few were small businessmen, employees, or students. As for the females, about 80% were housewives. The remaining 20% worked as casual laborers whenever their household activities permitted them to do so. All of the females and 86% of the males were married. Slightly more than half of the respondents lived in extended families of two or three generations; the rest lived in nuclear families. More than three-fourths of the male and female respondents lived in rural areas; only about one-fourth lived in urban areas.

Data were collected by means of a questionnaire administered in a face-to-face situation and covering (1) general items; (2) family items, including socialization patterns, marital relations of the respondents, and parent-child interactions; (3) occupational items; and (4) crime items.

Familial violence was analyzed within the context of extramarital relations and of domestic quarrels within the family of orientation or of procreation.

Familial violence tends to take place in families in which the victim and the offender have had a longtime association with each other. Each one of them thinks that he has been harassed, cheated, harmed, insulted, neglected, and/or charged with certain allegations by the other. Thus, personal criticism, arguments, and counterarguments escalate past and present conflicts. These "volcanic" domestic quarrels sometimes become so serious that one or both spouses are hurt or even killed by the other.

## Violence Related to Extramarital Relations

Sex and love intrigues constitute one of the important causes of murder among various respondents in the present study. Initially, one spouse may make a verbal attack on the other. It is directed toward a particular issue, like the specific actions of the marital partner or toward social, psychological, emotional, or physical defects in the spouse. When one spouse learns that the other has been unfaithful, it is seen as a high provocation. In the heat of passion one may even kill the spouse.

For example, when Mrs. B. discovered her husband was having illicit sexual relations with a woman in their own village, she said she would not stand for that and asked her husband to sever his relations with the other woman. Instead, he stopped giving her money for household expenses and starting drinking, abusing, and beating her. She said that her anger reached a peak when her husband did not return home for two nights. On the third day, when her husband returned at night, she became wild with anger, and they had a heated argument. Her husband abused her and began beating her with a stick. This, she said, she could not stand, and in a fit of rage she picked up an ax lying in the house and killed him.

Similarly, Mrs. C. reported that her husband was too dominating, demanding, very irresponsible, and inconsiderate, and he never took an interest in her or in the children. After some time, he started drinking a lot and coming home very late at night. She came to know that her husband had been unfaithful to her, that he used to roam with another woman in the village while telling her that he had to go out for business reasons. One day she said that "her husband came home at about 2 A.M. drunk. As soon as he entered the house, he started abusing her for asking why he was so late, became violent and started beating her." She said she could not tolerate this anymore as he had been very harsh and cruel to her. Infuriated, she took an ax and struck him on the head, killing him instantly.

Males also used the defense of provocation to explain or justify their violent reactions. Mr. I. said that his wife showed little interest in family matters. She did not have any wifely interest in him. Her attitude of disregard toward his demands and expectations "was a highly frustrating experience for him." She did not even care for the child. She used to go out alone in the evening, which made him suspicious. Once he saw her talking to an unknown man, with whom she had developed illicit relations. He insulted them and asked her to come back home. She got wild at being chased. She abused him verbally and admitted that she disliked him, which created more frictions between the two. This continued for some time until, in a state of emotional disequilibrium, he picked up an ax and gave her a hard blow on the head, which killed her.

In the first two cases cited here, the women had killed their husbands because of their illicit relations with other women. They had failed to conform to the normative expectations of faithful husbands. Besides, the husbands were also verbally and physically aggressive toward their wives, which further severed their relation with each other. In the third case, the male was convicted for murdering his wife, who had illicit relations with another man. She had thus failed to fulfill her obligation as a faithful wife. She was unable to conform to the normative expectations of a wife. This was the main source of marital disappointment and dissatisfaction, leading to maladjustment and friction in married life.

The above three cases reveal how marital maladjustment was experienced on account of the spouse's complete or partial sexual promiscuity, unfaithfulness, or sexual perversion. Fidelity from a spouse is expected because it is part of the social values and also because marriage leads to a strong sense of possession. When an individual learns that his or her spouse has been unfaithful, this creates jealousy, rivalry, and desire for revenge. The conflict ends when one provokes the other physically to such an extent that the other retaliates, and in the tussle one is finally killed by the other.

## Violence Related to Domestic Quarrels

Some other reasons for family violence are domestic quarrels, problems related to maladjustment among family members resulting in serious tensions between husbands and wives, parents and children, siblings and also between in-laws and their married children. Some cases may be cited to illustrate the point.

Mr. L. was an unmarried man who had been arrested for killing his mother. He reported that his mother used to constantly find fault with her children and criticized them. After the marriage of his brothers, his mother became more and more quarrelsome in nature. He said that his mother always complained "that her sons and daughters-in-law were inconsiderate, unjust and lazy. This created unpleasantness and bitterness in the family." One evening when he came home from work, he saw that his mother and his sister-in-law were quarreling with each other. He intervened and stopped them from doing so, but, as he reported, his mother started fighting with him, saying that he took the side of his sister-in-law and was not concerned about her. She abused him badly for being inconsiderate to her. This, he said, made him lose his emotional balance at that time. He took a stick lying nearby and hit his mother with it. His mother fell down and later collapsed.

This indicates how domestic quarrels lead to strained relations and to violent outbursts even between the closest of kin, like mother and son. Similarly, siblings also resort to violence due to rivalry or jealousy on account of land or property disputes. This violence is more common among males because they are legal heirs to their parental property. None of the females committed violent acts in their family of birth. The study reveals that of the total 50 male and 50 female family offenders, only 14% of the males had resorted to violence in their family of orientation. The males had been violent toward their mothers and brothers. No female had killed her mother or father, brother or sister.

The circumstances in which one is placed after marriage have a bearing on an individual's personality and behavior, and influence relations with the other individuals in the family. Similarly, interpersonal and other elements with which one has to live after marriage may have a bearing on one's marital relationship and the overall adjustment with family members. The overt circumstances refer to the external environment in which one has to live after marriage and include the financial conditions, problems of alcoholism, type of family, the bearing of children, the relation with in-laws and husband and other living conditions. These circumstances, can affect marital relations and thus create tensions leading to violence.

Mrs. P. said that she was married when she was 17 years old to a man who was 3 years older. She said that her relations with her husband were not cordial because he was a heavy drinker. He used to drink every night and came back very late. When he was asked to stop drinking, he often abused and beat her. This irritated her a lot, and marital discord followed. She also reported that "her husband spent most of the money he earned on drinks. He used to ask her to get money from her parents if she wanted to satisfy any of her requirements." This annoyed her a lot, and she felt miserable. On the fateful day of the crime she said that her husband had abused her and beaten her severely on being questioned why he was so late and why he could not stop taking alcohol. She felt disgusted and disillusioned at that time and, in a fit of exasperation, took a kitchen knife and shoved it in his stomach. He fell down and was soon dead.

There were many such cases where the problem of alcoholism became the focal point of familial violence and the victim precipitated the violent act.

In some cases the in-laws also created problems of utter maladjustment for the women who had to live with them.

Mrs. R. related that her husband was very harsh to her, right from the beginning of her married life. Her mother-in-law also treated her very badly. She was asked to do the entire cleaning, sweeping, washing, and cooking for the whole family. Sometimes when she was not well and refused to do so much work, she was abused and beaten by her mother-in-law. Her mother-in-law was partial to her own daughters and her other two daughters-in-law. What irritated her most, she said was that "her husband always took his mother's side and humiliated her in front of everyone."

Even during her pregnancy she was neglected. She said that "no consideration was shown to her by her husband and mother-in-law, and she had to do all of the household work." Her mother-in-law criticized her for being inefficient. This made her even more irritable. Finally, she was looked down upon by husband and in-laws for giving birth to a female child. They said that she was not capable of giving birth to a male child. This she could not tolerate, and sometimes she argued with her mother-in-law about it.

On the day of the crime, as she recalled, they had come to the point when frictions took place very frequently over trivial matters. She said that she was preparing the meals when her mother-in-law came and complained that the food was never ready in time. She explained that she had not been well and so was a little slow. But her mother-in-law exploded and not only abused her but also assaulted her. Her husband was away, and her father-in-law refused to intervene. Thus, she felt extremely neglected. She could not control herself, and in a fit of rage she struck her mother-in-law with a stick lying nearby. Her mother-in-law fell unconscious on the floor and later was declared dead.

We repeatedly heard respondents relate incidents of how the victims tried to cut them down verbally and physically. This eventually led to physical assault and violence. It seems evident that what one family member said often precipitated the violence. On the basis of the foregoing discussions, one may conclude that crimes of violence occur with the highest frequency in relationships characterized as relatively close and intimate or personal and direct, in short primary contacts.

## CONCLUSION

The study shows that most of the violent criminal acts were committed as a result of unconscious motivation, deep emotional needs, or sudden unconscious emotional outbursts. The predominant motive of violence resulted from altercations and family quarrels due to marital problems of adjustment, jealousy, dislike for spouse, infidelity of the spouse, or maltreatment by in-laws or husband or both. Familial maladjustment was thus a major cause of familial violence.

Crises in family relations occur between family members because of (1) extramarital relations, (2) severely strained relations between husband and wife, (3) nonfulfillment of mutual expectations, (4) disputes related to land and property, and (5) unkind and inconsiderate in-laws. These crimes are aggravated when the family members are overly stimulated or tempted, exceptionally provoked or also emotionally disturbed because of the continuous stress and strain. These incidents of extreme provocation produce a desire to deviate from social or legal norms and resort to violent behavior. It has been found at times that some people are more dominating, demanding, abusive, aggressive, critical, and possessive. These negative qualities may not be tolerated by the other family member. This gives rise to conflicts and tensions. When the gulf becomes wider, the other person also retaliates with greater force. This at times ends in violent behavior. It appears that the contribution of the victim is vital in many cases of familial violence. Sexual deviance, alcoholism, and beatings are the triggering point for the violent reaction.

The family has been historically a strong social institution in Indian society. Thus, it is a great source of both psychological and social support for the individual family members. It is in this context that one must examine the violence and its nature, and emphasize that an institution which is so close and important for its individual members can itself at times become a source of violence. While extreme family violence is still relatively rare, spouse abuse, psychological harassment, and physical torture are quite common. Social scientists have often stressed the study and analysis of uniform patterns and not of rare occurrences. However, it should be kept in mind that "rare" is as important and worthy of study as "uniform" and "general."

## REFERENCES

Ahuja, R. (1969). *Female offenders in India*. Meesut: Neenakshi Prakashan.
Kumari, R. (1989). *Brides are not for burning: Dowry victims in India*. New Delhi: Radiant Publishing.

# 9

# An Analysis of Cases Involving Elderly Homicide Victims and Offenders

*Peter C. Kratcoski*

---

As the 20th century draws to a close, an ever-growing percentage of the U.S. population will be made up of persons age 60 and above. Life expectancy has increased for both men and women, and the problems related to aging, including decreased physical strength and mental alertness, lack of economic resources to meet medical expenses or increased living costs, and reduced contacts with or even isolation from the community are now affecting more and more Americans. Victimization of older persons by criminals is also an important concern. When such individuals are victimized, they are more likely than younger crime victims to face offenders armed with guns and to be accosted in or near their own homes (U.S. Department of Justice, 1987).

Although we tend to relate older persons to violent crime as victims rather than perpetrators, the elderly do commit violent crimes. In 1989, for example, 375 persons arrested for murder and nonnegligent manslaughter in the United States were age 60 and over (FBI, 1990). When such violence occurs, the circumstances surrounding the events need to be examined, with the purpose of answering the following questions: Do violent older persons prey upon relatives and friends, or are their victims likely to be strangers to them? Where is the violence most likely to occur? Is violence an incidental outcome of the commission of other offenses, or directly intended? Are older persons who commit violent offenses situational offenders, or do they have histories of criminal activity? What types of weapons are used? Is alcohol or drug use a factor? Do the victims of such violence help to bring about the event by their behavior toward the offenders at the time of the incidents or over a long period of time? Such inquiries are of great importance when the violent offense considered is homicide.

To address the questions about violent crimes by the elderly posed above, a study of older homicide offenders and their victims was developed. Cases involving offenders who had reached the age of 60 before committing a homicide offense for which they were arrested were abstracted from 12,885 homicide cases recorded in Chicago during 1965-1981 and 2,600 cases of nonjustifiable homicide recorded in the coroner's office in Cuyahoga County (Cleveland), Ohio, for the years 1970 through 1983.[1] A total of 383 homicides by persons age 60 and older was identified. The data provided information on both the homicide assailants and the victims in regard to the victim-offender relationship, location of the offense, type of weapon used, use of alcohol prior to the incident by the offender and/or the victim, and other circumstances surrounding the acts. The homicide incidents were also analyzed with regard to their being related to domestic violence or occurring in a stranger-to-stranger confrontation. Those that happened in domestic settings were examined to identify possible victim precipitation, patterns of domestic violence culminating in the homicide, and patterns of alcohol abuse by the offenders and/or the victims.

Since crimes are largely committed against persons of social characteristics similar to those of the offender (social class, race, age), it was expected that many of the victims in these homicides by older offenders would be elderly persons. Feinberg and Khosla (1984) stated:

> The limited evidence on the subject of victim-offender relationships suggests that they are often similar in race, age, social background and even previous arrest history. It logically follows that the victims of elderly criminals may themselves be elderly persons. (p. 40)

## THEORETICAL FOCUS

Historically, the field of criminology has shown little interest in involvement of the elderly in crime as offenders or victims. The social structure of American

---

[1]. The Chicago data were collected by Franklin E. Zimring, Richard L. Block, and Carolyn Rebecca Block and maintained by the Illinois Criminal Justice Information Authority. The Cuyahoga County data was collected by Peter C. Kratcoski and Donald B. Walker.

society has been dominated by the young, and the culture has been youth-oriented. Now, the trend toward an aging population has produced a significant interest in the area of gerontology and an increased awareness of elderly involvement in the problem of crime. Criminologists have begun to devote more attention to the older population, and the role of the elderly as offenders is emerging as a significant topic of interest (Newman, Newman, & Gerwirtz, 1984).

It was noted earlier that one problem commonly associated with aging is degenerating health. A number of researchers have related mental illness or deterioration to violent, aggressive activity by older persons. Gewerth (1988) noted that pathological changes produced by such disorders as cerebral arteriosclerosis and senile dementia can reduce inhibitions or cause delusions that trigger violent episodes. Whiskin (1968) also found cases of depression, functional psychosis, personality disorder, alcoholism, and paranoid schizophrenia among the elderly offenders he studied.

Stress theory is also advanced as an explanation for violent behavior by the elderly. There is no doubt that older persons experience many stressful life events, including personal illness or the illness or death of a spouse or close friends, reduced income and financial pressures, dependence on others for assistance that may be grudgingly provided, worry about the future, or fears for physical safety in a deteriorating neighborhood or public housing project or because of dependence on public transportation. Stress theory holds that violent behavior is a possible outcome when persons are subjected to high levels of stress without adequate defenses. The increased close contact that occurs when retirement places an elderly couple constantly in each other's company may also produce such stress.

Disengagement theory has also been related to violence by the elderly. This theory notes that elderly persons are frequently forced by circumstances to reduce their contacts with persons outside the home, and they experience loss of status and feelings of uselessness when they have retired and no longer hold active positions in the community. As their contacts with others are reduced, they become more and more isolated. If retirement was mandatory, rather than chosen, feelings of bitterness or failure can trigger violent outbursts. As spouses spend more and more time in each other's company, tensions build up that can ultimately result in a violent striking out of one spouse against the other.

Gelles (1972), in a study of family violence, found that 18% of the husbands and 14% of the wives age 51 years or older that he studied reported that violence occurred frequently in their homes. He concluded that the potential for intrafamily violence does not decrease with age, although the factors precipitating the violence may change as the years go by. A statewide study of elder abuse in Massachusetts (O'Malley, Segars, Perez, Mitchell, & Kneupfel, 1984) confirmed Gelles's finding that spouses continue to react violently to each other in later life. In more than half of the cases of elderly abuse, alcohol and drugs were used by either the offender or the assailant, or both. In the majority of the cases, physical abuse of the elderly by the elderly was an ongoing matter. In some such instances, the ultimate outcome is a homicide.

## THE RESEARCH STUDY

This research study was developed to explore the circumstances surrounding homicides committed by older offenders. Elderly homicide offender cases were abstracted from two sources. Cases involving 286 offenders age 60 or older were taken from 12,885 homicide cases recorded in Chicago from 1965 through 1981. Ninety-seven cases involving offenders in the same age group were taken from 2,600 cases recorded in the Coroner's Office of Cuyahoga County for the years 1970-1983.

In the Chicago cases, 91% of the assailants were male, and 9% were female. Seventy-one percent of the victims were male, and 29% were female. Eighty percent of the elderly assailants were nonwhite, and 20% were white. For the Cuyahoga County cases, 81% of the assailants were male, and 19% were female. Eighty percent of the victims were male, and 20% were female. Eighty-nine percent of the elderly assailants were nonwhite, and 11% were white. Seventy-two percent of the victims were nonwhite, and 28% were white. In both data sets, therefore, the vast majority of both the assailants and the victims were nonwhite males.

The ages of the victims and their relationships to the elderly homicide offenders were determined. For the Chicago sample, 25% of the victims were age 60 or older; for the Cuyahoga County sample, 44% of the victims were age 60 or older. For the Chicago group, approximately one-third (32%) of the victims were related to the offenders, and among the victims who were age 60 and older, 41% were family related to the offender. For the Cuyahoga County sample, 32% of the victims were related to the offenders, and in an additional 57% of the cases the victims were acquainted with the offenders.

If disengagement theory applies to homicides by older offenders, one would expect many of the incidents to occur in the home. In the Chicago sample, 74% of the incidents occurred in the residence of the victim or of the offender. When the victim and the assailant were family-related, 85% of the offenses occurred in the residence. For the Cuyahoga County data set, 68% of the homicides by those 60 and older occurred in the home.

Previous research studies have established that homicides are often the result of domestic fights or quarrels. For the Cuyahoga County set, 67% of the homicides by persons age 60 and older occurred during or after a quarrel, 7% happened as felony murders, and the circumstances surrounding the other homicides involved other events or were not specifically known. However, for the Chicago data, only 64 (22%) of the 286 cases involved a domestic quarrel.

This is a surprisingly low figure. This finding suggests that the contexts and circumstances in which quarrels occur are broader than the domestic setting.

Stress theory would lead one to speculate that older homicide offenders would tend to be situational offenders whose aggressive violence was triggered by the pressures of events, rather than persons with criminal records. This supposition held true for the Cuyahoga County group. Only 16% of those homicide offenders age 60 and older had previous criminal records. However, for the Chicago group there was an indication of more extensive earlier criminal behavior. Twenty-three percent of the offenders who were related to their victims and 51% of the offenders who were not related to their victims had criminal records. The older offenders in the Chicago sample who had previous criminal records tended to be concentrated in the group whose victims were not family members.

The weapon most frequently used by elderly homicide offenders, regardless of the circumstances surrounding the event, was a firearm. For the Chicago set, 63% used firearms; for the Cuyahoga County set, 89% used firearms. The availability of a lethal weapon is of particular importance when the assailant is elderly because the use of other weapons (knives, heavy objects, or fists) by this type of offender may not result in a fatality, whereas use of a firearm most often inflicts a fatal wound.

Alcohol use at the time of the homicide incident was examined to determine its relation to the occurrence. The full impact of alcohol use on the event cannot be ascertained, because information on alcohol use by the elderly person who committed the homicide was not available in either set of data. However, the presence of alcohol in the body of the victims was noted. As shown in Table 9.1, the percentage of alcohol use by the Chicago and Cuyahoga County victims was virtually identical.

As shown in Table 9.1, 33% of the victims in the Cuyahoga County group and 32% of the victims in the Chicago group had been using alcohol at the time the homicide occurred. One can speculate that, in cases in which the victims and the offenders were related or acquainted and in which they were interacting at

TABLE 9.1 Alcohol Use by Victims in Homicides Committed by Persons Age 60 or Older

| Presence of Alcohol | Cuyahoga County Group[a] | | Chicago Group[b] | |
| --- | --- | --- | --- | --- |
| | N | % | N | % |
| Alcohol use by victim | 25 | 33 | 86 | 32 |
| No alcohol use indicated | 50 | 67 | 187 | 68 |
| Totals | 75 | 100% | 273 | 100% |

[a]Information on this item available for 75 of the 97 cases.
[b]Information on this item available for 273 of the 286 cases.

the time of the incident, there is a strong possibility that, if the victims were using alcohol, the offenders were also doing so.

Stress theory would hypothesize that, in addition to the pressures from life events experienced by elderly homicide offenders, provocation by the victims at the time of the incidents or over a more extended period of time would have an influence on the occurrence of the homicides. Information on the victim's participation in the homicide event in an active, aggressive role of precipitation of the event was not available for the Cuyahoga County data set. For the Chicago data, this information was available for the majority of the cases. Although the information available was not extensive enough to establish the circumstances of the victims' involvement or the degree to which the victims instigated or provoked the violent occurrence, it does provide enough details to lead one to conclude that in 91 cases in which the victim and the elderly offender were family-related, 64% (58 cases) involved victim participation in the incident by instigation or provoking of hostilities, either verbally or physically.

In 75 of the Chicago cases, the available information indicated victim precipitation of the homicide act. Table 9.2 details the relationship between the victim and the offender in these cases.

## DISCUSSION AND CONCLUSIONS

This research sought to examine the circumstances surrounding homicides in which the offenders were age 60 and older, to determine the characteristics of their victims, the locations where these events occurred, and the circumstances surrounding them. The criminal behavior histories of the offenders were examined to discover if these homicides were isolated instances or part of life patterns

TABLE 9.2 Relationship of Victim to Offender in Homicides Committed by Persons Age 60 or Older in Cases Involving Victim Precipitation (N = 75)[a]

| Relationship of Victim to Offender | N | % |
| --- | --- | --- |
| The victim was the spouse of the offender. | 16 | 21 |
| The victim was the boyfriend of the offender. | 4 | 3 |
| The victim was the ex-spouse or an immediate family member other than spouse. | 7 | 10 |
| The victim was another relative or an in-law. | 5 | 7 |
| The victim was a friend, neighbor, or close acquaintance. | 26 | 35 |
| The victim was a functionary in the offender's life. | 4 | 6 |
| The victim was not related to or acquainted with the offender. | 13 | 18 |
| | 75 | 100% |

[a]These 75 cases are taken from the 286 cases in the Chicago data.

of criminal behavior. The types of weapons used in the homicides and the possibility of alcohol use influencing the fatal occurrences were also studied. Finally, the roles the victims may have played in bringing about their own demise were investigated.

The findings of this research confirm a number of widely held beliefs about homicides by the elderly and victim-assailant relations. The homicides tended to involve persons of the same race and to occur in the residences of the assailants or of the victims, with the assailants and the victims related to or acquainted with each other. Like homicides in general, the vast majority of elderly homicide offenses were committed by males. The presence of alcohol in the bodies of approximately one-third of the victims would indicate that alcohol use had some effect on the homicide event. The availability of firearms to the elderly offenders was of great importance.

The pattern of the homicide incidents occurring in the home, during or after a quarrel, in a spontaneous rather than a planned manner, with the male most frequently the aggressor, would tend to confirm the applicability of stress theory to homicides by the elderly. The presence of alcohol in the victims' bodies in one-third of all of the incidents also suggests that the stress and disengagement theories apply. As older persons retire or decrease their social activities, they tend to spend more and more time with their spouses, sexual companions, or close acquaintances, or they are alone for long periods of time. Increased use of alcohol by the elderly as a result of boredom or its use as a way to combat loneliness or depression could have a bearing on the occurrence of aggressive violent behavior in persons of this age group.

As couples age, they may encounter many stressful situations in which they turn to each other for emotional support because resources outside the home are no longer open to or meaningful to them. As a result of disengagement, this increased dependency often creates a highly stressful climate for the spouses and also for close friends or acquaintances who are aware of the problems. For some older persons, it appears that the needs for assistance and companionship from spouses and close acquaintances intensify at exactly the time when such persons are less likely to be able to satisfy these needs. A violent act brought on by frustration or resentment can result. Pity may also bring about a decision to commit an act of violence. This occurs most frequently when a person decides to end the suffering of a spouse who is suffering from an incurable illness. The loved one is thus victimized by the very person who has been a trusted and loved companion, although in some instances the victim has appealed to the offender to end his or her suffering and may consent to or even actively encourage the commission of the violent act. The motives of the assailants in these cases are obviously far different from those of the elderly persons who commit homicides with motivations of anger or revenge, and such tragic cases present dilemmas for the criminal justice system.

The influences of physical illnesses and mental deterioration caused by aging on the occurrence of violent aggressive behavior by elderly persons is an important area where more extensive research is needed. As an ever increasing percentage of the population falls into the 60 and older age group, methods of dealing with these problems take on increased significance. The growing public awareness of Alzheimer's disease and the difficulties it creates for its victims and for those who must care for them is an indication that the mental health problems of older persons need to be given more attention. The potential for victimization of the elderly in their own homes or living situations is enormous. The complete dependence of many of the elderly on other persons for housing, nursing care, transportation, and social interaction can prove to be a burden for which those who must provide these services are ill prepared to cope. This is a compelling social problem that requires immediate attention. Mistreatment may take the form of physical violence, withholding of needed medication or physical activity, forcing an elderly person to sign over funds or property to others, or pressuring an elderly person to enter a nursing facility against his or her will. Protecting elderly persons from such abusive activity can be extremely difficult because those suspected of abuse can contend that the elderly person is confused, senile, and incapable of accurately describing what is happening within the home situation.

Even when the reasons for violent aggressive reactions by the elderly are understood, legal and mental health professionals may not take them into consideration when dealing with such offenders. The case files used in this research revealed that many of the offenders were known to the police and social service agencies through previous contacts. Those involved incidents of domestic violence, mental health difficulties, and applications for welfare or home nursing services. If the agency personnel who interacted with these elderly persons in earlier contacts had perceived the potential explosiveness or hopelessness of their situations, more extensive and intensive attention to their needs might have prevented the violence that ultimately occurred. There is a need for community efforts to establish rapport with elderly persons through church groups, nursing home visits, or interface with other agencies that have contact with the elderly.

The possibility of drawing disengaged older persons back into active community life through volunteer work should be more intensively explored. Older Americans have a wealth of knowledge and experience that could be tapped into by agencies and groups that are sorely in need of assistance. Possibilities for such volunteer involvement by the elderly include community, church, and civic endeavors, tutoring or providing clerical services at schools, and working with juvenile and adult offenders. Some programs, such as Foster Grandparents, may provide small subsidies for those who need them. Involvement with others, carefully geared to older persons' physical health conditions, abilities, and interests, can help diffuse the tensions that can develop in their lives and promote feelings of well-being and self-worth.

# REFERENCES

Federal Bureau of Investigation. (1990). *Crime in the United States*. Washington, DC: U.S. Government Printing Office.

Feinberg, G., & Khosla, D. (1984). Sanctioning elderly delinquents. *Trial, 21*, 46.

Gelles, R. J. (1972). *The violent home*. Beverly Hills, CA: Sage Publications.

Gewerth, K. E. (1988). Elderly offenders: A review of previous research. In B. McCarthy & R. Langworthy (Eds.), *Older offenders* (pp. 14-34). New York: Praeger.

Newman, E. S., Newman, D. J., & Gerwirtz, M. L. (1984). *Elderly criminals*. Cambridge, MA: Oelgeschlanger, Gunn and Haim.

O'Malley, H., Segars, H., Perez, B., Mitchell, V., & Kneupfel, G. M. (1984). Elder abuse in Massachusetts: A survey of professionals and paraprofessionals. In J. J. Costs (Ed.), *Abuse of the elderly* (pp. 57-88). Lexington, MA: Lexington Books.

U.S. Department of Justice. (1987). *National Crime Survey 1986*. Washington, DC: U.S. Department of Justice.

Whiskin, F. (1968). Delinquency in the aged. *Journal of Geriatric Psychiatry, 1*, 240-249.

# Part III
# The Child Victim

The mistreatment of children is not a new phenomenon. It has taken place in many ways throughout history. Infanticide, abandonment, mutilation, beating, painful initiation ceremonies and ritualistic killing of children have been practiced in different parts of the world for centuries.

There is no question that violence has always been a part of the lives of families and individuals, that it is a widespread and enduring feature of human society, and that it has occurred in all social levels. There is much of it in our contemporary society, which certainly considers itself civilized.

Violence is a difficult term to define with precision. Following Gelles and Straus (1979), for example, one could define violence as "an act carried out with the intention or perceived intention of physically hurting another person." However, there is more to violence than that. Family violence may include physical maltreatment (slapping, hitting, and burning), sexual abuse (rape, incest, molestation), verbal abuse (threats, insults, harassment, denigration), and psychological or physical neglect.

During recent years a vigorous rights movement, particularly in the United States, has fought for the recognition and redress of the injustice, exploitation, and degradation against various groups victimized because of their race, gender, religion, sexual identity, handicap or age. The rights of children have received increasing attention. However, the focus has been mostly on "protection" rather than on "choice" rights.

The awareness and recognition of child abuse and neglect on the part of professionals and the general public have played an important role in the establishment and growth of the children's rights movement. Initially pediatric radiology and then other advances in medical science and practice during the second half of the twentieth century have provided a solid foundation for the definition, detection and diagnosis of physical child abuse and neglect. In other words, it became possible to establish through medical procedures that some physical injuries or damage suffered by children were not caused by accidents as maintained by their parents or caretakers, but rather by purposeful actions on the part of the adults. Nevertheless, many deaths of children due to abuse and neglect go undetected or are conveniently but wrongly ascribed to the sudden infant death syndrome (SIDS). Lack of funds, training, time, or interest lead to many children being buried every day with their true cause of death hidden or overlooked. In the tiniest of victims, even the best investigators miss clues. For example, shaking a baby to death can leave no obvious trace. This grim situation is particularly true in rural areas where the coroners are elected without regard to professional knowledge or training. Some are local funeral directors, janitors, bus drivers, or are functionally illiterate. Moreover, where neighborliness and familiarity are strong, like in small communities, investigators sometimes bypass child autopsies because they sympathize with a grieving family or cannot believe them capable of murder. Autopsy rates vary widely in the United States, ranging from 23 percent in Tennessee to 67 percent in Rhode Island. They are consistently the lowest in the South. At the same time reported child abuse fatalities are rising. In 1989, a record 1,237 children are known to have died in the United States from abuse, up 39 percent in four years. Experts are convinced that many more were murdered.

Since physical abuse and neglect can be more easily recognized, verified and quantified, they have received the most attention and elicited the most intervention. There is growing awareness, however, of the existence and devastating impact of psychological maltreatment, often described as emotional abuse and neglect or mental injury. The National Center on Child Abuse and Neglect (1981) defines emotional abuse as "verbal or emotional assault (e.g., threatening, belittling); close confinement (e.g., tying, locking in closet); other or unknown (e.g., attempted physical or sexual assault)." Emotional neglect is defined as "inadequate nurturance/affection (e.g., failure to thrive); knowingly 'permitted' maladaptive behavior (e.g., delinquency, serious drug or alcohol abuse); and other (e.g., refusal to allow needed remedial care for diagnosed emotional problem)." Others (Jacobsen, 1986) have identified the following concepts from which operational definitions can be developed: rejecting, degrading, terrorizing, isolating, corrupting, exploiting, and denying emotional responsiveness. In short, psychological maltreatment deprives children of their normal emotional development and "psychological rights."

Psychological maltreatment is the most difficult type of child abuse and neglect to deal with because of problems with definitions, standards of evidence, research methodologies and intervention strategies. The major handicap is that, unlike physical abuse and neglect where the evidence may be all too evident, psychological problems and scars are subtle and may not surface for a long time. Thus, unless it accompanies physical or sexual abuse, psychological mistreatment is rarely addressed by the courts or by child protective services. The increased involvement, awareness, and advocacy on the part of the child development specialists, psychologists, and educators will be essential to the recognition of child psychological maltreatment as a legitimate problem to be addressed just as the contributions of medical doctors, especially pediatricians, and of social workers were instrumental in establishing the existence of child physical abuse and neglect and in developing prevention and intervention models.

Child sexual abuse entails both physical and emotional abuse but most often the second over a protracted period of time. The so-called child sexual abuse accommodation syndrome consists of secrecy; helplessness; entrapment and accommodation; delayed, conflicting and unconvincing disclosure; and retraction. It has a long-term and often undiscovered negative impact on the affective and cognitive development of the victims particularly because the offenders are frequently adults or siblings in direct proximity to or in a legitimate relationship with them (e.g., as teacher, clergy, coach) over a long period of time.

It is these long-term, delayed consequences of child abuse and neglect that are currently attracting society's interest and concern, especially when they manifest themselves as criminal behaviors. The dramatic increase of violence in our society; the surge in juvenile delinquency; and the progressively younger age of people involved in prostitution or serious crimes are forcing society to become more aware of child abuse and neglect as the possible root cause of crime and to recognize that in many cases yesterday's victims are today's victimizers. A childhood devastated by abuse and neglect is increasingly being used as a defense in criminal cases, particularly capital ones.

All the chapters in this section of the book contribute significantly to our understanding of child abuse and neglect and of society's reaction to it. Esin Konanc, Sezen Zeytinoglu, and Seyda Kozcu in chapter 10 present the results of a 2-year investigation of child abuse and neglect cases tried in the criminal courts of Ankara, Istanbul, and Izmir, the three biggest cities in Turkey. The cases are analyzed in terms of the different types of child abuse and neglect, the characteristics of the victim (age, sex, handicaps) and of the perpetrators (age, sex, relationship with the victim), and the sentences imposed by the tribunals. The results are presented within the context of sociocultural factors in Turkey.

Irving Kaufman (chapter 11) discusses the long-term aftereffects of child abuse and incest experiences on adults who have been victimized as children and repressed their memories of that experience. Later in life the trauma can result in a wide range of physical and mental symptoms as well as affect their character structure. Although the dyad power–powerlessness is not the only major factor in abuse, it has a special role that is addressed in this chapter.

In chapter twelve, Carol Bryant argues that while child victimology is a multilevel problem requiring a comprehensive, multidimensional assessment and treatment, traditional treatment methodologies overlook, and thus do not treat, the human spirit. The basis of her transpersonal model is the recognition of the human spirit and the subsequent treatment of the whole person. This metaperspective is based upon Erickson's developmental goals, the yogic seven-chakra system, and an inclusive multilevel treatment approach.

Seth Kalichman, Mary Craig, and Diane Follingstad (chapter 13) focus on the mental health professionals' treatment of child abuse and why they may not report it, notwithstanding the fact that all states in the United States have enacted laws requiring human service professionals to report suspected child abuse.

Finally, in chapter 14, Michael Robin addresses the problem of false allegations of child abuse and their consequences. Being falsely accused of abuse is a source of personal shame and social stigmatization. Robin states that people who have been falsely accused of abuse often experience the same type of symptoms as those who have actually been abused, like trauma, betrayal, powerlessness, and stigmatization. He maintains that our ethical obligation to "above all else, do no harm" requires us to respond to those who suffer the trauma of false accusation.

# REFERENCES

Gelles, R. J., & Straus, M. (1979). Determinants of violence in the family: Toward a theoretical integration. In W. R. Burr et al. (Eds.), *Contemporary theories about the family* (vol. 1, pp. 549–581). New York: Free Press.

Jacobsen, J. J. (Ed.). (1986). *Psychiatric sequelae of child abuse*. Springfield, IL: C. C. Thomas.

National Center on Child Abuse and Neglect. (1981). *Executive summary: National study of the incidence and severity of child abuse and neglect*. Washington DC: National Center on Child Abuse and Neglect.

# 10

# Analysis of Child Abuse and Neglect Court Cases in Three Cities in Turkey

*Esin Konanç, Sezen Zeytinoğlu, and Seyda Kozcu*

---

In Turkey, the social, psychological, and legal aspects of the child abuse and neglect problem have recently started to be systematically studied. It is believed that preventive and therapeutic measures can be effective only if they are based on a proper understanding of the phenomenon.

Although wide-scale incidence and prevalence data about child abuse and neglect are not available yet, a number of studies have been (and are being) done, approaching different aspects of the problem. In a study (Günçe & Konanç-Onur, 1983) comparing abuse histories of juvenile delinquents with a group of matched controls, it was found that more delinquents had received physical punishment from their families. It was also found that both groups had experienced a great amount of labor exploitation.

Two other studies related to physical abuse were done in different regions of Turkey (Bilir, Ari, Atik, & Pinar, 1987; Zeytinoğlu & Kozcu, 1987). The common results of these studies showed that although many children were frequently punished through physical means, a majority of them did not receive physical injuries. Physically punished children were more often males and they were above the age of 4 years. The reason frequently given for physical punishment was the child's disobedience to the parents. It was also found that, of the people who had witnessed incidents of serious beatings, a majority tended to interfere personally but very few reported them to the officials.

At present, there are several ongoing research projects in various cities of Turkey related to other types of child abuse and neglect, such as emotional abuse, problems of street children, and exploitation of child labor.

Approaching the issue from a cultural-definitional perspective, Zeytinoğlu (1988) inquired about types of behaviors that are considered child abuse in Turkey by the professionals working in various sectors related to children or child abuse (e.g., professionals in health, social services, education, and law). It was found that emotional abuse (e.g., rejecting, threatening, giving a lower value to female children in some regions, expecting extreme obedience from children) and physical abuse were considered the major forms of child abuse in Turkey. Additionally, a considerable number of the responses were related to the exploitation of children in the labor force. The rest of the answers were related to educational neglect (35%), instigation of children to commit certain crimes (28%), physical neglect (24%), and sexual abuse (9%). When the professionals were asked about specific abuse incidents they had encountered in their careers, these categories of responses appeared in the same order.

In another study, Konanç-Onur (1988) has analyzed how the problem of child abuse and neglect was treated in the Turkish legal system. Because there is not a separate code regulating child abuse and neglect, she analyzed the provisions of all of the relevant acts in the legal system, namely, the Social Welfare and Child Protection Act, the Juvenile Court Act, the Labor Act, and the Penal Code. She concluded that the treatment of the problem in the legal system did not require a new arrangement. Rather, the main problem seemed to be implementation of these laws in the face of societal attitudes, traditions, and insufficiency of preventive and therapeutic institutions.

In the Turkish legal system, penal courts are one of the institutions that deal with the problem of child abuse and neglect. In the Turkish Penal Code (T.P.C.) many types of physical abuse, physical neglect, and sexual abuse are considered crimes. In this regard, it was believed that analyzing the child abuse and neglect cases referred to the penal courts might shed some light on efforts to identify and understand several aspects of the problem.

## THE CASES

In this study, child abuse and neglect cases brought to 39 penal courts in Istanbul, Ankara, and Izmir during 1985–1986 have been analyzed. The courts were selected from the regions of the cities in which each socioeconomic status was represented. The cases were selected on the basis of two criteria: the articles of the Turkish Penal Code and the age of the victims. In the articles of the Penal

Code the following acts related to sexual abuse, physical abuse and neglect are considered crimes: rape of children (T.P.C. 414), kidnapping of children (T.P.C. 431), murdering of children (T.P.C. 449, 450), infanticide for preserving one's reputation for chastity (T.P.C. 453), abandonment resulting in death or serious bodily or mental damage to children (T.P.C. 473), instigation of children to prostitution (T.P.C. 435), carnal abuse of children (T.P.C. 415), child neglect resulting in death or bodily or mental damage (T.P.C. 459), and the abuse of disciplinary or educational measures endangering the children's physical and psychological health (T.P.C. 473, 477).

The other criterion in selecting the cases was related to the age of the victims. Although 18 years was decided to be the upper age limit, in some cases, because of considerations related to sociocultural factors, the upper age limit was decreased to 15. Although legally all are defined as rape, some cases of rape of girls between the ages of 15 and 18 were not considered sexual abuse cases in our study. Detailed court investigations have shown that some of the incidents that we excluded were motivated by certain marriage traditions that, especially in the most recent decades, have turned into problems difficult to overcome by the concerned parties. For example, some sexual abuse incidents were seen to be initiated consensually and resulted in the marriage of the victim with the offender. It is a well-known marriage tradition in some regions of Turkey that the boy's family is expected to give money, goods, or land to the girl's family. Unfavorable economic factors may cause some couples to elope or start living together in order to avoid this obligation. When such incidents were referred to the courts, the boy was usually acquitted by the court provided that he legally married the girl. In this study, if the kidnapping or raping incidents were seen to have this motive, they were not treated as cases of child abuse.

The cases were analyzed with the purpose of identifying the ratios of different types of child abuse and neglect, characteristics of the victims (age, sex, handicap), characteristics of the offenders (sex, age, relation to the victim), characteristics of the people who referred the cases to the courts, and the sentences given by the courts.

## RESULTS

Of a total of 48,165 court cases that were screened, 701 (1.46%) were found to be related to child abuse and neglect. When these cases were categorized into different types of child abuse and neglect, it was seen that a majority (68.3%) was related to sexual abuse incidents such as rape, carnal abuse, or kidnapping for sexual reasons. Although 20.7% of the cases were related to incidents of negligence or carelessness resulting in the death of or injury to the children, physical abuse (7.6%), abandonment (2%), and instigation to prostitution (1.4%) were found to be rare.

## Characteristics of the Victims

The age and sex of the victims in various abuse and neglect categories are presented in Table 10.1. An interesting finding related to gender was found in sexual abuse cases: the number of male victims (45.93%) was very close to the number of female victims (54.07%). When gender and age were analyzed together, it was seen that more boys were sexually abused before the age of 7, and more girls were the victims of sexual abuse after 7. Another important finding related to sexual abuse was that more than half of the victims (55%) were below the age of 12.

In neglect cases, 53% of the victims were infants. This was an expected finding considering the fact that infancy is a period of life that necessitates a great deal of adult care and attention. It seems that the uneducated mothers of the lower socioeconomic class, overburdened with the care of many children in houses not having the necessary safety precautions, fail to prevent their infants from running into bizarre accidents. The finding that more male children (66%) were victims of neglect is more difficult to explain. One reason for this may be the expectation of and the freedom given to the boys to be more active. This may increase their chances of incurring accidents. Another reason may be the different values attributed to the sexes in Turkey. It is known that male children are given higher value than female children, especially in some segments of Turkey (Kağitçibaşi, 1982); therefore, it is possible that the neglect incidents with male victims might have been referred to the courts more often. The finding that a majority of the abandoned babies were female (79%) can also be explained by the different values given to male and female children in Turkey.

It was found that almost all of the victims of physical abuse were above the age of 4 and that their numbers increased with age. This finding, which parallels the results of other Turkish studies (e.g., Zeytinoğlu & Kozcu, 1987), is in contrast with many Western findings, which indicate that a majority of physical abuse victims are infants and young children. The reasons for this discrepancy may lie in the cultural differences in the kinds and degrees of parental expectations from and the discipline directed to infants and young children. Several research findings and professional experiences in Turkey have pointed out that parents generally have rather low expectations of proper performance from their infants and young children. These youngsters seem to be typically treated with care and indulgence without experiencing any appreciable amount of discipline. At this stage of parenthood, the parents' status in society seems to be affected not by the performance or competence of their children but merely by having children (and especially having male children). Additionally, mothers of infants generally seem to enjoy a wide range of social support from their families, relatives, and neighbors, and thus they may not experience a high level of stress as a result of caring for their infants. Further cross-cultural research is needed to understand the nature of these differences and their effects on the child abuse problem.

TABLE 10.1 Characteristics of Victims

| Types of child abuse and neglect | N | % | Sex | | | | Age | | | | | | | | | | |
|---|---|---|---|---|---|---|---|---|---|---|---|---|---|---|---|---|---|
| | | | M | % | F | % | 0-3 | % | 4-7 | % | 8-12 | % | 13-15 | % | 16-18 | % |
| Rape or carnal abuse | 479 | 68.33 | 220 | 45.93 | 259 | 54.07 | 9 | 1.88 | 102 | 21.29 | 150 | 31.32 | 185 | 38.62 | 33 | 6.89 |
| Neglect | 145 | 20.68 | 95 | 65.52 | 50 | 34.48 | 77 | 53.10 | 28 | 19.31 | 10 | 6.90 | 23 | 15.86 | 7 | 4.83 |
| Physical abuse | 53 | 7.56 | 23 | 43.4 | 30 | 56.6 | 2 | 3.77 | 9 | 16.98 | 10 | 18.87 | 17 | 32.1 | 15 | 28.3 |
| Abandonment | 14 | 2.00 | 3 | 21.43 | 11 | 78.57 | 11 | 78.57 | — | — | 3 | 21.43 | — | — | — | — |
| Instigation to prostitution | 10 | 1.43 | 0 | — | 10 | 100 | — | — | — | — | 1 | 10 | 3 | 30 | 6 | 60 |

## Characteristics of the Offenders

In this study, age, sex, relation to the victims, education, and occupation of the perpetrators were to be analyzed. However, in many cases, information about education and occupation was not present in the files. In a majority of the cases in which this information was available, the perpetrators were seen to be uneducated people of the lower socioeconomic class. The age and sex of the perpetrators in different abuse and neglect categories are presented in Table 10.2.

It was interesting to see that all of the physical abuse incidents (100%) and almost all of the sexual abuse incidents (99.58%) were committed by male offenders. The finding that 64% of offenders guilty of neglect were female was not surprising because women are the main caregivers of young children in Turkey.

Related to the age of the offenders, a very important finding appeared in sexual abuse incidents. Of all of the sexual abuse cases, one-third was found to be committed by adolescents. Fourteen percent of them were below the age of 15. Although the terms of imprisonment given to these young offenders are reduced by law, we believe that the definition of sexual abuse crimes in the Turkish legal system needs to be reconsidered in terms of the ages of the offenders and the age differences between the victims and the offenders.

Parallel to the previous findings in the literature, a majority of child abuse and neglect perpetrators (66%) were people who were known to the victims prior to the incidents (such as neighbors, friends, parents, relatives, employers). The finding that only 14% of the incidents were committed by the victims' parents may be a reflection of two different phenomena. Either many of the offenders in Turkey are people outside the nuclear family or more probably, intrafamily incidents are not often referred to the courts (because of societal attitudes toward the rights of the family institution).

## Characteristics of People Who Referred the Cases to the Courts

A majority (68%) of the abuse cases were referred to the courts by either one or both of the victim's parents and 14% by either the victims themselves, their friends, or their relatives. Eleven percent were referred by the police and only nine cases by people working in educational or health institutions. This result clearly shows that the article in the Penal Code that obligates government and health personnel to report child abuse cases is not applied in practice.

## Sanctions Applied to the Offenders

A majority of the parents who were accused of child negligence were either acquitted by the courts (70%) or their imprisonment was converted to fines (29%). This was also the pattern in the physical abuse cases. However, severe

TABLE 10.2 Characteristics of Perpetrators

| Types of child abuse and neglect | N | % | Sex | | | | Age | | | | | | | | |
|---|---|---|---|---|---|---|---|---|---|---|---|---|---|---|---|
| | | | M | % | F | % | 11-15 | % | 16-18 | % | 19-21 | % | 22-40 | % | 40- | % |
| Rape or carnal abuse | 479 | 68.33 | 477 | 99.58 | 2 | 0.42 | 65 | 13.57 | 92 | 19.21 | 72 | 15.03 | 149 | 31.11 | 101 | 21.09 |
| Neglect | 145 | 20.68 | 52 | 35.86 | 93 | 64.14 | 2 | 1.38 | 4 | 2.76 | 9 | 6.21 | 114 | 78.62 | 16 | 11.03 |
| Physical abuse | 53 | 7.56 | 53 | 100 | — | — | — | — | 7 | 13.2 | 5 | 9.43 | 29 | 54.72 | 12 | 22.64 |
| Abandonment | 14 | 2.00 | — | — | 14 | 100 | — | — | — | — | 2 | 14.29 | 12 | 85.71 | — | — |
| Instigation to prostitution | 10 | 1.43 | 5 | 50.00 | 5 | 50.00 | — | — | — | — | — | — | 5 | 50.00 | 5 | 50.00 |

imprisonment was imposed on sexual abusers. This punishment was not converted to fines. Here, it should be stressed that 65 (14%) of sexual abuse offenders were between the ages of 11 and 15, and 92 (19%) were between the ages of 16 and 18. Moreover, in most of these cases it was reported that the victim had given consent in the act. However, the Turkish Penal Code punishes the rape of children under 15 years of age by imprisonment for not less than 5 years (T.P.C. 414). Although this sentence is reduced if the offender is younger than 15, he is still imprisoned according to the penal code. Unfortunately, this situation has been found to start new abuse incidents for the young offenders. A study done in a children's correctional institution in Ankara showed that, of the children who had committed sexual crimes between the ages of 11 and 15, 72% had been imprisoned in the children's sections of the adult prisons. Many of these children reported that they were themselves subjected to various types of sexual abuse in these prisons (Günçe & Konanç-Onur, 1983).

## CONCLUSION

It should be stressed that the findings of this study should not be evaluated as representing all of the child abuse and neglect incidents that took place in the three cities during 1985 and 1986. It is believed that there are several factors that may have a bearing on whether or not a child abuse or neglect incident is referred to the courts. One factor seems to be related to the value systems of society. For example, the very high ratio of sexual abuse cases that were referred to the courts might be caused by the high value given to concepts such as chastity and virginity in Turkey. It is also possible that many physical abuse incidents, especially when committed by the victim's parents and even by teachers or employers, may not be referred to the courts because of toleration of such treatment as a disciplinary measure in some segments of society.

The apparent inadequency of the societal institutions to take proper action for the victims and the offenders of child abuse and neglect seems to be another factor that may affect the referral of such incidents to the courts. Especially in cases of child neglect and sometimes in cases of physical abuse, considerations of institutional inadequacies and the general socioeconomic levels of these families apply, and even the judges seem to refrain from taking the actions that the laws require. For example, results show that in a majority of the neglect incidents, the offenders were acquitted by the courts. In contrast, the offenders in sexual abuse cases were punished by several years of imprisonment, as required by the laws. The differential treatment of the cases by the courts constitutes another reason for the difference between the referral rates for abuse and neglect offenses.

In summary, it can be stated that the referrals to the penal courts and the decisions of the courts seem to be affected by an interplay of several socioeconomic and cultural factors, such as societal values, the socioeconomic levels of the people involved, and the insufficiency of the relevant institutions that treat the abused children and the abusers. It is believed that the development of effective mechanisms to combat the problem of child abuse and neglect should be based on a proper consideration of several factors, among which the ones mentioned above should have close attention. More research is certainly necessary to illuminate the individual and interactive effects of these factors in an all-encompassing manner.

# REFERENCES

Bilir, Ş., Ari, M., Atik, B., & Pinar, N. P. (1987). Konya, Kayseri ve Denizli il merkezlerinde 4–12 yaş grubu 4003 çocuk, çocuk üzerinde dövülme sikliği ve bununla ilgili bazi duygusal sorunlarin taranmasi. *Çocuk Gelişimi ve Eğitimi Dergist, 2,* 3–5.

Günçe, G., & Konanç-Onur, E. (1983). Child abuse in Turkey. *Child abuse and neglect: Research and innovation* (NATO, ASI series). Boston: Metinus Kijhoff.

Kağitçibaşi, Ç. (1982). The changing value of children in Turkey. *Current studies on the value of children,* Paper no. 60-E. East West Population Institute. Honolulu, HI.

Konanç-Onur, E. (1988). *Legal aspects of child abuse in Turkey.* Paper presented at the Fifth National Psychology Congress, Izmir, Turkey.

Zeytinoğlu, S., & Kozcu, Ş. (1987). *A study of physical child abuse in Turkey.* Paper presented at the First European Congress of Child Abuse and Neglect, Rhodes, Greece.

Zeytinoğlu, S. (1988). *Sağlik, Sosyal Hizmet, Hukuk ve Eğitim Alanlarinda Çalişanlarin Türkiye'de Çocuk İstismari ve İhmali ile İlgili Görüşleri.* Paper presented at the Fifth National Psychology Congress, Izmir, Turkey.

# 11

# Aftereffects of Childhood Abuse and Incest

*Irving Kaufman*

---

This chapter will discuss the long-term aftereffects of childhood abuse/neglect experiences on adults who have been victimized as children and have repressed their memories of that experience. Later in life the trauma can result in a wide range of physical and mental symptoms as well as affect character structure.

Included will be (1) a review of some representative examples of the studies of other researchers in this area of the aftereffects of abuse, (2) a brief description of the personality of the abuser-victimizers and the associated "family system," and (3) clinical examples. Although power–powerlessness is not the only major factor in abuse, it has a very special role, which will be addressed here. The in-depth case presentation includes the use of hypnosis on an adult patient who relived her incest experiences, which occurred when she was a 5-6-year-old child. It became clear how her later life-styles, anxiety, and physical symptoms relate to the recaptured memories of the actual assaults.

## LITERATURE

Reports on the incidence of physical and sexual abuse vary. Dr. Steel (1987) referred to over 2 million cases a year in the United States, which is considered a conservative estimate. Lukianowicz (1972) found incest to be an international problem, generally starting at a mean age of 11 and lasting for 6 months or longer, with similar family patterns. The definitions of incest according to Lloyd (1979) include a consideration of (a) the age of the victim, (b) whether sexual penetration occurred, (c) whether sexual contact occurred, and (d) the circumstances surrounding the episode.

Much of the literature on the aftereffects of abuse/incest considers the coincidence between the observable current problems or the lack thereof in the context of a history of such victimization. The question of the relationship between the two phenomena—symptoms and a history of abuse/incest—is assumed in a "post hoc, ergo propter hoc" way.

Emslie and Rosenfeld (1983) studied 65 hospitalized children and adolescents. About 37% of the nonpsychotic girls, 10% of the psychotic girls, and 8% of the boys had histories of incest. The authors concluded that social and psychological pathology serious enough to warrant hospitalization is not a simple effect of incest itself but a consequence of severe family disorganization and the resulting ego impairment. I agree with this conclusion.

These authors illustrate the problem of determining whether pathology such as phobias, psychoses, psychosomatic disorders, and the like are specifically related to incest or the incest itself is another expression or facet of the family pathology. Later in this chapter, some of the dimensions of symptom specificity will be outlined.

Husain and Chapel (1983) studied 437 adolescent girls admitted to a psychiatric hospital for emotional problems. About 14% reported incestuous experiences. As Kaufman (1987) also reported, the mean age of the first encounter was around 11 years. The major perpetrator was the father, but other family members, such as stepfathers, brothers, uncles, and grandfathers, were also involved. There was no clear connection in this study between the occurrence of the incest and the illness of the patient. The emphasis in this study was on how frequently one finds incest in the history of such patients.

Sedney and Brooks (1984) surveyed a nonclinical population of 300 college women. Thirteen percent of the subjects reported having had sex with a family member. The authors reviewed the long-term consequences of women who "did" and those who "did not" have childhood sexual experiences. The study revealed that of those who "did" 51% had sleep problems, 65% had depression, 59% had nervousness/anxiety, 30% had nightmares, and 41% had extreme tension. Among those who "did not" have early sexual experiences 29% had sleep problems, 41% had nervousness/anxiety, and 27% had nightmares. They concluded that women with early childhood sexual experiences had significantly more problems in the depression-anxiety areas and consulted doctors or were hospitalized 2½ times more often than those who did not have early childhood sexual experiences. Their sample was made as comparable as possible in reference to age, ethnic and religious background, and other variables. This study revealed the negative traumatic impact of early childhood abuse and sexual experience on later mental, emotional, and physical health.

Carmen, Rieker, and Mills (1984) studied 188 male and female inpatient psychiatric patients. Almost half of the patients had histories of physical and/or sexual abuse. In addition to the consequences of such victimization described above, these patients had difficulty in coping with aggression and anger, impaired self-esteem, and inability to trust. This study also emphasized the high frequency of alcoholism in the abusers. The experience of child abuse was also found to make the victims more vulnerable to later abuse by spouses or to rape than were nonabused individuals.

A study by Herman (1986) of 190 consecutive psychiatric outpatients revealed that one-third of the female patients and 29% of the male patients had been victimized. The majority of these patients were white, working class, urban, single persons in their 20s and 30s. Most of the victimization (88%) was intrafamilial. The diagnosis of borderline personality disorder and substance abuse disorder was particularly common in the violent female patients. Antisocial personality disorder, not psychosis, was more common in the males.

Male and female victims manage their aggression differently. Male victims tend to direct their anger outward; female victims, inward. The female patients in this sample also were frequently and repeatedly victimized, whereas the males directed their aggression outward, including 10% who later became sex offenders themselves. When females did become assaultive, they more frequently were psychotic and/or substance abusers.

The above research reveals a significant relationship between child abuse/ incest and later mental illness.

## PERSONALITY OF THE VICTIMIZERS

In separate chapters in the book *Father and Child*, Steele (1982) and Kaufman (1982) discuss the personality characteristics of parents who abuse their children physically and sexually and the "family systems" inherent in the victimization (Kaufman, Peck, and Tagiuri, 1959).

Steele (1982) discusses the following characteristics of the abusing fathers: (1) a poorly developed sense of identity and very low self-esteem overcompensated by exaggerated self-assurance and braggadocio, (2) a sense of emptiness associated with excessive neediness and dependency, (3) little trust that the world is safe and a "pseudoparanoid" attitude toward authorities, (4) difficulty in finding pleasure for themselves or their offspring, (5) expecting too much compliant behavior too soon from their children, (6) a strong belief in the value of punishment and a corresponding lack of empathy and resulting inability to respond sensitively and correctly to the child's needs and age-appropriate behavior, (7) misperception of the child as the bad part of the parent.

I am in total agreement with Dr. Steele's observations of this type of insensitive, narcissistic person demanding compliance with his or her own needs. There is a major similarity between the mothers and fathers. Although there is insensitivity to the child's needs, the thesis here is that the pathology is not just an absence of caring for or about the child's needs. It moves beyond that to an awareness of what will most hurt, frighten, and overpower the child. I also agree with Dr. Steele's observation that the parent is trying to cope with his or her feelings about having been abused and that the abusive family is a "system" needing a victim to abuse. There is a role reversal in which the child is viewed as a source of comfort and satisfaction of narcissistic needs.

I would add that children also are used by abusers as defenses against being overwhelmed by their own terror. The abusers may be male or a female. Galdston, (1965) agreeing with Kaufman stated that the abusers feel a terror inside and instill it into their victims. He sees this as a form of schizophrenia. Neither Herman (1986) nor Steele (1987) refer to this personality structure as a subtype of schizophrenia. Steele (1987b) also described these fathers as follows: (1) some are sociopaths who have trouble with the law; (2) some are mostly similar to the general cross-section of the population; (3) some have a poorly developed sense of identity with low self-esteem, compensated for by exaggerated self-assurance and braggadocio. Aside from the conceptualization of schizophrenia, Kaufman (1987) mostly agrees with Steele (1987c) on the personality of the abusing fathers.

Another interesting dimension in all kinds of abuse, especially sexual, is the choice of the age of the victim. Mohr, Turner, and Jerry (1964) pointed out that men choose to abuse children at an age relevant to their own developmental-level fixation.

## CLINICAL EXAMPLES

As the clinical examples will illustrate, power is one frequently occurring dimension of the physical abuse-incest gestalt. Even though the production of physical pain and stimulation that has sexual components are inherent elements in it, it is my belief that certain major core issues leading to this kind of abuse reside in power-dominance and in rendering the victim powerless. There is often a sense of relentless pursuit by the victimizer and attempts to entrap the victim.

In one case, the father would regularly enter the child's bedroom. Even though she knew "it" might occur, she would try to go to sleep and shut out that awareness. This shutting out occurs in many cases and in itself becomes a part of the ongoing pathological and self-preservative pattern. It enables many of the victims to function in enough areas of their lives so that the damage caused by the experience is not always overtly and explicitly manifest in all-encompassing ways.

A patient, age 40, came for marital counseling, having repressed all memory of her incestuous experiences. She had a feeling that in her marriage she had to submit to her husband's uncaring and often brutal authority and became extremely anxious when she was told that she failed to meet his requirements.

After several years of conventional therapy, including a great deal of support and ego building, it was agreed that she would be hypnotized. Under hypnosis, she recalled and relived an abusive sexual assault. She remembered herself as a little 5-6-year-old child lying in bed and faintly hearing a frightening sound. She covered her ears, saying in a little girl's voice, "I want to sleep—let me sleep," trying to shut out the terrifying experience she knew was about to happen again. Her father grabbed her and threw her around like a rag doll. In a dazed, overwhelmed, bruised state, she felt her legs lifting and spreading apart. Her father licked her genitals and then inserted his penis into her mouth to orgasm. During none of this time did she experience "sexual" sensations. Fear, terror, and helplessness dominated her. During the hypnotic session, she cried and feebly tried to call out. She recalled that during the day her father would pinch her or pull her hair so that she would be in a state of anxiety, thus reminding her that she was his prey awaiting his assault.

She felt that he wanted to totally take her over, day and night, and constantly remind her that she had no self that was not his to use. He had had a domineering and physically abusive mother. His need to overpower his daughter seemed to be related to his own terror of being so overwhelmed, first by his mother, then by his intense internal anxiety, which he felt could destroy him. By attacking his daughter, he used identification with the aggressor and repetition compulsion to try to master his fear.

This abusive behavior went on for years until the daughter reached an age where the father became afraid he would be discovered. Then his wife died rather mysteriously, and he married a woman with whom he could live out his pathological needs.

There are several issues to be considered in this not unusual case. A little child is the ideal target for this kind of pathological behavior. The developing child's first ego need for survival is to contain his or her anxiety; such containment normally would liberate the conflict-free energy needed to master the environment.

The overpowering sensory stimulation caused by a physical beating or by the discharge of the sexual excitement an adult feels has an enormous, overwhelming impact. The victimizer's goal is to create intense fear and anxiety. Freud (1905/1953) described in his early writings how the child who is sexually stimulated and cannot discharge his or her feelings sexually, as the adult does, experiences the assault as intense anxiety. This leaves the victim particularly prone to later development of anxiety symptoms such as phobias.

The estimates of the very large number of children who have been excessively stimulated by pain-producing beatings and sexual encounters could well be a major factor in the large number of cases in which anxiety is a major symptom.

The patient discussed above never was psychotic. Some patients, not the majority, can become psychotic because the overwhelming stimulation breaks down their stimulus barrier, and they have to retreat from facing their terrifying reality world.

Like a large number of abuse/incest victims, the patient had been a very constricted person. She is a woman of exceptional intellect, creative talent, and executive abilities. When she first came into therapy, most of these skills were not available to her. She was a typist and could also manage some filing and routine housework. Now she is an executive with a staff of several employees, owning and running her own business and home. She has begun to develop her creative interests in art, music, and literature and has become involved in community issues. She saved herself from becoming totally engulfed by walling off a large part of herself, including repressing conscious awareness of what she had experienced as a child. This repression enabled her to function marginally but also kept her in a cage of limited activities. She said she felt she was on a short tether and dared not venture too far into the "light." She had within her the imprint of the terrorizing experiences and the constant reminder that she was her father's possession. The price she would pay for her freedom was too threatening.

The therapy, including the hypnosis, was a mixed blessing. It has been necessary to help her to confront the demons and how they assaulted her through her father and could appear in her fantasy in any situation where she dared to be a separate self. The therapy has alternated between such horrendous reliving and other periods of consolidating and emerging, finding beauty in music, poetry, friendships, and a career—as well as repeatedly living through the horror in order to gain more freedom.

I have regularly found specific symptoms associated with the traumas inherent in the particular parent-child assault. One case of bulimia was found to be connected to oral sex experiences with the father. Not all cases of bulimia have this origin, but in this case it reflected the way the father forced his daughter to serve his need for sexual excitement and literally flooded her with sensations that left that imprint. In another case, the mother terrorized her son, not only by her brutality but also by threatening to cut off his penis if he touched himself. She prefaced her threats and abusive dominance of him with the following phrase: "By virtue of the authority invested in me as your mother, you will do what I say." He later became prey to bullies in high school and then developed severe phobias. He too would shut out contact and literally fall asleep during an altercation with his wife.

Another adult patient had seen many therapists for help with her anxieties, nightmares, pains in her chest, and shortness of breath. She became increasingly constricted and after high school was unable to continue her education or go to work. With the help of therapy, she recalled that when she was a child her father and mother treated her as a major incompetent. For example, they would not allow her to choose her clothing or put them on by herself long after such behavior was appropriate. She was in a state of panic, rage, and helplessness when she started therapy. Now she has begun to become increasingly autonomous. She gave up her promiscuity, alcohol, and drugs. She has discovered and is developing her artistic skills; she has married and runs her own home.

One of the problems in therapy is that it is necessary, whenever possible, to bring to consciousness the details of the interpersonal patterns of dominance and power that rendered the child helpless. This knowledge, while necessary, may not be sufficient to resolve the symptoms because the interpersonal component of power-powerlessness leaves the child and later the adult with no other functional way to manage the terror. There is often a paradoxical pattern in which the victim either reenacts the victimization (as did the first patient discussed above, who married a man who tried to "take her over" as her father did) or becomes the victimizer.

Either role can be so terrifying that the patient remains entrapped in his or her symptoms. The ruthless, relentless rage lying behind the victimization is not only terrifying to behold but also threatening as a potential solution for the desired freedom. Unless this area of being a potential victimizer is addressed and the associated guilt identified, the patient may remain stuck.

## CONCLUSION

Power as a dimension of normal human development is a complex issue. Initially, the infant is powerless, and the parent has to determine his needs and assume the executive functions necessary to preserve and sustain life. Later the child feels that he is in control. The child makes a noise, and the parents intervene to do whatever is necessary. The slightly older child, as Piaget (1930) said, feels that the universe is under his control, and the moon is moving in relation to him. When the child becomes aware of the parents' contribution to his life, the parent becomes overinvested with power, and then "my daddy can beat your daddy" kind of thinking develops. Ultimately, the growing child has to go through a period of disillusionment and turn against the parents in order to take on the autonomy and power needed to manage his own life. Somewhere in that sequence something can go wrong, especially if the individual does not have the appropriate object constancy and support needed to develop his own sense of self and feeling of power in relationship to a potentially overwhelming world.

It is these damaged individuals who remain terrified and need to terrify others, through abuse or incest or as terrorists, in order to feel able to function.

In future research into victimology, it will be necessary to devote time to a closer scrutiny of the normal sequence leading to an appropriate sense of power as well as to study what creates the pathology of a need to ward off the fear of powerlessness by making others feel helpless. This pathology is manifested in such ways as terrifying and abusing a child or a spouse or other people by becoming a terrorist.

# REFERENCES

Carmen, E., Rieker, P., and Mills, T. (1984). Victims of violence and psychiatric illness. *American Journal of Psychiatry, 141,* 378-383.

Emslie, G., & Rosenfeld, A. (1983). Incest reported by children and adolescents hospitalized for severe psychiatric problems. *American Journal of Psychiatry, 140,* 708-711.

Freud, S. (1953). Three essays of the theory of sexuality. *The standard edition of the complete psychological works of Sigmund Freud* (Vol. 7, pp. 135-230). London: Hogarth Press. (Original work published 1905)

Galdston, R. (1965). Observations on children who have been physically abused and their parents. *American Journal of Psychiatry, 122,* 440-444.

Herman, J. (1986). Histories of violence in an outpatient population: An exploratory study. *American Journal of Orthopsychiatry, 56*(1), 137-141.

Husain, A., & Chapel, J. (1983). History of incest in girls admitted to a psychiatric hospital. *American Journal of Psychiatry, 140,* 591-593.

Kaufman, I., Peck, A., & Tagiuri, C. (1954). The family constellation and overt incestuous relationships between father and daughter. *American Journal of Orthopsychiatry, 24*(2), 266-279.

Kaufman, I. (1982). Father-daughter incest. In Cath, S., Gurwitt, A., & Ross, J. (Eds.), *Father and child* (pp. 491-507). Boston: Little, Brown.

Kaufman, I. (1985). Child abuse—family victimology. *Victimology, 10:* 62-71.

Kaufman, I. (1987). Crime and its victims: Interactory roles of victim, victimizer and society. In E. Viano (Ed.), *Crime and its victims* (pp. 17-23). New York: Hemisphere.

Lloyd, D. (1979). Medical-legal aspects of sexual abuse. *Pediatric Annals, 8*(5), 88-99.

Lukianowicz, N. (1972). Incest: 1. Paternal incest. *British Journal of Psychiatry, 120,* 301-308.

Mohr, J. W., Turner, R. E., & Jerry, M. B. (1964). *Pedophilia and exhibitionism.* Toronto: Toronto University Press.

Piaget, J. (1930. *The child's conception of physical causality.* New York: Harcourt Brace.

Sedney, M., & Brooks, B. (1984). Factors associated with a history of childhood sexual experience in a nonclinical female population. *Journal of the American Academy of Child Psychiatry, 23*(2), 215-218.

Steele, B. (1982). Abusive fathers. In Cath, S., Gurwitt, A., & Ross, J. (Eds.), *Father and child* (pp. 481-490). Boston: Little, Brown.

# 12

# The Victimology of Children: A Transpersonal Conceptual Treatment Model

*Carol L. Bryant*

## INTRODUCTION

Child victimology is a multifaceted problem requiring a multilevel treatment approach (Anderson, 1979; Martin, 1976; Sgroi, 1982). A transpersonal paradigm provides a multilevel treatment model for victimized children. Violence in the lives of children often has a disabling impact upon their normal psychological, physiological, spiritual, and symbolic development. Therapists who treat child victims must take into consideration what Alice Miller (1981) has labeled "soul murder" (the killing of feelings). Since the victimized child is initially dependent upon the perpetrator and/or primary caretaker(s) for "whatever reality is assigned to the experience," the therapist's acceptance and validation of the child's reality (good and bad) is crucial to the healthy psychospiritual survival of the victim (Summit, 1983). A transpersonal paradigm attempts to validate, understand, and examine the relationships of the traumatizing experience(s) and treatment to facilitate and support growth beyond the ego (Walsh & Vaughan, 1980).

In this context, the term *transpersonal* refers to a perspective that acknowledges and learns from all treatment models. It does not seek to impose a new belief system but rather to see relationships between existing treatment modalities. More important, it acknowledges the existence of the human spirit (soul) and provides a context for the emotional shock of abuse. Trauma or abuse can also be a precursor to transpersonal experiences.

Shock is not just a psychological and physical response to trauma. Frequently, during a state of shock, the individual also may have a transpersonal experience. A transpersonal experience is an additional dimension of awareness that exists beyond what is considered one's "conditioned" normal consciousness ("that which is conscious of itself, thinks, has experience of and determines the outside world"; the image of oneself that includes "the boundary between instinctual and purposive processes," the ego boundary). In transpersonal experiences the ego boundaries dissolve, and awareness is extended beyond the ordinary confines of time and space (Grof, 1975).

Ego boundaries can also dissolve when trauma disturbs the mental stability of one's conditioned experience of oneself. As a result, the stable sense of a solid self is pierced through by a direct experience of existence beyond normal consciousness. For example, one's sense of time is altered where events may appear to be happening in slow motion; one's sense of self may be that of an observer watching a movie, rather than an active participant in a traumatic event; one's sense of physical location may be outside of the body, in midair; and one's sense of vision and hearing may come from another visual angle and auditory location other than one's eyes or ears. The senses are enhanced and extend beyond what is considered normal perception.

Dissolving ego boundaries to experience transcendental spiritual experiences is often a goal of many adults on spiritual paths. Bypassing both past mental conditioning and/or trauma, the adult on a spiritual path who engages in specific spiritual practices (e.g., meditation) is making a conscious decision to allow himself or herself a direct experience of expanded consciousness (transpersonal experiences).

However, for the child exposed to and/or victimized by violence there is no known frame of reference in which to place such an experience. As a result, the sequence of internalized emotional and physical responses that the child is aware of is overwhelming. Through the child's natural shock response to trauma, ego boundaries are attacked and collapsed. When consciousness is expanded beyond the normal range of time and space, a direct transpersonal experience along with body-mind split can occur. The conditioned sense of self regresses and/or withdraws. The child may become preverbal, and if not allowed to express feelings related to the trauma and/or integrate the added transpersonal experience, he or she may continue in a chronic shock state.

To the child, feelings of emotional abandonment translate into feelings of unworthiness, self-blame, shame, and fear of death. Left unsupported, the child's unconscious ego defenses take over, and soul murder occurs. The child thinks something is wrong with him or her. Depending upon the child's immediate support system, the traumatizing experience may be relegated to the realms of the unconscious. If so, predictable psychosomatic behaviors result. To compensate for feeling separated from the inner self (soul), a false self is erected to protect the child from internalized feelings of abandonment and shame. Because the child's ego is too immature to comprehend, resist, and/or contain the full impact of the violent experience, both the child's ego and soul may be traumatized or damaged. In cases of very young victimized children, in whom the ego is yet undifferentiated, the process of healthy ego development may be blocked and fragmented (Steele, 1983). This is particularly evident in extremely traumatic sexual abuse cases involving extreme trauma of very young children, who subsequently developed multipersonality disorders (Coons, 1986; Putnam, 1985).

A transpersonal focus supports the developmental level of the victim's ego. It recognizes the phenomenon of spirit and spiritual experiences related to body-mind splits and acknowledges the soul as a critical healing factor in the therapeutic process. It also assists the victim in developing a healthy ego to return to. Only then can the trauma and/or experience be integrated and the victim come to a unifying psychospiritual experience. In this unifying experience, the child is ultimately one with his or her environment, good or bad.

The experience of being "one with his or her environment" (Wilber, 1979) can be likened to the experience of the fetus in the mother's womb. Although the fetus is a separate entity with its own awareness, it is also intimately connected to the mother and her awareness. The therapeutic process can recreate this phenomenon in a safe therapeutic context. By descending into the depths of the psyche in what Dora Kalff (1980) calls "the free and protected space," the victimized child's body and mind polarities (good and evil) are eventually reconciled and tend to disappear.

## THE TRANSPERSONAL TREATMENT MODEL

The transpersonal treatment model is divided into seven sequential categories of increasing variability and complexity. Although treatment methodologies have been categorized for victims at each psychospiritual developmental level, the categories themselves represent a contradiction to therapists, challenging their most common assumptions about treatment. It is this writer's assumption that the soul's consciousness, as compared to Piaget's (1932, 1967, 1970, 1977) cognitive developmental stages of growth, also goes through specific developmental stages. The soul's developmental stages correspond to the opening of psychospiritual somatic centers, also identified as the yogic seven chakra centers (Rama, Ballentine, & Ajaya, 1976).

When a child loses trust in the world and feels emotionally abandoned by the adults who are most important to the child's protection and recovery, he or she is driven further into regression, alienation, powerlessness, shame, embarrassment, humiliation, self-blame, and self-hate (Summit, 1983). A psychospiritual somatic crisis, a body-mind split (Sanford, 1987) ensues, which leads victims into assuming disabling emotional responsibility for a situation in which they had no control. Energetically, such losses cause the lower chakras to contract. The ability to trust and the sense of survival are threatened (first chakra), autonomy and initiative are blocked (second chakra), thinking and sense of power are distorted (third chakra), and feelings are introjected—Alice Miller's (1981) "soul murder"—(fourth chakra). The four lower chakras are all impaired. The higher, unimpaired levels can be used to treat the lower, impaired levels. In therapy, this involves directly accessing the lower levels at their unique psychospiritual somatic cores where corrective psychoenergetic interventions are most effective. The seven levels of treatment, corresponding to chakra centers (Rama et al., 1976) and Erikson's (1963a, 1963b) augmented goals of developmental stages are as follows:

Level 1 of Treatment
   Crisis intervention, containment
     Chakra of survival and undifferentiation
     Erikson's goal: Resolution of the immediate crisis
     Establish trust versus mistrust

Level 2 of Treatment
   Structure building, psychotherapy
     Chakra of emotionality and sexual drives
     Erikson's goal: Autonomy versus shame and doubt

Level 3 of Treatment
   Uncovering techniques, psychoanalysis
     Chakra of cognition, power with self and others
     Erikson's goal: Identity and maintaining primary faithfulness to onself versus guilt and inferiority

Level 4 of Treatment
   Script analysis, humanistic therapy
     Chakra of compassion, family and community-mind
     Erikson's goal: Intimacy versus isolation

Level 5 of Treatment
   Existential therapy, introspection
     Chakra of concrete operational, self-esteem, and creative communication
     Erikson's goal: Generativity versus stagnation and recognition of spiritual integrity

Level 6 of Treatment
  Transpersonal therapy, spiritual practices
    Chakra of integration of formal operational and self-actualization, conceptual intuitive knowledge
    Erikson's goal: Integrity versus despair and integrity integration
Level 7 of Treatment
  None, transcendence
    Chakra of self-realization, actualization, and enlightenment
    Goal of consciousness: Spiritual integrity and wisdom

## Level 1: Crisis Intervention—First Chakra

The developmental task of Level 1 is based upon instinctual conditioning to stay alive. Assessment of lethality and safety factors must be taken into consideration. Stopping the victimization and crisis containment are the therapist's primary responsibilities at Level 1. This can be done through a multidisciplinary community approach, which may involve hospitalization or providing a safe shelter for the victim and incarceration, detoxification, or hospitalization for the perpetrator.

The first chakra is associated with the anal area and is identified as the body region where basic instinctual drives and feelings are located. It is the center of instinctual, reflexive behavior. It is also connected with feelings of fear, the instinct for self-preservation, attacking, being aggressive, and searching out prey. Signs of chakra impairment at this level are excessive fear (real and/or imagined), loss of locus of control, withdrawal, fantasy, or infantile behavior.

The victimized child must first feel safe and experience stability before he or she is ready for treatment. Treatment at this level is based on victims' relearning to identify themselves through their sensations and emotions. Creative, nondirective play that allows for safe emotional and tactile expression, such as sandplay therapy, is most effective at this stage and can be used as the primary medium on all levels of treatment to make contact with unconscious fragmented introjections. Once trust with the therapist and/or environment is established, therapy can move forward.

## Level 2: Structure Building—Second Chakra

The developmental function of this level is to build a sense of self and social network. During this developmental phase, the child, with prompting as well as on his or her own initiative, learns to control emotional impulses and redirect this energy to move toward autonomy and/or differentiation. Internal shifts generally occur through clients' experiences of their own mobility and emotionality in treatment. Attraction and repulsion issues are worked on through the bonding process with the therapist and in various therapeutic group settings.

This type of therapeutic relationship sets the stage for corrective interactions necessary to change previous introjected distortions.

Situated in the neighborhood of the generative organs, the second chakra is the center of sexuality, accepting self, energy, relationship to people, mobility, and emotionality. Because it is also the center of physical/emotional reactions and responses, the second chakra is considered the source of irresistible and impulsive sensate gratification needs. Addictions, along with dysfunctional addictive behaviors, such as battering, substance abuse, and child molestation, are chronic symptoms of second-level fixations. Second-level impairment is identified by numerous psychosomatic complaints. These include psychoneurotic reactions, behavior extremes, developmental lags, gastrointestinal dysfunctions, bedwetting, and nightmares. Interpersonal relationships are impaired.

With teens or adults, treatment would focus on the following structure-building techniques: journal writing, behavior modification, role playing, unisex peer support groups, and coed peer therapy groups. The therapist acts as a role model by setting limits and is often directive during treatment. Treatment tends to be psychotherapeutic, rather than psychoanalytic. The underlying treatment focuses on challenging dysfunctional thinking and assisting the ego in restructuring and/or incorporating a new set of reality-based psychospiritual ideas, attitudes, and beliefs.

At Level 2, indirect expressive projective methodologies using play therapy work best for victimized children. Some Level 2 therapeutic techniques include drawing; storytelling (age 4 and up); sand-play therapy (age 5 to 12); dollhouse play (ages 4 to 10); and puppet play. Adults who are fixated at this level can effectively participate in sand play and creative art therapy.

At the onset of moving from Level 1 to Level 2, the ego is still in crisis shock because the crime is too terrible for the child to talk about and/or remember. Therefore, play therapy may still follow the lead of the victim. The therapist's role is to provide the container for the child's feelings and to witness the child's reenactment of the crime through his or her symbolic play.

## Level 3: Uncovering Techniques—Third Chakra

The developmental focus at Level 3 is to move beyond the role confusion associated with the individual's multiple interpersonal relationships and to establish an identity based upon a sense of one's own personal will. In this context, will is defined as self-determination based upon personal desire, intention, and discretion. This process is the result of recognizing and acting upon individual initiative (power) to move toward change (organization of new concepts, attitudes, ideas, and beliefs) and becoming a conscious, active (industrious) participator in the development of one's own growth process. The ego is developing to the point where individual drives, including the sex drive, are subordinated to a person's goal or purpose in life. One begins to question authority, become self-governed, and think for oneself.

The third chakra is located over the solar plexus and is related to ego, will, emotional telepathy, vitality, and personal power. It is the center where truth (gut feelings) is psychosomatically experienced. Chakra impairment at this level is experienced as a split between thinking and feeling. One tends to think about how one might feel rather than have a direct experience of one's own repressed emotions. Victimized children experience body-mind splits (Sanford, 1987) at this level of chakra impairment. Other psychosomatic symptoms include stomach complaints, which are often side effects of suppressed rage, anger, resentment, and hostility.

Treatment focuses on uncovering the unconscious alienated aspects of self and subsequent reintegration with the central self. Therapeutic techniques may include psychoanalysis, psychophysiological release techniques (e.g., adults abused as children may be encouraged to kick a ball and to think of it as the abuser), revenge fantasies, Gestalt therapy, transactional analysis, and integrating-the-shadow aspect of Jungian therapy, along with physical forms of self-regulating disciplines (dance, yoga, Tai Chi, etc.). Bodywork may be very effective at the third stage of ego-somatic restructuring. It allows the client's consciousness to energetically connect with and release the body's contracted psychosomatic blocks. The environment and the role of the therapist plays a crucial role in this healing process. For perhaps the first time, the victim may experience physical touch in a safe, structured, contained, and caring atmosphere.

Play therapy can be expanded to include acting out against the crime within a contained "free and protected space." Very young children (ages 2 to 5) may assist in the life-size drawing of the perpetrator and be coached in aggressive play in which the drawing becomes the internalized abuser. The child learns to express blocked feelings about the abuser through interactive role modeling. The therapist's role may alternate between letting the client lead, being directive, and/or maintaining the role of coach.

## Level 4: Script Analysis—Fourth Chakra

The developmental task of Level 4 is for the ego-self to experience feelings. As the full range of repressed, disowned, and/or projected feelings are consciously reexperienced and assimilated, compassion develops for oneself and others. Viktor Frankl (1959) describes this stage as a "will to meaning." There is a strong desire to be authentic and genuine. At this stage, the victim consciously reexperiences a direct confrontation with existence. At this phase of development, the victim detects the deeper inner spiritual truths about humankind and integrates this on a personal level and in relationships.

The fourth chakra is located at the heart and considered the center of nurturance. The heart chakra is the container of all feelings of love and compassion, empathy, and concern for others. The solid sense of self ("I AM") experienced at Level 3 is the foundation for reaching out and experiencing connectedness with others at Level 4. When the fourth chakra is impaired, the child is self-protective, emotionally armored, suicidal, and withdrawn. There may also be symptoms of chest constriction and/or chest pain, which could extend up toward the throat.

Once stimulated, the heart chakra is transformed. Relationships take on a new quality. There is an interchange of playfulness between individuals. Creativity blossoms, and the family views their relationships with each other as interdependent.

The therapeutic focus moves to script analysis—family therapy, psychodrama, and other humanistic approaches. The role of the therapist in essence is neutral. This flexibility allows the therapist to alternate between psychodynamic probing, compassionate understanding, challenging family and sociocultural myths, coaching, role playing, symbolic mirroring, relabeling, family sculpting, and so on. Logotherapy is also helpful when making the transition from Level 4 to Level 5.

For example, a 14-year-old boy, residing in a residential treatment setting, learned that his mother had moved to another state without notifying him that she was leaving. Realizing that he had been abandoned, he lost control and became violently aggressive. He requested the staff to put him in leather wrist restraints so that he wouldn't hurt himself or punch holes in the walls. His therapist took hold of his clenched fist and asked him to feel the feelings he was experiencing there. He was angry. Then he was asked to trace the anger from his fist into his chest and experience what he felt there. At this point he felt his pain, identified his grief, and began to sob. He cried out that no child should have to feel this kind of heartbreak. Yet the pain was his experience, and he couldn't escape it. The empathic presence of his therapist allowed him to fully experience the depth and range of his feelings and gave him the support necessary to assimilate the trauma into his consciousness. Subsequently, he released his previously held distortions about himself and his relationship with his family and replaced them with an integrated reality of his situation without exhibiting further dysfunctional behavior.

## Level 5: Existential Therapy—Fifth Chakra

The developmental task of Level 5 is self-expression and communication through creativity. The goal of this stage is for the victimized child to identify with the creative principle before facing the reality of his or her victimization. By taking charge of the creative process in a therapeutic setting, the child begins to feel empowered and more alive. Rather than staying fixated with the psychospiritual somatic experience of a creation that is now viewed as "damaged goods," the child begins to identify with the role of creator.

The fifth chakra is located at the throat level. When the underlying feelings of pain resulting from the trauma are overlaid with feelings of anxiety, fear, and anger, the fifth chakra may be contracted but not impaired. Impairment of the fifth chakra is identified by chronic depression and stagnation.

A Level 5 therapeutic approach helps children release cathected energy of the preceding chakras. Therapy revolves around exploring symbolic content by observing the child's play in a variety of media. Through expressive nonverbal creative play, the child learns to call into being repressed energy (positive and negative) and develops both a sense of mastery and balance of divergent energies through a slow process of stimulation and assimilation. Because of this, it is useful to explore existential and transpersonal therapeutic techniques when the ego-self is damaged at the lower levels. The role of the therapist is to be caring, open, respectful, empathic, and trusting. An atmosphere in which the child feels free to be in honest agreement or disagreement with others is crucial.

Effective therapeutic approaches for adults at this level of dysfunction can begin with altering the environment. Walks in nature, near rivers, lakes, and the ocean, seem to be particularly healing. Eventually, clients may be encouraged to paint, draw, and write poetry and/or songs about their feelings. Again, much of the initial work focuses on integrating the symbolic content level with normal everyday experiences. The sense of belonging that began at Level 4 is expanded upon at Level 5. A successful outcome of treatment is the development of a personal integrated metaperspective about psychospiritual reality.

## Level 6: Transpersonal Therapy—Sixth Chakra

The developmental goal of Level 6 is cultivation of intuition as opposed to instinct. The individual is farsighted, intuitive, inspirational, and pragmatic. As a result of trauma at Level 6, both instinct and intuition may temporarily fuse. The child's ego is too immature to assimilate the crisis shock and therefore regresses. Crisis shock is the child's initial psychospiritual somatic reaction to trauma. Impairment may be organic (as the consequence of physical abuse) or nonorganic (as a result of prolonged chakra contraction).

The sixth chakra is located between the brows and is associated with the pineal and pituitary glands. It is considered the center of inward seeing or vision-logic (Wilber, 1980). Here the task is one of synthesizing metaperspectives, coordinating ideals, seeing truth at a glance, integrating concepts, and experiencing the self as a "whole" rather than a "hole."

It would be unusual for persons to seek treatment if they were functioning at this developmental level. However, those who have evolved to this stage are likely to engage in meditation, spiritual practices, transpersonal self-realization techniques, and perhaps follow the guidance of a spiritual teacher. Level 7 is enlightenment, which also transcends treatment as most therapists would understand it.

## PSYCHOSPIRITUAL SOMATIC DYNAMICS OF VICTIMIZATION

Crisis shock tends to be a precondition to the victimization of the child, whereas chronic shock tends to be the postcondition to child abuse. Crisis shock, the first phase of this process, is initially experienced as a mental and/or emotional death that occurs both immediately preceding the threatening experience and within the immediate time frame of the experience. Chronic shock, the second phase, is the exhibition of dysfunctional ego-defending/ego-dissolving behavior, which can involve the dissociative reactions that Kubler-Ross (1983) has described as "a slipping out of the cocoon," and somatic distress.

During the crisis shock phase, children experience being flooded by feelings of fear, hopelessness, helplessness, and terror. Children consciously aware of the violence and the victim's vulnerability initially defend against the nature of the catastrophic event through gearing their physical and emotional aspects to a survival mode. Adrenalin enters the system, leading to shortness of breath and rapid heartbeat (Kritsberg, 1985).

Although images of the violence become crystallized (fixated) in the child's memory, his or her emotional system shuts down, leading to "numbness" (Pynoos & Nader, 1987) and symptoms of crisis shock (crisis shock has also been described as an "out-of-body" experience by many victims of sexual abuse). In dysfunctional family systems, most adults "need to insulate themselves from the painful realities of childhood victimization," so victimized children are emotionally abandoned by the very adults who are most crucial to their protection (Summit, 1983). The child is left unable to talk about his or her feelings. As a function of this type of dilemma, what subsequently emerges is a typical behavior pattern of chronic shock symptoms that allow for the ongoing survival of the child (Summit, 1983).

## CONCLUSION

Child victims experience "a loss of innocence," feelings of helplessness, hopelessness, and despair. During an act of violence, most children's automatic responses may be twofold: attempt to help stop the crime and/or retreat emotionally. If immediately after the trauma they are unable to talk about their distress with someone who is emotionally nurturing and supportive, they may succumb to a predictable pattern of aberrant behavior (Mrazek & Mrazek, 1987).

Disassociation, self-blame, bedwetting, depression, withdrawal into fantasy, regression, somatic conditions, night terrors, and denial are some of the coping strategies children exhibit when dealing with tragedy. In this regressed state, the child may block out the memory of the trauma and relive the crime via symbolic play, dreams, and somatic dysfunctions. Unable to free themselves from internalized introjections, children continue to exhibit their distress through unique psychosomatic symptoms. Without external support during the crisis and immediately following the murder, the children in the aforementioned situation retreated further to a preverbal state and inability to talk about what had happened with a professional (Faller, 1984).

Chronic shock can subsequently damage the victimized child's ego and/or make it inaccessible during the initial stages of treatment. The child's sense of self continues to be distorted. This can also be compared to the child victims experiencing a quasi-death (Sanford, 1987). The therapist may have to bypass the damaged ego-self through the preverbal treatment modalities and begin with Level 5 or 6 therapeutic approach.

The transpersonal treatment model provides a metaperspective that includes all treatment modalities. The usefulness of this system is that it combines psychospiritual somatic realities in a practical developmental model, allowing for accurate diagnosis and treatment planning for victimized children.

## REFERENCES

Anderson, L. (1979). The character disordered family: A community treatment model for family sexual abuse. *American Journal of Orthopsychiatry, 49*, 436-444.

Coons, R. (1986). Child abuse and multiple personality disorder: Review of the literature and suggestions for treatment. *Child Abuse and Neglect, 10*, 455-462.

Erikson, E. (1963a). *Childhood and society.* New York: Norton.

Erikson, E. (1963b). *Insight and responsibility.* New York: Norton.

Faller, K. (1984). Is the child victim of sexual abuse telling the truth? *Child Abuse and Neglect, 8*, 473-481.

Frankl, V. (1959). *Man's search for meaning: An introduction to logotherapy.* Boston: Beacon Press.

Grof, S. (1975). *Realms of the human unconscious: Observations from LSD research.* New York: Viking Press.

Kalff, D. (1980). *Sandplay: A psychotherapy approach to the psyche.* Santa Monica, CA: Sigo Press.

Kritsberg, W. (1985). *The adult children of alcoholic syndrome.* Pompano Beach, FL: Health Communications.

Kubler-Ross, E. (1983). *On children and death.* New York: Macmillan.

Martin, H. (Ed.). (1976). *The abused child: A multidisciplinary approach to developmental issues and treatment.* Cambridge, MA: Ballinger.

Miller, A. (1981). *The drama of the gifted child.* New York: Basic Books.

Mrazek, P., & Mrazek, D. (1987). Resilience in child maltreatment victims. *Child Abuse and Neglect, 11*, 357-366.

Piaget, J. (1932). *The moral judgment of the child.* New York: Free Press.

Piaget, J. (1951). *Play, dreams and imitation in childhood*. New York: Norton.
Piaget, J. (1967). *Six psychological studies*. New York: Random House.
Piaget, J. (1970). *Structuralism*. New York: Basic Books.
Piaget, J. (1977). The essential Piaget. (H. Grugber & J. Voneche, Eds.) New York: Basic Books.
Putnam, F. W. (1985). Dissociation as a response to extreme trauma. In R. Kluft (Ed.), *Childhood antecedents of multiple personality* (pp. 65-97). Washington, DC: American Psychiatric Association.
Pynoos, R., & Nader, K. (1987). Children who witness assault. *Preventing Sexual Abuse* (Newsletter of the National Family Life Institute), 2(1), p. 8.
Rama, S., Ballentine, R., & Ajaya, S. (1976). *Yoga and psychotherapy: The Evolution of Consciousness*. Honesdale, PA: Himalayan Institute.
Sanford, L. (1987). Pervasive fears in victims of sexual abuse: A clinician's observations. *Preventing Sexual Abuse* (Newsletter of the National Family Life Education Network), 2(2), 1-3.
Sgroi, S. (1982). *Handbook of clinical intervention in child sexual abuse*. Lexington, MA: Lexington Books.
Steele, B. (1983). The effects of abuse and neglect on psychological development. In J. Call, E. Galenson, & R. Tyson (Eds.), *Frontiers of infant psychiatry* (Vol. 1, pp. 235-244). New York: Basic Books.
Summit, R. (1983). *The child sexual abuse accommodation syndrome*. Torrance, CA: Community Consultation Service, Harbor-UCLA Medical Center.
Walsh, R., & Vaughan, F. (1980). *Beyond ego: Transpersonal dimensions in psychology*. Los Angeles: J. P. Tarcher.
Wilber, K. (1979). *No Boundary*. Boulder, CO: Shambala Publications.
Wilber, K. (1980). *The Atman project*. Wheaton, IL: Theosophical Publishing House.

# 13

# Mental Health Professionals' Treatment of Child Abuse: Why Professionals May Not Report

*Seth C. Kalichman, Mary E. Craig, and Diane R. Follingstad*

---

Child abuse is a prevalent problem in the United States, with as many as one in five children being abused yearly (De Jong, Hervada, & Emmitt, 1983; Haugaard, 1986). The psychological effects of child abuse suggest that many victims and families seek mental health services (Browne & Finkelhor, 1986; Gelinas, 1983; Peters, 1976), and studies have indicated that a large percentage of mental health clients have been abused as children (Browne & Finkelhor, 1986; Courtois, 1979). Mental health professionals are therefore likely to have contact with victims of child abuse.

All states in the United States have enacted legislation that requires human service professionals to report suspected child abuse. Although these laws explicitly state that reporting suspected cases is mandatory, several studies have indicated that many professionals choose not to report cases of child abuse (James, Womack, & Stauss, 1978; McPherson & Garcia, 1983; Muehleman & Kimmons, 1981; Nightingale & Walker, 1986; Swoboda, Elwork, Sales, & Levine, 1978; Williams, Osborne, & Rappaport, 1985). Concerns about disrupting treatment processes and questions about the effectiveness of child protection agency interventions have been found to influence clinicians' tendency to report (James et al., 1978; Kalichman & Craig, 1990; Swoboda et al., 1978). Also, professional specialization, case-specific situational factors, and levels of training have been shown to influence reporting (Craig & Kalichman, 1986; Nightingale & Walker, 1986).

Kalichman & Craig (1990) found significant differences between licensed and nonlicensed professionals in reporting incestuous abuse. Twenty-five percent of the nonlicensed mental health professionals sampled from mental health centers indicated that they would do things other than to report incestuous abuse, whereas all of the licensed professionals surveyed stated that they would report such a case. Among nonlicensed clinicians, rationales for not reporting were similar to those in other studies in that they centered around the protection of the child/victim and feeling that treatment would be disrupted if they reported abuse.

The results of Kalichman and Craig's (1990) study are inconsistent with other studies of licensed professionals in the child abuse reporting literature. Swoboda et al. (1978) indicated that many licensed psychologists were unlikely to report a hypothetical case of child abuse, whereas Kalichman and Craig found complete compliance with reporting laws by licensed clinicians. Differences between these results may be explained by differences in sampling procedures, measurement instruments or both. Although Swoboda et al. and others (James et al., 1978; Nightingale & Walker, 1986) have sampled clinicians through professional associations, Kalichman and Craig sampled subjects from mental health centers, where clinicians may have been held responsible for reporting by agency policies as well as the law.

With regard to measurement instruments, Swoboda et al. (1978) utilized cases described in vignettes, and Kalichman and Craig (1990) developed a questionnaire that specifically investigated incestuous abuse as opposed to Swoboda's use of child abuse in a general sense. Because of these differences, comparisons between studies of child abuse reporting have been difficult to interpret.

Another dimension of professional treatment of child abuse is attribution of responsibility. Kalichman and Craig (1990) found that subjects attributed 20% of the responsibility for father–daughter incest to mothers in incestuous families. Although mothers in abusive families are of interest in both the treatment and understanding of abuse, few studies have investigated the mothers as a source of attributed responsibility. Kalichman and Craig also indicated that the responsibility attributed to daughter/victims was significantly greater for adolescent victims (8%) than for child victims (2%). These results appear important in light of the relationships found between responsibility attribution and treatment of clinical populations (Alexander, 1980).

In another study of responsibility attribution, Doughty and Schneider (1987) found that clinicians sampled from mental health centers attributed significantly less blame to incest victims and fathers than did a sample of college students. Doughty and Schneider's results suggest that the attitudes of clinicians may differ from those of the general population. Although Kalichman and Craig's (1990) and Doughty and Schneider's findings have potential clinical implications, these results are specific to incestuous abuse and may not necessarily generalize to other types of child abuse.

There are a number of potential factors that may affect clinical decisions to report cases of child abuse and responsibility attribution. For example, the age of the victim may influence responsibility attribution and reporting. Older victims may be held more responsible, as indicated by Kalichman and Craig (1990) and may also be less likely to be reported. The type of abuse that is suspected may play a role in decisions to report (Nightingale & Walker, 1986). Finally, how the child describes her situation and behaves during an interview may have substantial impact on how clinicians respond (Pierce & Pierce, 1985).

The purpose of the present study was to investigate professionals' tendency to report and their patterns of attribution of responsibility for child abuse as a function of victim age, type of abuse, and the victim's reactions to discussing the abuse. Subjects were sampled from both clinical settings and professional associations to allow for preliminary comparisons between these two sampling procedures.

## METHOD

### Subjects

The subjects were 103 clinicians working within three community mental health centers in Florida, 16 nurses who attended a national conference for student nurses, and 25 psychologists who attended a state psychological association meeting (see Table 13.1). All subjects provide clinical services and have had at least one clinical experience involving child abuse. Subjects were randomly represented across experimental conditions.

### Procedure

Each participant completed an experimentally controlled vignette with three systematically manipulated variables (Alexander & Becker, 1978): the victim's age (5, 10, or 15 years old); the type of suspected abuse, operationalized as a teacher's report of either suspected physical or sexual abuse; the child's reaction

TABLE 13.1 Percentages of Educational Backgrounds among Participants (N = 144)

| Professional group | Educational background | | | |
|---|---|---|---|---|
| | Bachelor's level | Master's level | PhD Psychologists | Psychiatrists |
| Nursing association | 81% | 19% | 0 | 0 |
| Psychological association | 0 | 52% | 48% | 0 |
| Mental health clinicians | 50% | 40% | 7% | 3% |
| Total | 44% | 40% | 13% | 3% |

when questioned about her relationship with her father; whether the child described the abuse in detail during an interview or cried and refused to discuss the suspected abuse. The independent variables were the only aspects of the vignettes changed across conditions to control for possible confounding (Alexander & Becker, 1978). Subjects were randomly assigned to one of 12 vignette conditions within a 3 × 2 × 2 factorial design. The case vignette read as follows:

Amy is a [5/10/15]-year-old girl who lives at home with her mother, father, and younger brother. She has been referred to see you by her physical education teacher. The teacher is concerned because Amy became upset and said that she did not want to be touched when a teacher patted her on the back, and she has also been refusing to change into her swimsuit for swimming class. Her teacher tells you that her concern is over the possibility of Amy being [physically/sexually abused] at home.

Upon first meeting her you notice that Amy appears neat and clean and seems to be in reasonably good health. When you begin to ask Amy about her home life, specifically about her relationship with her father, Amy begins to cry and seems upset. (However, she opens up to you and reveals a full and detailed description of her home situation in which her father sexually abuses her.)

Subjects rated their tendency to report the abuse and how confident they were that abuse was occurring on a 6-point Likert scale. Subjects were also asked to identify factors that they believed were most influential in their decision to report. Assignments of relative percentages of responsibility were then made to the father/offender, mother/spouse, daughter/victim, and society (Alexander, 1980).

## RESULTS

Participants' tendency to report and confidence responses were converted to categorical variables. Converted responses reflect a tendency either to report or not to report and either a high or low degree of confidence that abuse is occurring. Nonparametric analyses indicated that confidence level and tendency to report did not differ between samples. Subjects were therefore combined for further analyses.

## Tendency to Report

Eighty-one percent of the clinicians stated that they would tend to report the presented case of child abuse. Victim age and type of abuse did not significantly affect tendency to report. However, tendency to report was significantly affected by the descriptions of the child's reactions ($\chi^2 = 22.42, p <.001$). Subjects in the condition where the child cried and refused to talk were less likely to report than in the condition where she described the abuse (see Table 13.2).

## Confidence in Abuse

Results indicated that victim age and type of abuse did not significantly affect subjects' degree of confidence that abuse was occurring. There was, however, a significant effect of the child's reactions during the interview on the professionals' confidence that abuse was occurring ($\chi^2 = 6.47, p <.01$). The child who cried during the interview was less likely to be viewed as a victim of abuse than the child who described the abusive situation. In addition, 84% of the subjects indicated that the child's reactions during the interview were more important in determining their level of confidence than the teacher's suspicion of abuse or the child's appearance.

## Resorting and Confidence

Subjects' confidence that abuse occurred was significantly associated with their tendency to report ($\chi^2 = 26.28, p <.001$). All subjects strongly suspecting abuse responded that they would report the case. Of the subjects who would report, 56% indicated that the factor most influential in their decision was their legal obligation to report. In contrast, 81% of the subjects not reporting indicated that the factor most influential in their decision not to report was the lack of confidence they had that abuse was occurring.

TABLE 13.2 Tendency to Report as a Function of Victim Reactions

| Tendency to report | Victim reactions | |
|---|---|---|
| | Child cries during interview | Child describes the situation |
| Would report case | 51 (66%) | 66 (99%) |
| Would not report case | 26 (44%) | 1 (1%) |

TABLE 13.3 Tendency to Report as a Function of Educational Background

| Tendency to report | Education | | | |
|---|---|---|---|---|
| | Bachelor's level | Master's level | PhD Psychologists | Psychiatrists |
| Would report case | 61 (95%) | 41 (72%) | 13 (68%) | 2 (50%) |
| Would not report case | 3 (5%) | 16 (28%) | 6 (32%) | 2 (50%) |

## Clinician Characteristics and Reporting

The relationship between education and reporting was investigated. Table 13.3 presents the relationship between participants' tendency to report and educational background. Of the professionals not reporting, 19 were bachelor's- and master's-level counselors, 6 were doctoral-level psychologists, and 2 were psychiatrists. Significance tests were not performed due to disproportionate cell sizes.

## Attribution of Responsibility

Preliminary analyses indicated that there were no significant differences in attribution of responsibility to the father/offender, daughter/victim, mother/spouse, and society between the professionals sampled from mental health centers and those from professional associations. Participants were therefore combined for further analyses.

A multivariate analysis of variance indicated that there were no significant effects of victim age and victim reactions on responsibility attribution. However, there was a significant effect of the type of abuse on responsibility attributed to the father ($F = 3.68, p < .05$). Sexually abusive fathers were blamed significantly more than physically abusive fathers. Also, mothers of physically abused daughters were blamed significantly more than mothers of sexually abused daughters ($F = 5.79, p < .02$; see Table 13.4).

TABLE 13.4 Mean Percentages of Responsibility Attribution as a Function of Type of Abuse

| Type of abuse | Source of Responsibility | | | |
|---|---|---|---|---|
| | Father (%) | Mother (%) | Daughter/victim (%) | Society (%) |
| Sexual abuse | 69 | 17 | 3 | 11 |
| Physical abuse | 63 | 33 | 3 | 1 |
| Total | 66 | 25 | 3 | 6 |

The relationship between levels of responsibility attribution and reporting was investigated by regression analyses, with percentages of responsibility entered as the predictor variables and tendency to report as the criterion. There were no significant relationships indicated.

## CONCLUSIONS

Results of this study replicate those of previous investigations of mental health professionals' tendency to report and attitudes toward child abuse (Kalichman & Craig, 1990). Clinicians likely to have contact with victims of child abuse and their families tend to report cases of suspected abuse, but decisions to report are affected by situational factors. Clinicians in this study were less likely to report when they felt uncertain that abuse was occurring. The victim's reactions to discussing the abuse had the strongest impact on clinicians' confidence that abuse was occurring and on their tendency to report. Because many children are likely to react to questions about their abuse with signs of fear and emotional distress (Pierce & Pierce, 1985), confidence that abuse was occurring should have been the same across conditions, and each case should have been reported.

There are several reasons clinicians may fail to report child abuse when they feel uncertain that abuse is occurring. For example, they may be concerned about making false accusations toward the fathers in these situations. Concerns over errors in reporting may include beliefs that one will be held liable for misjudging the occurrence of abuse, despite the fact that statutes specify that persons mandated to report are immune from liability for filing an unsubstantiated report. Further research is needed to clarify the factors contributing to mental health professionals' decisions to report, such as the effects of agency policy and professional training.

As indicated in previous studies (Craig & Kalichman, 1986; Kalichman & Craig, 1990; Nightingale & Walker, 1986), the importance of training clinicians in identifying and reporting cases of child abuse is suggested. The effects of educational level on reporting indicated by Kalichman and Craig (1990) were replicated in this study; professionals with more advanced degrees were more likely to report. Of particular interest are the 12% of subjects not reporting the abuse but stating that they were relatively confident that abuse was occurring. Contrary to previous research (James et al., 1978; Muehleman & Kimmons, 1981; Swoboda et al., 1978), clinicians in this study were not especially concerned over the effects that reporting might have on the therapeutic relationship. Subjects not reporting were more concerned with the accuracy of their perception of abuse. Continuing education and workshops are needed for professionals, focusing on identification of abuse, signs of abuse as they are related to developmental levels of children, and the realistic outcomes that may result from reporting.

Levels of responsibility attributed to the father were replicated in this study, and contrary to earlier findings (Craig & Kalichman, 1986), there was no effect of victim age. Fathers were blamed more, however, for sexual abuse than for physical abuse. This result may be due to professionals' perceiving sexual abuse as a more serious type of abuse and therefore blaming the sexually abusive father more for his actions. Although the differences between types of abuse were statistically significant for father responsibility, the actual difference between means was only slight, suggesting that clinical implications may be limited.

Results also replicated relatively high levels of responsibility attributed to mothers in abusive families (Kalichman & Craig, 1990). Interestingly, there were no effects of victim age on mother responsibility. Mothers were perceived as being equally responsible for their 5-, 10-, and 15-year-old daughters' abuse. However, mothers were blamed significantly more in suspected physically abusive situations than in suspected sexually abusive cases. One possible reason for this difference may be that sexual abuse is often viewed as a more covert process in a family and may occur without physical evidence that would be apparent to mothers. Given the treatment implications of responsibility attribution (Alexander, 1980; Schneider, Hastorf, & Ellsworth, 1979), further research is needed to clarify the mother's perceived role in father–daughter abusive families. Also, the roles of fathers in families where the mother is the offender deserves careful attention.

This study did not replicate Kalichman and Craig's (1990) finding that victims were blamed more as adolescents than as children. It is possible that this discrepancy may be an artifact of measurement procedures. Kalichman and Craig utilized a within-subjects manipulation of victim age. Subjects judged relative levels of responsibility for a case of abuse when the victim was described as a child, an adolescent, or of no specific age. In contrast, the present results were based on a single case, in which subjects assigned responsibility to a victim of one particular age. The effect of victim age was therefore analyzed between subjects. Clinically, the present situation appears more meaningful, in that clinicians are likely to approach cases based on the situational factors unique to a case rather than relative to other possible situational factors. However, Kalichman and Craig's results may have been tapping some level of clinical judgment not measured in the present instrument. Future research is needed to determine the clinical implications of each of these methods.

Levels of responsibility attribution were not significantly related to tendency to report. While reporting is only one of many treatment problems involved in child abuse, it is one that has direct implications for perpetrators of abuse. This aspect of reporting provided the basis for our prediction that patterns of responsibility attribution may have influenced reporting. The potential treatment effects of responsibility attribution in cases of child abuse, therefore, remain unclear. Results indicating high levels of responsibility attribution and changes in attribution over different conditions may have important treatment implications, but future research is needed to clarify these relationships.

Finally, future research should investigate the potential effects of other situational factors and types of abuse that may affect professionals' decisions to report (Melton & Corson, 1987; Nightingale & Walker, 1986). The use of controlled vignettes in this research provides valuable information by allowing researchers to manipulate variables systematically (Alexander, 1980; Alexander & Becker, 1978). However, there is also a need for more ecologically valid studies to identify factors related to reporting as they are found in clinical settings. As more information about the factors that may affect professionals' reporting and responsibility attribution becomes available, it will be important to determine their clinical implications as well.

## ACKNOWLEDGMENTS

The authors wish to thank Tony Broskowski, Northside Community Mental Health Center, Hillsborough Community Mental Health Center, Broward County Mental Health Division, The National Student Nurses Association, The South Carolina Psychological Association, Rita Kalichman, and Syd Kalichman for their support in this study. This research was supported by a fellowship from the University of South Carolina.

## REFERENCES

Alexander, C. (1980). The responsible victim: Nurses' perceptions of victims of rape. *Journal of Health and Social Behavior, 21*, 22-23.

Alexander, C., & Becker, H. (1978). The use of vignettes in survey research. *Public Opinion Quarterly, 42*, 93-104.

Browne, A., & Finkelhor, D. (1986). Impact of child sexual abuse: A review of the research. *Psychological Bulletin, 99*, 66-77.

Craig, M., & Kalichman, S. (1986). *The mental health professional and the incest victim: Who we blame and when we report*. Paper presented at the meeting of the Southeastern Psychological Association, Orlando, FL.

Courtois, C. A. (1979). The incest experience and its aftermath. *Victimology, 4*, 337-347.

De Jong, A. R., Hervada, A. R., & Emmitt, G. A. (1983). Epidemiologic variations in childhood sexual abuse. *Child Abuse and Neglect, 7*, 155-162.

Doughty, D., & Schneider, H. (1987). *Attribution of blame in incest among mental health professionals*. Paper presented at the meeting of the Southeastern Psychological Association, Atlanta.

Gelinas, D. J. (1983). The persisting negative effects of incest. *Psychiatry, 46*, 312-332.

Haugaard, J. J. (1986). *Defining a victim group: The effects on child sexual abuse research*. Paper presented at the meeting of the American Psychological Association, Washington, DC.

James, J., Womack, W., & Stauss, F. (1978). Physician reporting of sexual abuse of children. *Journal of the American Medical Association, 240,* 1145-1146.

Kalichman, S., & Craig, M. (1990). Victims of incestuous abuse: Mental health professionals' attitudes and tendency to report. In E. Viano (Ed.), *The Victimology Handbook.* New York: Garland.

McPherson, K., & Garcia, L. (1983). Effects of social class and familiarity on pediatricians' responses to child abuse. *Child Welfare, 62,* 307-313.

Melton, G., & Corson, J. (1987). Psychological maltreatment and the schools: Problems of law and professional responsibility. *School Psychology Review, 16,* 188-194.

Muehleman, T., & Kimmons, C. (1981). Psychologists' views on child abuse reporting, confidentiality, life, and the law: An exploratory study. *Professional Psychology, 12,* 631-637.

Nightingale, N., & Walker, E. (1986). Identification and reporting of child maltreatment by Head Start personnel: Attitudes and experiences *Child Abuse and Neglect, 10,* 191-199.

Peters, J. J. (1976). Children who are victims of abuse and the psychology of offenders. *American Journal of Psychotherapy, 30,* 398-421.

Pierce, R., & Pierce, L. (1985). Analysis of sexual abuse hotline reports. *Child Abuse and Neglect, 9,* 37-45.

Schneider, D. J., Hastorf, A., & Ellsworth, P. (1979). *Person perception.* Reading, MA: Addison-Wesley.

Swoboda, J., Elwork, A., Sales, B. D., & Levine, D. (1978). Knowledge of and compliance with privileged communication and child-abuse-reporting laws. *Professional Psychology, 9,* 448-458.

Williams, H., Osborne, Y., & Rappaport, N. (1985). *Child abuse reporting law: Differences among professional groups in tendency to report and knowledge of the law.* Paper presented at the meeting of the Southeastern Psychological Association, Atlanta.

# 14

# The Trauma of False Allegations of Sexual Abuse

*Michael Robin*

---

In the early 1960s, all of the states in the United States passed child abuse reporting laws. These laws have clearly played a positive role in protecting abused and neglected children from unnecessary suffering. The problem with these laws, however, is that they tend to be so sweeping and vague that they may encourage the reporting of situations that represent marginal or inappropriate child care rather than actual abuse (Daro, 1988). Or they may encourage false or malicious reporting of altogether innocent persons. Because existing standards for case reporting and case assessment are so ill-defined, there is an increased risk of unwarranted intervention in family life (Besharov, 1985).

So far, little consideration has been given to the potential negative effects a child abuse investigation might have on family relationships. As Faller (1985) has written,

> ... the protective service investigation itself can increase the level of stress in the home and place the child at greater risk than before. Thus, the system we have instituted to enhance our ability to identify children and intervene to help them may have very negative consequences for parents and their children. These consequences impact not only on the guilty but the innocent as well. (p. 65)

## SEXUAL ABUSE INVESTIGATIONS

Historically, children's reports of sexual abuse have been discounted. It was believed that children made unreliable witnesses because of their difficulties in distinguishing real events from what they may have imagined, and because of their propensity to fantasize sexual events (King & Yuille, 1987). By the early 1970's, the pendulum shifted, and there has since been a significant increase in public awareness about the reality of child sexual abuse. Public sensibilities are offended by the large numbers of children who are said to be sexually abused. What is particularly disturbing is that children are being abused, in many instances by their own parents, or by other trusted members of the community such as teachers, doctors, and even clergymen.

It is widely assumed that the sexual abuse that has been identified so far is only the "tip of the iceberg." This metaphor suggests that sexual abuse is greatly underreported and may be much more widespread than people realize. As public awareness of child sexual abuse has increased, there has been a large increase in case reporting to child protective service agencies which has helped contribute to a crisis atmosphere. According to Schuman (1984), there is "such a degree of sensitivity or outrage about possible child abuse that a presumption exists that such abuse has occurred whenever it is alleged" (p. 1).

## CHILDREN'S STATEMENTS

From the early belief that children were incapable of giving an honest and accurate accounting of a sexual abuse experience, contemporary child abuse professionals have created an equally untenable hypothesis, that "children don't lie about sexual abuse." According to Berliner and Barbieri (1984),

> There is little or no evidence indicating that children's reports are unreliable, and none at all to support the fear that children often make false accusations of sexual assault or misunderstand innocent behavior by adults . . . not a single study has ever found false accusations of sexual assault a plausible interpretation of a substantial portion of cases. (p. 127)

Faller (1984) likewise states, "We know that children do not make up stories asserting that they have been sexually molested. It is not in their interest to do so. Clinicians and researchers in the field of sexual abuse are in agreement that false allegations by children are extremely rare" (p. 475). The notion that "children don't lie about sexual abuse" is based, according to Summit, on the assumption that most children lack the motivation and personal experience required to make a false allegation (Summit, 1983).

Terr (1986) says that it is naive to believe that false reports of child abuse are rare. Although it may be true that children do not frequently lie about sexual abuse, they will, at times, make "false" reports (Goodman, 1984). The trouble with the idea that "children don't lie about sexual abuse" is that it confuses the distinction between truth and truthfulness (Bok, 1978). Even though a child may not be lying, it does not mean that they are necessarily telling the truth. Many children give inconsistent accounts of abuse. Their reports frequently lack clarity and often contain omissions, distortions, and misperceptions of events (deYoung, 1986). In addition, sometimes children are unduly influenced by third parties on statements about abuse. It has been noted that children in custody disputes have, on occasion, been "coached" on statements about abuse (Yates & Musty, 1988; Green, 1986).

# DENIAL OF FALSE ALLEGATIONS

Many of those who work in the child protection field have considerable difficulty accepting the possibility that some alleged offenders are innocent, that some children give inaccurate reports of abuse, and that some "significant" (i.e., meaningful) percentage of child abuse reports involve "false" allegations. Jones and McGraw (1987) say that false allegations can only be recognized and responded to effectively, however, if the clinician and the public considers such a situation to be a possibility.

Gardner (1987) has suggested that the reluctance of many child protection professionals to accept the possibility of a false allegation is rooted in certain psychological factors that are related to their choice of careers. Gardner has written that a large number of those who work in the child sexual abuse field have been victimized themselves. Many of these persons are attracted to the abuse field because it provides them opportunities to work through earlier traumas. Gardner says that many of these workers use their experience in healthy ways, much to the benefit of their clients. However, there are some who maintain unresolved anger and resentment toward the original abuser, and fear that to acknowledge that some alleged offenders are innocent would call into question the authenticity of their own experience.

It seems that the reluctance to accept the possibility that a "significant" percentage of cases involve false allegations is also based, in part, on the fear that to give attention to false allegations might undermine public support for abused children and the child protective system. What is not fully appreciated, however, is the extent to which children are harmed by false allegations. Children can be harmed when they have to go through extensive medical and psychological examinations for abuse that did not occur. They also suffer when family relationships are strained or disrupted and when they are unnecessarily placed in foster care (Benedek & Schetky, 1987b).

## SACRIFICE OF CHILDREN

Despite the rhetoric that our society is "child-centered," the 1980s began a period of major cutbacks in programs specifically designed to meet the needs of children. Programs that were cut included Aid to Families with Dependent Children, child care, food programs, child abuse programs and many others that affect the well-being of children. These program cuts resulted in considerable hardship for children (Edelman, 1987). Publications at this time began to wonder if there was "an unconscious national conspiracy against children" (Rothenberg, 1980) or "do we really hate our children?" (Pogrebin, 1983). According to Scheper-Hughes and Stein (1987), it was a great paradox that

> the time of greatest public outtcry against child abuse is also the time of the widespread, official planning of the sacrifice of children in public policy. Americans, while giving their consent to abusive social policies, simultaneously expressed renewed horror against child abuse, and exercise a grim moralism toward individuals suspected of harming their children. (p. 342)

As Scheper-Hughes and Stein (1987) suggest, when our society focuses its attention on identifying and punishing individuals who abuse their children, these persons become "social scapegoats" for what is a "normative pathology." Through the scapegoating process, the rest of society is able to avoid confronting its collective responsibility and guilt for supporting abusive social policies for children (Scheper-Hughes & Stein, 1987). As literary critic Kenneth Burke (1945) once wrote, "criminals either actual or imaginary may thus serve as scapegoats in a society that 'purifies itself' by 'moral indignation' in condemning them" (p. 406).

## ASSIGNMENT OF STIGMA

There is considerable personal shame and social stigma for people accused of child sexual abuse. Many are frustrated by the inability to remove the "stain of accusation" that lingers over their reputation, even when charges are dropped or the case is determined to be unfounded.

Being accused of child abuse is a form of what Garfinkel (1956) refers to as a "degradation ceremony." A degradation ceremony involves the assignment of stigma, and by definition, a person with a stigma is not quite human (Goffman, 1963). The trauma of a child abuse accusation is that it violates a person's sense of self and redefines their moral status in the community. According to Garfinkel, "It is not that the new attributes are added to the old nucleus. He is not changed, he is reconstituted . . . the former identity stands as accidental; the new identity is the basic reality. What he is now is what 'afterall' he was all along" (p. 421). The accused person is "de-graded," and has in Goffman's term, a "spoiled identity" (Goffman, 1963).

Persons who are falsely accused of child sexual abuse often fail to receive needed social support, as they find that others tend to believe that something must have happened when a report is made. The underlying atmosphere of many investigations, therefore, is one of implied guilt. Many of those who claim to be falsely accused say that they were unable to get the investigators to talk to them about their side of the story. Thus, a child abuse investigation becomes a crisis, that is extremely frightening and devastating to one's sense of well-being. As Faller (1985) suggests, a child abuse accusation can result in considerable stress, loss of self confidence, mistrust, fear of losing one's children, and anger at those who are perceived as responsible for the report.

Being falsely accused of child abuse is ultimately a form of victimization. People who have been falsely accused of abuse often experience the same types of symptoms as those who have been abused. These symptoms include: (1) trauma—the sense of being overwhelmed by an uncontrollable, terrifying life event, (2) betrayal—the awareness that someone on whom one depended or trusted caused them harm, (3) powerlessness—being out of control of one's life, and (4) stigmatization—the sense of shame at having one's identity and reputation called into question (Finkelhor, 1984).

Schultz (1986) surveyed 100 families who claimed to be falsely accused of child sexual abuse. Respondents were defined as innocent when charges were dropped or if there was an acquittal in a jury trial. Schultz noted that many of the respondents reported significant personal stress surrounding the entire situation. Among the symptoms reported were anxiety, fear, difficulty in resuming normal activities, obsessive thoughts about the events, eating and sleeping difficulties, and depression. Many respondents also reported financial stress, job losses, and social isolation.

## CASE EXAMPLES
### No. 1

In 1984, in Jordan, Minnesota, twenty-five children were taken from the custody of their parents and were placed in foster homes outside of Jordan for over one year. Most of the children were not allowed to have contact with their parents during this time. After a lengthy trial, two parents were acquitted, the charges were dropped against the others, and the state attorney general's office eventually assumed responsibility for the investigation. The attorney general concluded that the

> manner in which the Scott County cases were handled resulted in it being impossible to determine, in some cases, whether sexual abuse actually occurred, and if it did,

who may have done these acts. . . . The tragedy of Scott County goes beyond the inability to successfully prosecute individuals who may have committed child sexual abuse. Equally tragic is the possibility that some are unjustly accused and forced to endure long separations from their families." (Humphrey, 1985)

The attorney general's report criticized the repeated questioning of children. In some cases, children were interviewed dozens of times. Most of the children were separated from their parents and placed in foster care prior to being interviewed. A number of them initially denied being abused by their parents. Disbelieved by county officials, they were told "the sooner you tell the truth, the sooner your parents will be able to get help, and the sooner you can go home." The children eventually told elaborate stories of sexual abuse.

The broad range of children's responses was interpreted narrowly and only in the context of supporting the sexual abuse allegations. Promises that families would be reunited if the children accused their parents of sexual abuse, were ignored as factors in shaping the children's responses. Some of the children reported feeling pressured by the county prosecutor to implicate their parents. One child, who admitted lying about being abused, said, "I could tell what they wanted me to say by the way they asked the questions" (cited in Benedek & Schetky, 1987a, p. 915).

According to two University of Minnesota child psychiatrists, the manner in which the children were questioned caused them considerable stress and anxiety. In an unpublished paper, Drs. Jensen and Garfinkel wrote,

in the Scott County system the procedure of removing the child from the home for a long period of time, changing the child's identity with a new name, separation from siblings, change of religion, and instructions not to reveal any identifying information about themselves produced a strong undermining of the children's personality structure. These procedures were undertaken presumably to protect the children from further abuse by the parents, but in this overzealous approach, produced violations of the children's basic identity. An entire county organization failed to understand the impact of these procedures on child development. (Jensen & Garfinkel, 1987)

## No. 2

In December 1983, Ms. Doe (a pseudonym) received a call from the local police that an anonymous caller had alleged that her husband had been sexually abusing their 2- and 4-year-old daughters. The substance of the allegation was based on the fact that the 2-year-old, while playing on the male neighbor's lap, tried to unbutton his shirt. As it turned out, the neighbor's wife was irate that her husband made the report, as she felt that he had misperceived the little girl's behavior.

Several days before Christmas, without warning, four policemen came to the

Doe home for the two children. The mother, in a letter to the Minnesota state attorney general, described their horrifying experience. She wrote,

> try to imagine your home invaded without warning by armed policemen and to watch helplessly as your frightened, screaming, crying children are whisked off in the dark of night by strangers. There is not a thing you can do to save them from their nightmare, though their eyes plead with you to protect them. That kind of violation does not ever fade from your lives. (cited in Besharov, 1988, p. 4)

When the police arrived, the four year old, experiencing her removal from her parents as a "kidnapping," clung to her mother crying hysterically, "I don't want to go, I didn't do anything." After being returned home, she had frequent nightmares, all with common abandonment themes, such as being lost in snowstorms or department stores, unable to find her parents. Angry at her parents for failing to prevent her "kidnapping," the little girl would get hysterical when she heard police cars and repeatedly asked if she would be taken away again.

The two young girls were removed from the home without county investigators ever meeting with the parents to discuss the allegations. The parents believed the agency responded in this way because of its "policy of treating as true all allegations of abuse, regardless of source and (the fact that) the County Child Protection's procedures manual has no reference to the possibility that the maker of a report may have improper motives" (cited in Besharov, 1985, p. 559).

Although the Does filed a multi-million dollar lawsuit, what they really wanted, according to the mother, was for

> someone to make these people say, sorry—not just to me but to the kids. I wanted them to let the kids know bad things do happen, but even if it is a mistake you live up to it. I think it's important to acknowledge if you have done something damaging to another individual, especially if it causes hurt, emotional or whatever. I think it's important to acknowledge it. That's how I was raised. (P. Doe, personal communication, July 20, 1988)

## ON FORGIVENESS

According to Robert ten Bensel, "compassion is the knowledge of harm to others and the ethical response to help in reducing pain" (R. ten Bensel, personal communication, Oct. 5, 1988). When a person is falsely accused of child sexual abuse, because that experience produces harm and suffering, then professionals or others who might be responsible have an obligation to make amends. After all, the primary ethical tenet of the medical profession and the other helping professions is "primum non nocere"—"above all else do no harm." The act of apology is a form of atonement and for it to effectively contribute to healing, it must be honest and genuine.

Much of the trauma associated with false allegations of child abuse is based on the unwillingness of the professional community to acknowledge its mistakes. This refusal is apparently based, in part, on the fear that an apology might be interpreted as an admission of guilt in a potential lawsuit. The process of healing for victims of false accusations however, would be greatly enhanced if the professional community was more willing to acknowledge its mistakes, apologize, and listen to the accused's interpretation of their experience.

## CONCLUSION

As we face the future, it is crucial that we consider the possibility that a child has been abused when an allegation is made and also consider the possibility that the allegation is not true. False allegations not only hurt the adults and children involved, but they undermine public trust in the child protective system. In our effort to protect children, we must create a child protective system that is fair, responsible and worthy of public trust.

## REFERENCES

Benedek, E., & Schetky, D. (1987a). Problems in validating allegations of sexual abuse: Part 1. Factors affecting perception and recall of events. *Journal of the American Academy of Child and Adolescent Psychiatry, 26*(6), 912-915.

Benedek, E., & Schetky, D. (1987b). Problems in validating allegations of sexual abuse: Part 2. Clinical evaluation. *Journal of the American Academy of Child and Adolescent Psychiatry, 26*(6), 916-921.

Berliner, L., & Barbieri, M. K. (1984). The testimony of the child victim of sexual assault. *Journal of Social Issues, 40*(2), 125-138.

Besharov, D. J. (1985). Doing something about child abuse: The need to narrow the grounds for state intervention. *Harvard Journal of Law and Public Policy, 8*(3), 539-589.

Besharov, D. (1988). The central dilemma: Protecting abused children while protecting innocent parents. In H. Wakefield & R. Underwager (Eds.), *Accusations of child sexual abuse* (pp. 3-15). Springfield, Illinois: Charles C. Thomas.

Bok, S. (1978). *Lying*. New York: Vintage Books.

Burke, K. (1945). *A grammar of motives*. New York: Prentice-Hall.

Daro, D. (1988). *Confronting child abuse*. New York: Free Press.

deYoung, M. (1986). A conceptual model for judging the truthfulness of a young child's allegation of sexual abuse. *American Journal of Orthopsychiatry, 56*, 550-559.

Edelman, M. (1987). *Families in peril: An agenda for social change*. Cambridge, Mass.: Harvard University Press.

Faller, K. (1984). Is the child victim of sexual abuse telling the truth? *Child Abuse and Neglect*, 8, 473-481.

Faller, K. (1985). Unanticipated problems in the United States child protection system. *Child Abuse and Neglect*, 9, 63-69.

Finkelhor, D. (1984). *Child sexual abuse: New theory and research*. New York: Free Press.

Gardner, R. (1987). *The parental alienation syndrome and the differentiation between fabricated and genuine child sex abuse*. Cresskill, NJ: Creative Therapeutics.

Garfinkel, H. (1956). Conditions of successful degradation ceremonies. *American Journal of Sociology*, 61, 420-424.

Goffman, E. (1963). *Stigma: Notes on the management of spoiled identity*. Englewood Cliffs, New Jersey: Prentice-Hall.

Goodman, G. (1984). The child witness: Conclusions and future directions for research and legal practice. *Journal of Social Issues*, 40(2), 157-175.

Green, A. (1986). True and false allegations of sexual abuse in child custody disputes. *Journal of the American Academy of Child Psychiatry*, 25(4), 449-456.

Humphrey, H. (1985). *Report on Scott County investigations*. St. Paul, MN: Attorney General's Office.

Jensen, J., & Garfinkel, B. (1987). *Errors in abuse investigations in two countries*. Unpublished manuscript. University of Minnesota Medical School, Minneapolis, MN.

Jones, D., & McGraw, J. (1987). Reliable and fictitious accounts of sexual abuse to children. *Journal of Interpersonal Violence*, 2(1), 27-45.

King, M. A., & Yuille, J. C. (1987). Suggestibility and the child witness. In S. J. Ceci, M. P. Toglia, & D. F. Ross (Eds.), *Children's eyewitness memory* (pp. 24-35). New York: Springer-Verlag.

Pogrebin, L. (1983). Do Americans hate children? A challenging analysis of a national 'phobia'. *Ms*, 12(5), 47-50, 126-127.

Rothenberg, M. (1980). Is there an unconscious national conspiracy against children in the United States? *Clinical Pediatrics*, 19(1), 10-24.

Scheper-Hughes, N., & Stein, H. (1987). Child abuse and the unconscious in American popular culture. In N. Scheper-Hughes (Ed.), *Child survival* (pp. 339-358). Dordrecht: D. Reidel Publishing Co.

Schultz, L. (1986). *One hundred cases of wrongfully charged child sexual abuse: A survey and recommendations*. Unpublished manuscript. School of Social Work, West Virginia University.

Schuman, D. C. (1984). *False allegations of physical and sexual abuse*. Paper presented at the Annual Conference of the American Academy of Psychiatry and the Law, Nassau, Bahamas.

Summit, R. (1983). The child sexual abuse accommodation syndrome. *Child Abuse and Neglect*, 7, 177-193.

Terr, L. (1986). The child psychiatrist and the child witness: Traveling companions by necessity, if not by design. *Journal of the American Academy of Child Psychiatry*, 25, 462-472.

Yates, A., & Musty, T. (1988). Preschool children's erroneous allegations of sexual molestations. *American Journal of Psychiatry*, 145(8), 989-992.

# PART IV
# Sexual Harassment and Assault

During the past 20 years, the visibility of sexual violence and society's response to it have increased considerably. Police departments and hospitals have instituted special programs to increase the understanding of their staffs toward victims of sexual assault; 24-hour hotlines exist in many communities across the United States and elsewhere; self-help and other counseling groups have been formed to help victims, families, and friends cope with the consequences of assault. Considerable legal reform has taken place with the enactment of new laws redefining sexual assault, expanding the definition to include marital situations, lightening burdensome evidentiary requirements, and stiffening the penalties for those convicted of these crimes.

There is no question that sexual assault is a problem of great personal and social significance. In recent random surveys of the population of the United States, the lifetime prevalence of sexual assault has been estimated at between 13.5% and 44% of women (Kilpatrick et al., 1985; Koss, Gidycz, & Wisniewski, 1987). Sexual assault affects both the physical and psychological well-being of victims as indicated by the chronic use of medical and mental health services on the part of victims (Golding, Stein, & Siegel, 1988; Koss, 1988). Moreover, 44% of rape victims consider suicide in its aftermath, and almost 20% attempt it (Kilpatrick et al., 1987; Resick, Jordan, Girelli, Hutter, & Marhoefer-Dvorak,

1988). The reality of rape affects those not victimized as well, through increased fear of crime and limitations on one's life-style.

Rape is quite probably the most extensively studied single-incident crime, particularly when it comes to victim reactions. This, in part, is because it is considered the crime that induces the most trauma in an adult, exclusive of murder.

In the United States, it was in the early and mid-1960s that crime rates began to rise dramatically. Between 1960 and 1970 the number of reported rapes and aggravated assaults doubled. Reported robberies almost tripled. Between 1970 and 1980, reported rapes doubled again. Law-and-order groups and victims' rights groups were quick to capitalize on growing crime rates for their lobbying activities, supporting capital punishment and the establishment of services for victims.

The women's movement also understood the importance and usefulness of data on crime, particularly on rape, a subject that rapidly became a rallying point for organizing and spurring women into action. Especially at that time when the common law definition of rape clearly identified women as its sole victims and men as its exclusive perpetrators, the usefulness of rape as a symbol for a movement focused on the status of women in society was and still is immense.

It was particularly in the 1970s that the women's movement in the United States seized on rape as its central issue. A major goal of the antirape movement was to show how rape was a violent act more similar to other crimes of violence than to other sex crimes. In rapid succession, in 1972 the first rape crisis centers opened in Ann Arbor, Michigan; Los Angeles; and Washington, DC, with funds provided by the U.S. Department of Justice. In 1975 the National Center for the Prevention and Control of Rape was established as a source of funding for research and treatment projects. In 1974, Michigan enacted the first completely revised sexual assault statute, which greatly influenced subsequent similar legislation in many other states. Consciousness-raising groups and hotlines were established; rape cases were brought to the attention of the media; grass-roots organizations providing services multiplied. By the late 1970s, people in the United States had become familiar with the antirape movement and were steadily accepting its presentation of rape as a serious social problem deserving society's attention (Rose, 1977).

All new research on rape that developed at this time adopted a feminist outlook, which gives social structure and social context a dominant role in explaining and describing rape. Feminist theoreticians consider rape as an extreme on a continuum of sexual exploitation, a clearly forceful way to keep women submissive. Rape is the outcome of patriarchalism, in which beliefs that support rape are bolstered by institutional arrangements that perpetuate men's control over women. These values, beliefs, and practices are passed on from one generation to the next during sex-role socialization.

According to this approach, rape is not the isolated, unexpected act of a sick, sexually dissatisfied or inadequate male. It is a form of aggressive behavior that is an inescapable element of the social environment where men are in control. It is a variation or slight exaggeration of socially approved, normal sexual relations. Normal sex, according to this perspective, is often forced or nonconsensual sex. It follows that such sex goes unnoticed and does not elicit social punishment (Bourque, 1989).

Thus, the major contribution of the feminist movement to rape research and intervention has taken two forms: first, it has made society aware of rape as a social problem worthy of research and intervention; second, it has cogently exposed the sexual stereotypes supporting the mythology surrounding rape. Generally accepted assumptions about rapists, their victims, and the act itself were labeled "rape myths" to be debunked by research.

An important consequence of the attention focused on rape by the women's movement has been legislative and court reform. Between 1974 and 1980, all state legislatures in the United States debated and the majority enacted changes in the laws on rape, with Michigan in the lead. The most important goal of the reform movement was to shift the burden of proof from the victim to the offender (Bienen, 1976, 1983).

The utilization of sex and gender as a stratifying social variable when analyzing the relationships between men and women in our society allows us to focus on a variety of behaviors that are consistent with society's views of feminine and masculine behaviors. Males are socialized into the role of aggressive seducer; females, into that of passive prey. Although rape represents the most violent manifestation of male aggression, there are several other forms or gradations of behaviors that manifest the same unequal distribution of power by sex under the rubric of sexual harassment. Richard Barickman, Michele Paludi, and Vita Rabinowitz, in chapter 15, point out that women experience sexual harassment in many forms, from sexist remarks and covert physical contact (patting, brushing against their bodies) to blatant propositions and sexual assaults. They outline and discuss five categories developed by researchers to encompass the range of sexual harassment: gender harassment, seductive behavior, sexual bribery, sexual coercion, and sexual imposition. Although their particular focus is on the victimization of college students, the circumstances they describe and the remedies they propose apply to faculty and staff as well.

Rita Gunn and Candice Minch explore in chapter 16 the problems confronted by victims of sexual assault in Canada. Data from interviews with victims, a review of police charges and case processing, and a survey of cases tried under the 1983 Canadian sexual assault legislation provide a social-legal analysis. Conclusions drawn from the research demonstrate ongoing discrimination toward sexual assault victims.

Lita Furby, Baruch Fischhoff, and Marcia Morgan report in chapter 17 the results of their study examining how women perceive the repertoire of possible strategies for preventing rape. In particular, they focus on strategies for defending oneself during an assault.

Carol DiCenso writes in chapter 18 about the adolescent sexual offender as both victim and perpetrator. Utilizing information collected from offenders involved with the Juvenile Sex Offender Program of the Rhode Island Training School for Youth, the relevant data are presented as they relate to the victim/offender cycle. The results suggest that early victimization of the offender is the most significant factor contribuing to their offending.

## REFERENCES

Bienen, L. (1976). Rape I. *Women's Rights Law Reporter, 3,* 45-57.
Bienen, L. (1983). Rape reform legislation in the United States: A look at some practical effects. *Victimology, 8*(1-2), 139-151.
Bourque, L. B. (1989). *Defining rape.* Durham, NC: Duke University Press.
Golding, J. M., Stein, J. A., & Siegel, J. M. (1988). Sexual assault history and use of health and mental health services. *American Journal of Community Psychology, 16,* 625-644.
Kilpatrick, D. G., Best, L., Veronen, A., Amick, E., Villeponteaux, L., & Ruff, G. (1985). Mental health correlates of criminal victimization: A random community survey. *Journal of Consulting and Clinical Psychology, 53,* 873-886.
Kilpatrick, D. G., Veronen, L. J., Saunders, B. E., Best, C. L., Amick-McMullen, A., & Paduhovic, J. (1987). *The psychological impact of crime: A study of randomly surveyed crime victims. Final Report.* Washington, DC: National Institute of Justice.
Koss, M. P. (1988). *Criminal victimization among women: Impact on health status and medical services usage.* Paper presented at the annual meeting, American Psychological Association, Atlanta, GA.
Koss, M. P., Gidycz, C. A., & Wisniewski, N. (1987). The scope of rape: Incidence and prevalence of sexual aggression and victimization in a national sample of higher education students. *Journal of Consulting and Clinical Psychology, 55,* 162-170.
Resick, P. A., Jordan, C. G., Girelli, S. A., Hutter, C. K., & Marhoefer-Dvorak, S. (1988). A comparative outcome study of behavioral group therapy for sexual assault victims. *Behavior Therapy, 19,* 385-401.
Rose, V. M. (1977). Rape as a social problem: A by-product of the feminist movement. *Social Problems, 25,* 75-89.

# 15

# Sexual Harassment of Students: Victims of the College Experience

*Richard B. Barickman, Michele A. Paludi, and Vita C. Rabinowitz*

---

Sexual harassment in U.S. colleges and universities is a major barrier to women's professional development and a traumatic force that disrupts and damages their personal lives (Betz & Fitzgerald, 1987). Dzeich and Weiner (1984) have reported that 30% of undergraduate women suffer sexual harassment from at least one of their instructors during their 4 years of college. When definitions of sexual harassment include sexist remarks and other forms of "gender harassment," the incidence rate in undergraduate populations nears 70% (Adams, Kottke, & Padgitt, 1983; Lott, Reilly, & Howard, 1982). These percentages translate into millions of students in our college system who are sexually harassed each year. The incidence rate for women graduate students and faculty is even higher (Bailey & Richards, 1985; Bond, 1988). Though there are few studies focusing on the sexual harassment of nonfaculty employees in the college/university system, there is no reason to suppose that the harassment of college staff is any less than the 50% rate reported for employees of various other public and private institutions (Fitzgerald, Shullman, et al., 1988; Fitzgerald, Weitzman, Gold, & Ormerod, 1988). Sexual harassment is thus a major form of victimization of women in our system of higher education, even though it is still largely a "hidden issue" (as the Project on the Status and Education of Women called it in 1978).

Women students and faculty who have been harassed often change their entire educational program as a result. And stress reactions—often severe—almost invariably follow sexual harassment, including depression, tension, anger and fear, insomnia, headaches, feelings of helplessness and embarrassment, and decreased motivation (Whitmore, 1983). Performance in course work suffers, and many students drop out of school altogether.

We propose in this chapter to (1) review the psychological literature that documents the impact of harassment, (2) describe the differing perceptions of sexual harassment commonly held by women and men, and (3) offer suggestions for curtailing sexual harassment through the institution of college policies and panels to enforce them, training of faculty and graduate students, and educational campaigns to inform the academic community of the nature and severity of the problem.

Although our particular focus will be on the victimization of students, the circumstances we describe and remedies we propose apply to faculty and staff as well. If we can heighten awareness of the nature of sexual harassment—especially the severe damage it inflicts on women—within the academic community, and if remedial action is taken, all members of the community will benefit (including potential and actual harassers).

## DEFINITIONS AND INCIDENCE OF SEXUAL HARASSMENT

Women experience sexual harassment in many forms, from sexist remarks and covert physical contact (patting, brushing against their bodies) to blatant propositions and sexual assaults. Researchers have developed five categories to encompass the range of sexual harassment (Fitzgerald, Shullman, et al., 1988): gender harassment, seductive behavior, sexual bribery, sexual coercion, and sexual imposition. These levels of sexual harassment correlate with legal definitions of sexual harassment.

*Gender harassment* consists of generalized sexist remarks and behavior not designed to elicit sexual cooperation but rather to convey insulting, degrading, or sexist attitudes about women. *Seductive behavior* is unwanted, inappropriate, and offensive sexual advances. *Sexual bribery* is the solicitation of sexual activity or other sex-linked behavior by promise of reward. *Sexual coercion* is the solicitation of sexual activity by threat of punishment, and *sexual imposition* includes gross imposition, assault, and rape.

Sexual harassment is clearly prohibited within the college/university system as a form of sexual discrimination, under both Title IX of the 1972 Education Amendments and, for employees, Title VII of the 1964 Civil Rights Act. A key definition of sexual harassment has been issued by the Education Department's Office of Civil Rights (OCR):

> Sexual harassment consists of verbal or physical conduct of a sexual nature, imposed on the basis of sex, by an employee or agent of a recipient of federal funds that denies, limits, provides different, or conditions the provision of aid, benefits, services, or treatment protected under Title IX.

In addition, guidelines first issued by the Equal Employment Opportunity Commission (interpreting Title VII) and adopted in 1981 by the OCR further specify the range of sexual harassment covered by these statutes. According to these guidelines, behavior constitutes sexual harassment when the person engaging in such behavior explicitly or implicitly makes your submission to it a term or condition of your employment or academic standing or makes decisions affecting your employment or academic life according to whether you accept or reject that behavior; or the person's behavior is an attempt to interfere, or has the effect of interfering, with your work or academic performance or creates an intimidating, hostile, or offensive working or learning environment.

The last condition—the creation of "an intimidating, hostile, or offensive working or learning environment"—is particularly significant because it covers the most pervasive form of sexual harassment, the form most often defended on the grounds of "academic freedom." In a 1986 decision, *Meritor Savings Bank v. Vinson*, the Supreme Court unanimously affirmed that "sexual harassment claims are not limited simply to those for which a tangible job benefit is withheld ('quid pro quo' sexual harassment), but also include those in which the complainant is subjected to an offensive, discriminatory work environment ('hostile environment' sexual harassment)" (Bennett-Alexander, 1987, p. 65). In doing so the Court explicitly adopted the EEOC's guidelines, which have been extended to the academic community—especially to students, who are not covered by the statutes governing employer/employee relations—by the OCR. These guidelines thus have a regulating force supported by the U.S. Department of Education that is crucial to the effort to curtail the widespread sexual harassment now afflicting our colleges and universities.

In recent years, research has provided compelling evidence that sexual and gender harassment of students can result in serious psychological, emotional, physical, and economic consequences (Koss, 1990). Such harassment often forces students to forfeit research, work, and even their career plans. Research by Adams, Kottke, and Padgitt (1983) reported that 13% of the women students they surveyed said they had avoided taking a class or working with certain professors because of the risk of being subjected to sexual advances. Furthermore, a 1983 study conducted at Harvard University indicated that 15% of the graduate students and 12% of the undergraduate students who had been harassed by their professors changed their major or educational program because of the harassment. Wilson and Krauss (1983) reported that 9% of the female undergraduates in their study had been pinched, touched, or patted to the point of personal discomfort; 17% of the women in the Adams et al. survey received verbal sexual advances, 14% received sexual invitations, 6% had been subjected to physical advances, and 2% received direct sexual bribes.

Bailey and Richards (1985) reported that of 246 women graduate students in their sample, 13% indicated they had been sexually harassed, 21% had not enrolled in a course to avoid such behavior, and 16% indicated they had been directly assaulted. Bond (1988) reported that 75% of the 229 women members of Division 27 who responded to her survey experienced jokes with sexual themes during their graduate training, 69% were subjected to sexist comments demeaning to women, and 58% of the women reported experiencing sexist remarks about their clothing, body, or sexual activities.

All of these findings indicate that when definitions of sexual victimization include sexual and gender harassment, it becomes clear that the sexual victimization of women is pervasive: literally millions of women each year experience victimization in the college/university setting.

## EXPLANATORY MODELS AND INSTITUTIONAL STRUCTURE

Sexual harassment occurs, in most instances, when individuals exploit a position of power granted to them by their roles in an institutional structure. This is as true for the classroom setting as it is for the workplace. Yet the major impasse to a general acknowledgment that sexual harassment is a devastating force in our educational system probably continues to be the widespread view that this is a matter of personal relations outside the control of the institution and unrelated to its own powers and prerogatives. Zalk (1990) has accurately and eloquently raised the falseness and insensitivity of this view:

> All the power lies with the faculty member—some of it real, concrete, and some of it is imagined or elusive. The bases of the faculty member's almost absolute power are varied and range from the entirely rational into broad areas of fantasy. Professors give grades, write recommendations for graduate schools, awards and the like, and can predispose colleagues' attitudes towards students. (p. 145)

For certain student groups, professors are particularly powerful (Rabinowitz, 1990). Such groups include

- Graduate students, whose future careers are often determined by their association with a particular faculty member.
- Students in small colleges or small academic departments, where the number of faculty available to students is quite small.

- Women of color, especially those with "token" status.
- Students in male-populated fields (e.g., engineering).
- Students who are economically disadvantaged and work part-time or full-time while attending classes.

Thus, the structure of the academy interacts with psychological dynamics to increase women's vulnerability to all forms of sexual harassment. Professors' greatest power lies in the capacity to enhance or diminish students' self-esteem. This power can motivate students to learn course material or persuade them to give up. The tone and content of the student-professor interaction is especially important. Is the student encouraged or put down? Do the faculty members use their knowledge to let students know how "stupid" they are or to challenge their thinking? As Zalk, Paludi, and Dederick (1990) point out, this is *real power!*

## CONSENSUAL RELATIONSHIPS

Zacker and Paludi (1989) report that some campuses have adopted a policy statement that includes information about consensual relationships. For example, the University of Iowa's policy on sexual harassment includes such a statement, as does Harvard University's, which reads in part as follows:

> Amorous relationships that might be appropriate in other circumstances are always wrong when they occur between any teacher or officer of the University and any student for whom he or she has a professional responsibility. Further, such relationships may have the effect of undermining the atmosphere of trust on which the educational process depends. Implicit in the idea of professionalism is the recognition by those in positions of authority that in their relationships with students there is always an element of power. It is incumbent upon those with authority not to abuse, nor to seem to abuse, the power with which they are entrusted. . . . Even when both parties have consented to the development of such a relationship, it is the officer or instructor who, by virtue of his or her special responsibility, will be held accountable for unprofessional behavior. . . . Relationships between officers and students are always fundamentally asymmetric in nature.

Including consensual relationships as part of the definition of academic sexual harassment has been met with great resistance (Sandler, 1988; Zacker & Paludi, 1989). Faculty men are less likely than faculty women to include consensual relationships in their definition of sexual harassment (Fitzgerald, Shullman, et al., 1988; Kenig & Ryan, 1986). Faculty men are also less likely than faculty women to define academic sexual harassment to include jokes, teasing remarks of a sexual nature, and unwanted suggestive looks or gestures. Men are also significantly more likely than women to agree with the following statements: "An attractive woman has to expect sexual advances and learn how to handle them," "It is only natural for a man to make sexual advances to a woman he finds attractive," and "People who receive annoying sexual attention usually have provoked it" (Kenig & Ryan, 1986). Finally, faculty men are more likely than women to believe individuals can handle unwanted sexual attention on their own without involving the college or university. Male faculty thus may perceive sexual harassment as a *personal*, not an organizational issue.

The idea that sexual harassment is an inherently personal rather than an institutional matter is a variation on the explanatory framework called the "natural/biological model" by Tangri, Burt, and Johnson (1982). They have identified three explanatory models that individuals typically use to account for sexual harassment. The *natural/biological model* interprets sexual harassment as a consequence of natural sexual interactions between people, either attributing a stronger sex drive to men than to women (thus, men "need" to engage in aggressive sexual behavior) or describing sexual harassment as part of the "game" between sexual equals. This model obviously can't account for the extreme stress reactions suffered by victims of sexual harassment (and not suffered by their harassers). It is as fallacious as a racist theory that attributes the victimization of minorities to a "natural" prerogative or capacity of a superior race or to the "inevitable" workings of social forces.

The *sociocultural model* posits sexual harassment as only one manifestation of the much larger patriarchal system in which men are the dominant group. Therefore, harassment is an example of men asserting their personal power based on sex. According to this model, sex would be a better predictor of both recipient and initiator status than would organizational position. Thus, women should be much more likely to be victims of sexual harassment, especially when they are in male-populated college majors.

This model gives a much more accurate account of sexual harassment because the overwhelming majority of victims are women and the overwhelming majority of harassers are men—90%–95% in each case (Fitzgerald, Shullman, et al., 1988). Yet it can have the unfortunate effect of leaving women feeling nearly as powerless as the natural/biological model does. If sexual harassment is so ingrained in our whole culture, how can the individual withstand such a massive, systemic force?

The *organizational model* asserts that sexual harassment results from opportunities presented by relations of power and authority that derive from the hierarchical structure of organizations. Thus, sexual harassment is an issue of organizational power. Because work (and academic) organizations are defined by vertical stratification and asymmetrical relations between supervisors and subordinates and between teachers and students, individuals can use the power of their position to extort sexual gratification from their subordinates.

This model is most useful for understanding and opposing sexual harassment in the academy, in our experience. But to obtain the fullest explanatory range and corrective power, it should be combined with the sociocultural model. Organizational power is so pervasively abused—victimizing literally tens of millions of women in the workplace, schools, colleges, and universities—*because* sexual inequality and victimization are endemic to our patriarchal culture. Just as the frequency of rape in warfare is a consequence of general cultural values licensed by the extreme "organizational structure" of war, so the frequency of sexual harassment is a consequence of these same values empowered by the ordinary, routine structures of work and education. Again, the analogy to racial discrimination holds.

## IMPLICATIONS FOR EDUCATION AND POLICY

Recently, Dovan, Grossman, Kindermann, Matula, Paludi, and Scott (1987) reported that college women were more likely to label a faculty member's harassment of a woman student in terms of his abusing his power over the student as a professor instead of abusing his power as a man. They recognized sexual harassment as allowing professors to undermine students' positions in higher education. This finding supports the organizational model of harassment: women were able to explain harassment as resulting from the opportunities presented by power and authority relations that derive from the hierarchical structure of the academy. This echoes May's (1972) description of power in the academy.

Dovan et al. (1987) also reported that women's adherence to the organizational model promoted their empowerment. Women who espoused this explanatory model reported seeking redress for the victimization. Such a response would not be predicted from adherence to the sociocultural model: women would not be likely to take interpersonally assertive action or to act on an expectation that the organization will help them resolve the issue. Women are much more likely than men to assign a central role to the college for preventing and dealing with all levels of sexual harassment. Since the research indicates that men attribute more responsibility to women victims of sexual harassment, men would also be likely to minimize the potential responsibility of college/university officials (Paludi, 1990). As a male faculty member reported in the Fitzgerald, Shullman, et al. (1988) study, "It has been my observation that students, and some faculty, have little understanding of the extreme pressure a male professor can feel as the object of sexual interest of attractive women students" (p. 337).

Fitzgerald, Shullman, et al. reported that male faculty members typically do not label their behavior as sexual harassment despite the fact that they report frequent initiation of personal relationships with women students. Male faculty members denied the inherent power differential between faculty and students, as well as the psychological power conferred by this differential. In addition, women faculty were more likely than men to disapprove of romantic relationships between faculty and students.

These data thus suggest that education is needed in men's perceptions of the misuse of power, their perceptions about women who have been harassed, and their attitudes toward sexual interactions. Another focus of such training lies in the politics involved in the mentor-protégé relationship. Typically, mentors and protégés do not have a common understanding of their relationship; consequently, students and faculty have substantially different definitions. (Haring-Hidore & Brooks, 1986; Paludi, 1987).

Fitzgerald, Weitzman, Gold, and Ormerod (1988) reported that male faculty members who participated in their study typically denied that there is an inherent power differential between students and faculty. Women students, however, recognize this power differential. Thus, educational programs are needed to deal with women's and men's understanding of the concept of harassment and the social meanings attributed to the behaviors that legally constitute harassment. Truax (cited in Fitzgerald, 1986) claimed:

> . . . men's perceptions of what their behavior means are vastly different from women's. . . . We find, in working with victims of sexual harassment that there is often little disagreement with what has happened between student and professor, but rather, with what the conduct means. Professors will try to justify their behavior on the grounds that they are just friendly and trying to make a student feel welcome, or they thought that the student would be flattered by the attention. (p. 24)

However, the interpretation given to the professor's behavior by women students is not flattery or friendliness. The consequences to undergraduate and graduate women of being harassed have been devastating to their physical well-being, emotional health, and vocational development, including depression, insomnia, headaches, helplessness, and decreased motivation (Whitmore, 1983).

All of these experiences contribute to emotional and physical stress reactions. In recent years, the label "Sexual Harassment Trauma Syndrome" (Shullman, 1989) has been applied to the effects of sexual harassment on physical, emotional, interpersonal, and career aspects of women's lives. Research has indicated that depending on the severity of the harassment, between 21% and 82% of women report that their emotional and/or physical condition deteriorated as a result of sexual harassment (Koss, 1990). Furthermore, like victims of rape who go to court, sexual harassment victims experience a second victimization when they attempt to deal with the situation through legal and/or institutional means. Stereotypes about sexual harassment and women's victimization blame women for the harassment. These stereotypes center around the myths that sexual harassment is a form of seduction, that women secretly want to be sexually harassed, and that women do not tell the truth.

The behavior that legally constitutes harassment is just that, despite what the professor's intentions may be. It is the power differential and/or the woman's reaction to the behavior that are the critical variables.

Several kinds of intervention may be instituted in order to challenge attitudes that perpetuate harassment. As Biaggio, Brownell, and Watts (1990) suggest, key individuals within organizations—residence hall advisors in dormitories, department chairs—can be targeted for attendance at workshops at which they can be informed about the institutional policy and procedures dealing with harassment. In addition, new student orientations are another arena for disseminating information about institutional policies that prohibit sexual and gender harassment. Items relating to gender and sexual harassment can be placed on teaching evaluations.

Sandler (1988) has also offered suggestions for meeting this goal, including (1) establishing a policy statement that makes it clear that differential treatment of professional women on campus will not be tolerated, (2) establishing a permanent committee to explore and report on professional climate issues, and (3) publishing an annual report on progress in regard to women on campus.

Hunter College of the City University of New York has been involved in several educational programs for students, faculty, administrators, and staff. For example, a four-part workshop on sexual harassment for faculty was cosponsored by the Employees Assistance Program. The workshop objectives included learning how formal and informal power or authority in the university setting is perceived by workers; learning the politics involved in such nonverbal gestures as touch, body position, and personal space; and learning the social meanings attributed to behaviors that legally constitute sexual harassment.

Yet education, however successful, is not sufficient in itself to prevent sexual harassment or offer remedies when it occurs. Because sexual harassment occurs in this context of institutional power, individuals who have been victimized are often, understandably, reluctant to use the ordinary channels in the college or university for resolving complaints. It is important, therefore, that the means of hearing and resolving complaints of sexual harassment should be distinct from the regular departmental and administrative hierarchies. The panel operating at Hunter College since 1982 has successfully met this requirement. The members are appointed by the president of Hunter College, and the panel reports to both the president and the vice president for student affairs/dean of students, but it is independent of the administrative structures of the President's Office and the Office of Student Services.

The fact that the panel at Hunter guarantees that all procedures will be confidential and further guarantees that the individual bringing the complaint will decide whether to make a formal complaint also encourages individuals to contact panel members to discuss a problem. Unless people—faculty, staff, and students—feel that they will have these protections, they will seldom report the sexual harassment they have experienced. Research findings fully support this conclusion. Obviously, individual complaints cannot be resolved and the pervasive injury done to the college community by sexual harassment cannot be remedied unless complaints are actually reported.

In the 6-year experience of the panel at Hunter College, most people make initial contact with the panel for informal discussions about their discomfort in a situation that may have involved sexual harassment. Often they do not realize—because of general misunderstanding of the nature of sexual harassment and the lack of open discussion about it—exactly what constitutes sexual harassment and what their rights are. Often, too, informal discussions with a panel member enable the person to deal with the problem on his or her own or lead to an informal resolution.

To promote the effective and equitable resolution of problems involving sexual harassment, it seems necessary to have the following:

1. An explicit policy adopted by the college or university in compliance with the provision of Titles VII and IX, such as the policy of CUNY's board of trustees, applicable to all units of the system. Such a policy allows the university and college to uphold and enforce its policies against sexual harassment within its own community (including such severe penalties as loss of pay or position or tenure) without requiring victimized individuals to undertake the laborious, protracted, and costly process of seeking redress from the courts under Titles VII and IX.

2. One body of individuals, delegated by and responsible to the president of the college, who are specially educated about the nature of sexual harassment and trained to deal with both complaints and those accused of sexual harassment fairly, sensitively, and confidentially. The panel at Hunter has prepared extensive educational materials for new panel members and regularly engages in training sessions, attends conferences, consults with experts at other campuses, and so forth. The panel now includes two counselors and three psychologists whose research specializations include the areas of sexual harassment.

3. A body composed of faculty, staff, and students so that the whole college community is represented. To make access to the panel as easy and as comfortable as possible, it should represent the college community in terms of sex, sexual orientation, academic programs and ranks, racial and ethnic background. Research has indicated, and the panel's experience has confirmed, that many individuals feel more comfortable contacting someone they identify as a peer.

4. Common definitions of sexual harassment and common procedures for resolving conflicts applied equitably throughout the college, regardless of the status of the complainant or the person complained against. Without a common procedure, inequities can easily occur.

Hunter's panel has also offered advice for counselors, advocates, and educators in the area of academic sexual harassment:

1. Acknowledge women's courage by stating how difficult it is to label, report, and discuss sexual harassment.
2. Encourage women to share their feelings and perceptions.
3. Provide information to women about the incidence of academic sexual harassment. Also share with women the symptoms associated with the sexual harassment trauma syndrome.
4. Assure women that they are not responsible for their victimization.
5. Work with women in their search for the meaning in their victimization; support them while they mourn their losses.
6. Work with women in monitoring their physical, emotional, academic, and interpersonal responses to academic sexual harassment.
7. Provide a safe forum for women's expression of anger and resentment.
8. Work with women on ways to validate themselves so as to feel empowered.

A student, faculty, or staff peer counseling group can be an important resource for women who are understandably wary of the entire institution as a result of sexual harassment by a member of that institution.

As Mead (1978/1984) argued, we need a new taboo on campus that demands we make new norms and not rely on masculine-biased definitions of success, career development, and sexuality. We need an ethic of care and the restructuring of academic institutions so that caring can become a central and active value (Stimpson, 1988). Educational training will not be sufficient to reach this goal: the relative power of women in relation to men in the college/university system, which underlies sexual harassment, will need to be changed; and that means massive changes in the present institutional structures that dominate our college and university system.

# REFERENCES

Adams, J. W., Kottke, J. L., & Padgitt, J. S. (1983). Sexual harassment of university students. *Journal of College Student Personnel, 24,* 484-490.

Bailey, N., & Richards, M. (1985). *Tarnishing the ivory tower: Sexual harassment in graduate training programs in psychology.* Paper presented at the American Psychological Association meetings, Los Angeles.

Bennett-Alexander, D. D. (1987). The supreme court finally speaks on the issue of sexual harassment—what did it say?" *Women's Rights Law Reporter, 10,* 65-78.

Betz, N., & Fitzgerald, L. F. (1987). The career psychology of women. New York: Academic Press.

Biaggio, M. K., Brownell, A., & Watts, D. (1990). Addressing sexual harassment: Strategies for prevention and change." In M. Paludi (Ed.), *Ivory power.* Albany: SUNY Press.

Bond, M. (1988). Division 27 Sexual Harassment Survey: Definition, impact, and environmental context. *The Community Psychologist, 21,* 7-10.

Dovan, J., Grossman, M., Kindermann, J., Matula, S., Paludi, M. A., & Scott, C. A. (1987).

*College women's attitudes and attributions about sexual and gender harassment.* Symposium presented at the Association for Women in Psychology, Bethesda, MD.

Dzeich, B., & Weiner, L. (1984). *The lecherous professor: Sexual harassment on campus.* Boston: Beacon Press.

Fitzgerald, L. F. (1986). *The lecherous professor: A study in power relations.* Paper presented at the American Psychological Association meetings, Washington, DC.

Fitzgerald, L. F., Shullman, S., Bailey, N., Gold, Y., Ormerod, M., & Weitzman, L. (1988). The incidence and dimensions of sexual harassment in academia and the workplace. *Journal of Vocational Behavior, 32,* 152-175.

Fitzgerald, L. F., Weitzman, L., Gold, Y., & Ormerod, M. (1988). Academic harassment: Sex and denial in scholarly garb. *Psychology of Women Quarterly, 12,* 329-340.

Haring-Hidore, M., & Brooks, L. (1986). *Learning from the problems mentors in academe have perceived in relationships with proteges.* Paper presented at the American Educational Research Association, Washington, DC.

Kenig, S., & Ryan, J. (1986). Sex differences in levels of tolerance and attribution of blame for sexual harassment on a university campus. *Sex Roles, 15,* 535-549.

Koss, M. P. (1990). Changed lives: The psychological impact of sexual harassment. In M. A. Paludi (Ed.), *Ivory power: Sexual harassment on campus.* Albany: SUNY Press.

Lott, B., Reilly, M. E., & Howard, D. R. (1982). Sexual assault and harassment: A campus community case study. *Signs, 8,* 296-319.

May, R. (1972). *Power and innocence.* New York: Dell.

Mead, M. (1984). A proposal: We need new taboos on sex at work. In B. Dzeich & L. Winer (Eds.), *The lecherous professor.* Boston: Beacon Press. (Original work published 1978)

Paludi, M. A. (1987). *Women and the mentor-protege relationship: A feminist critique for the inadequacy of old solutions.* Paper presented at the Interdisciplinary Congress on Women, Dublin.

Paludi, M. A. (Ed.). (1990). *Ivory power.* Albany, NY: SUNY Press.

Project on the Status and Education of Women. (1978). *Sexual harassment: A hidden issue.* Washington, DC: Association of American Colleges.

Rabinowitz, V. (1990). Coping with sexual harassment. In M. Paludi (Ed.), *Ivory power.* Albany, NY: SUNY Press.

Sandler, B. (1988). *Sexual harassment: A new issue for institutions, or these are the times that try men's souls.* Paper presented at the Conference on Sexual Harassment on Campus, New York.

Shullman, S. (1989). *The sexual harassment trauma syndrome.* Paper presented at the Annual Meeting of the Association for Women in Psychology, Newport, RI.

Stimpson, C. (1988). *Overreaching: Sexual harassment and education.* Paper presented at the Conference on Sexual Harassment, New York.

Tangri, S., Burt, M., & Johnson, L. (1982). Sexual harassment at work: Three explanatory models. *Journal of Social Issues, 38,* 33-54.

Whitmore, R. (1983). *Sexual harassment at UC Davis.* Davis, CA: Women's Resources and Research Center.

Wilson, K. R., & Krauss, L. A. (1983). Sexual harassment in the university. *Journal of College Student Personnel, 24,* 219-224.

Zacker, M., & Paludi, M. A. (1989). *Educational programs dealing with academic sexual harassment.* Unpublished manuscript, Hunter College.

Zalk, S. R. (1990). The lecherous professor: Psychological profiles of professors who harass their women students. In M. Paludi (Ed.), *Ivory power.* New York: SUNY Press.

Zalk, S. R., Paludi, M. A., & Dederick, J. (1990). Consensual relationships between faculty and students. In M. A. Paludi & R. B. Barickman (Eds.), *Academic and workplace sexual harassment: A Resource Manual.* Albany: SUNY Press.

# 16

# Sexual Assault in Canada: A Social and Legal Analysis

*Rita Gunn and Candice Minch*

---

The central issue guiding our research was the treatment of female sexual assault victims. The criminal justice system becomes involved in a minimal proportion of sexual assault offenses. This chapter, based on our book *Sexual Assault: The Dilemma of Disclosure, the Question of Conviction* (Gunn & Minch, 1988) addresses this problem by examining the impact of social and legal barriers.

Sexual assaults are committed almost exclusively by males within the context of a patriarchal society. Most victims are female. The power imbalance resulting from this gender-based structure fosters a progression from male dominance to aggression, manifesting itself in sexual assault. Within this context there is a lack of support for the victim, except where she is held blameless for the offense as determined by socially prescribed behavior for women. By looking at the reaction to the offense, not only on the part of the victims but also significant others, the legal system, and the media, the barriers to reporting the offense and to due process become clear.

The research on sexual assault reported here represents the most comprehensive data available in Canada. The data base is a major urban center. The research encompasses the victims' responses to sexual assault and the filtering process of charges in the criminal justice system. Our intent was to facilitate a better understanding of the sociolegal and structural dynamics of sexual assault within a Canadian context.

Research at the victim level examines the decision to report (or not to report) sexual offenses to the police and the relevant factors associated with making that choice. Deciding to report a sexual assault is dependent on social factors in which circumstances and effects of the incident, as well as all facets of the victim's life experiences, must be examined. All victims do not react the same way in seemingly similar circumstances. Consequently, such a decision must be determined by factors other than just the assault itself.

Access to this information had to come from victims themselves so that we could study the victim's perception of her victimization as well as her actual response. Victims who were seen at the rape crisis center in Winnipeg were interviewed. The center offers information, advocacy, support, and crisis and long-term counseling to victims.

Interviews with women at the sexual assault center provided firsthand insight into their perceptions and experiences as victims of sexual assault. Factors quite apart from the offense itself were found to be paramount in the decision to report to police. The decision was greatly influenced by reactions from significant others that contributed to the victims' internalized guilt and discouraged them from reporting to the police. More precisely, we found that factors such as relationship between the victim and the offender, response from the first person to whom the victim disclosed the assault, attribution of guilt by the victim, and the extent of injury to the victim were the primary determinants of the decision whether or not to report a sexual assault to the police.

Data on the processing of sexual assault by the criminal justice system comprised two years of reports made to the police in the city of Winnipeg. The research involved 154 reports and 211 offenders. Information on the charges was obtained from police files and interviews with the Crown attorneys who had handled the cases. The methodology employed allowed for an analysis of the charges from the time a report was made to the final outcome.

Results indicate that the great majority of the offenders' charges (71%) were filtered out of the criminal justice system. The police level saw the greatest loss of offenders' charges (58%). This left 29% of charges that resulted in a conviction for the offender, comprising findings of guilt on the original sexual assault charges, reduced charges, and plea-bargained charges. In fact, the original sexual charge resulted in a finding of guilt at the trial in only 9% of the cases.

The criminal justice system is inhibited by social/structural limitations that place blame on the victim for the assault committed against her. The high rate of charges filtered out of the criminal justice system substantiates this claim. The number of victims choosing to withdraw their participation in the criminal proceedings is also indicative of the lack of support and credibility given to reports of sexual assault on social and legal levels.

The data clearly demonstrate that myths and stereotypes persist in social and legal responses to victims of sexual assault. There is a dilemma manifested by the occurrence of sexual assault: The victim can choose to remain silent and thereby deny the due legal process for a serious offense committed against her.

## CANADA'S SEXUAL ASSAULT LEGISLATION

An initial assessment of charges tried under Canada's new sexual assault legislation reveals that Criminal Code amendments that emphasize the violent rather than the less pertinent sexual aspects of the offense have not produced the far-reaching effects envisioned. A continuing reliance on a number of issues that essentially put the victim on trial confirms that societal perceptions and reactions have not kept pace with the revisions made to the sexual assault legislation.

Canada's sexual assault legislation came into effect in January 1983. It replaced the existing rape laws, which had been taken from the law of England and incorporated into the first Canadian Criminal Code in the 1890s. Prior to the new law, the rape legislation remained virtually unchanged in Canada. The new legislation saw the abrogation of the former offenses of rape, attempted rape, and indecent assault. The legislation brought about a major shift in the focus of the offense, emphasizing the assaultive rather than the sexual aspect. The necessity of penetration was eliminated, and instead the violence of the offense was used in designating a sexual assault. The authors have found that the old label of *rape* still persists and is prevalent in media reporting of sexual assaults, even 5 years after its replacement in the law by the revised term in the sexual assault legislation.

The 1983 legislation has addressed the issue of gender in most sexual offenses by classifying either a male or a female as a victim or an offender. However, a number of offenses found in the old legislation remain, including seduction of female passengers on vessels, sexual intercourse with a female under 14 years of age, sexual intercourse with a female 14-16 years of age, buggery, gross indecency, and incest. The sexual assault legislation provides a three-tiered system of classifying assaults, depending on factors such as the use of a weapon, victim injury, threat to a third party, the number of offenders, and the endangerment of life. The offenses are classified in terms of severity, beginning with sexual assault and followed by sexual assault with threats of bodily harm, and aggravated sexual assault.

We have examined cases tried under the new legislation and have prepared a preliminary assessment of the impact of the amendments on the processing and ultimately on the reporting of sexual offenses. We have included the following major areas of the legislation: the meaning of sexual assault, corroboration and recent complaint, the sexual background and reputation of the victim, and spousal sexual assault.

## The Meaning of Sexual Assault

The definition of sexual assault had to be clarified with the advent of the sexual assault legislation. The new law did not differentiate between assault and sexual assault in terms of necessary elements. The establishment of a clear definition of sexual assault was imperative so that there would be standardization in terms of appropriately designating the offense.

One of the first major court decisions was made by the New Brunswick Court of Appeal in R. v. Chase (1984). The judge ruled that sexual assault was not related to the touching of a woman's breasts and that the offense was restricted to an assault on the so-designated primary sexual organs or genitalia. In fact, the touching of breasts was deemed to involve secondary sexual characteristics akin to a man's beard, and the original conviction for sexual assault was replaced with common assault.

There were a number of subsequent appeals of sexual assault convictions made in Canadian appeal courts based on the Chase decision, and the New Brunswick decision was ultimately rejected by both the Ontario (R. v. Gardynik, 1984) and British Columbia (R. v. Cook, 1985) appeal courts. An appeal to the Supreme Court of Canada in R. v. Chase was heard in October 1987 and resulted in a much-needed final clarification, to the effect that touching a woman's breasts did constitute a sexual assault, regardless of whether the touching involved secondary sexual organs.

Yet another area requiring definition was the boundaries of defining a sexual assault so as not to minimize the seriousness of the offense. The case of R. v. Thorne (1985) posed a problem in that a youth was found guilty of sexual assault for forcibly kissing the hand of a young woman. An appeal of the case to the Ontario Court of Appeal resulted in a decision that the youth was not guilty of sexual assault but rather was given a conditional discharge for an assault. Appropriate parameters regarding the classification of sexual assault are crucial so that the offense does not become trivialized.

Reference to the old term *rape*, now absent from the sexual assault legislation, continues to be a problem and is used in Canadian courtrooms by legal personnel and the media. Widespread recognition in society of the new legislation and its intent in focusing on the violent aspect of the offense will not occur with continued use of the now defunct and legally incorrect term of *rape*. One trial in which the judge used *rape* in sentencing an offender was subsequently appealed in the case of R. v. Daychief (1985). The courts, in particular, have a responsibility to make the new legislation and its appropriate terminology clear, both in the courtroom and for the general public whose interests they are employed to serve. The outcome of the appeal in the Daychief case was to uphold the decision in referring to the sexual assault as "rape." The appeal court judge in effect stated that just because the legal designation of the offense had changed, it did not alter the fact that a "rape" had occurred. We see this type of judicial direction as very damaging to the integrity and effectiveness of the sexual assault legislation.

## Corroboration and Recent Complaint

The requirement under the old legislation for corroborative evidence is no longer present under the new legislation. Corroboration involves evidence independent of the victim's testimony that supports the allegation that a sexual assault has been committed, such as cuts, bruises, torn clothing, and the like. The new legislation does not require such independent evidence for a conviction. In essence, the victim will be listened to in court, and a preoccupation with her credibility will not be given the paramount importance it once had under the old legislation.

The corroboration requirement historically had its roots in the belief that the testimony of the sexual assault victim could not be solely relied upon because of stereotyped notions that victims might be driven by ulterior (and ultimately deceptive) motives such as revenge, notoriety, or blackmail. Motivations of this kind on the part of the victim have been dispelled by research indicating that false accusations are rare and no more common in sexual assault than in any other offense.

The issue of recent complaint has similarly been stricken from the new legislation. The need for it under the old legislation was premised on yet another stereotype: that a "genuine" victim would speak to someone about the offense at the first opportunity. Sexual assault centers have provided support to many women who do not speak about the offense for years, especially if the offender is someone related or close to them. Such an unreasonable expectation once again underlies a basic distrust of the victim and her allegation without regard for the effective way in which the criminal justice system can uncover false accusations, regardless of the offense alleged. Further, expectation of an immediate response from the victim to the first person she sees after the offense fails to acknowledge the very real emotions of fear, shame, isolation, and confusion that may inhibit revealing the assault.

Even with the abrogation of corroboration and recent complaint under the sexual assault legislation, we found instances where they were in fact used to bolster the case in an indirect way (R. v. Page, 1984). We contend that when these factors are used by the judiciary in reaching a decision in a sexual assault case, they are damaging to the intent of the new legislation. If they are deemed noteworthy, albeit not legally necessary for a conviction, then what will the absence of such information indicate?

## Sexual Background and Reputation of the Victim

The image of the courtroom scene of a woman being harassed on the stand as she is being viciously cross-examined about her past sexual activity has been a familiar fact associated with sexual assault reports. Although the law was amended in 1976, the victim could still be cross-examined on her sexual conduct but was not compelled to answer. The defense could not lead evidence to refute her testimony; but once a question was asked in court, the victim's credibility was at risk, and that could not be completely withdrawn from the minds of a judge and jury. No response also could be seen as an admission of guilt. Furthermore, it was left to the judge to decide whether this type of evidence was relevant to the facts of the case, with judges having complete discretion in this determination.

The new sexual assault legislation has provided clear boundaries for questioning as to sexual background. Defense is no longer allowed to go on a "fishing expedition" in order to discredit the victim. The new amendments prohibit any mention of the victim's sexual past, with three exceptions (and these exceptions must be preceded by written notice to the prosecutors): (1) if it pertains to evidence (or absence) of sexual activity that was introduced by the Crown; (2) if it pertains to evidence that must establish the identity of the accused as the person who had sexual contact with the victim; (3) if it pertains to sexual activity that occurred on the same occasion as the incident that is the subject of the charge and relates to the defendant's belief in the consent of the victim.

Although these amendments provide an element of protection that previously was not there for victims, there is still considerable discretion allowed the judge in determining relevance. For example, in the case of R. v. J.A. (1984), a suspended sentence was given to a brother for the sexual assault of his 16-year-old sister. The judge's commentary on the "sexual sophistication" of the victim revealed his standards of expected sexual behavior for young females. He said:

> ... if the sister involved in that incestuous relationship with a brother is not of previously chaste character ... that previous sexual experiences encountered by a sister do not allow a brother to take advantage of that, but one must realize that the damage ... the psychological trauma may not be the same.

That sort of attitude will impact on judicial procedure and perpetuate the double standards of sexual behavior that have traditionally been applied to males and females.

However, if Crown prosecutors are vigilant and appeal decisions that have been based on an erroneous application of the legislation, these cases can be brought to a higher court and can also serve as an educational device for the judiciary. An illustrative case, R. v. Cormier (1985) was taken to appeal court to appeal a sentence for which the judge had minimized the seriousness of the offense because of the victim's sexual background. The two offenders had their sentences increased from 6 months and 3 months to 4 years and 2 years, respectively. The court appropriately considered the sexual assault charge rather than the life-style of the victim.

## Sexual Assault of a Spouse

From 1891 to 1983, immunity from prosecution for rape was guaranteed to husbands in Canadian law. With the advent of the sexual assault amendments has come protection of wives, regardless of whether or not the married couple is cohabiting. Although the new law is gender-neutral, this section refers predominantly to protection of wives who are sexually assaulted by their husbands. Embedded in the former law was a legal acknowledgment of wifely duty to provide sexual service to her husband. The first Canadian case heard in a courtroom (R. v. McDonald, 1983) was that of an estranged husband who pled guilty and received a 1-year sentence in prison. On sentencing, the judge commented that although the assault did take place, he was of the opinion that the victim could not have experienced the same extent of trauma as she might have, had she been assaulted by a stranger. Although some decisions have been favorable to wives, sentences have been comparatively less severe than in nonspousal cases, even though injuries are often serious. These injuries serve as proof of the assault, although corroboration is no longer required for a conviction. In not a single instance in our survey of the new legislation was there a case between two married persons in which there was not overt evidence that corroborated the wife's accusation. A 1-year sentence with varying probationary periods appears to be the norm (R. v. A., 1985; R. v. Ryan, 1985), although one extremely violent case resulted in only a 6-month sentence (R. v. Guiboche, 1983).

Treating the sexual assault of wives as a less serious crime strengthens traditional beliefs that contradict the spirit of the amendments. So far, judicial decisions have not provided universal support to the unacceptability of violence toward women. Many decisions are still couched in old rules of conduct for women (e.g., expected to be submissive) and belief in stereotypes (e.g., women want to be overpowered).

Because spousal immunity has only recently become codified in law, more cases must proceed to trial before the problem will be regarded as a serious one. As more cases are publicized and wives begin to realize their right to self-determination, more women will also realize their right to be safe from sexual attack, no matter what their marital status and relationship to the attacker. As more women in cohabiting and marital relationships declare their victimization, we will begin to see the extent of spousal assault.

## CONCLUSION

The foregoing synopsis of research on the sociolegal impact of sexual assault and the new sexual assault legislation indicates that many of the harmful stereotypes surrounding the offense still persist. The research illustrates that the victim is traumatized by the offense in her relationship with significant others, especially in those cases where the offender is known to the victim and to her family and friends. The dilemma faced by the victim in choosing to disclose the offense becomes increasingly clear when the reaction of the criminal justice system is examined and, once again, the victim receives less than a supportive response and the mandated "due process" within the legal system in the prosecution of the charge(s). A filtering out of charges in the criminal justice system of just over 70% supports this contention.

The preliminary analysis of the impact of the new sexual assault legislation reveals that it is not achieving its stated intentions in a substantive manner. The role of societal attitudes within a patriarchal society is seen as the major impediment to achieving widespread recognition of the realities of sexual assault as an offense involving power and domination as opposed to an uncontrollable sexual desire. These attitudes have been found to exist across society and include family, friends, the criminal justice system, and the media.

# REFERENCES

Gunn, R., & Minch, C. (1988). *Sexual assault: The dilemma of disclosure, the question of conviction*. Winnipeg, Canada: University of Manitoba Press.
R. v. A., 14 Western Criminal Bulletin (Yukon Territorial Court, 1985).
R. v. Chase, 40 Criminal Report, 3d (New Brunswick Court of Appeal, 1984).
R. v. Cook, 46 Criminal Report, 3d (British Columbia Court of Appeal, 1985).
R. v. Cormier, Canadian Criminal Law (New Brunswick Court of Appeal, 1985).
R. v. Daychief, 6 Western Weekly Review (Alberta Court of Appeal, 1985).
R. v. Gardynik, 42 Criminal Report, 3d (Ontario Court of Appeal, 1984).
R. v. Guiboche. (1983, September 9). *Winnipeg Free Press*.
R. v. J. A., Northwest Territorial Report (Northwest Territorial Court, 1984).
R. v. McDonald, (Alberta, 1983).
R. v. Page, 40 Criminal Report (Ontario Superior Court, 1984).
R. v. Ryan, Canadian Criminal Law (British Columbia Court of Appeal, 1985).
R. v. Thorne, 13 Western Criminal Bulletin (Ontario Court of Appeal, 1985).

# 17

# Preventing Rape: How People Perceive the Options of Defending Oneself during an Assault

*Lita Furby, Baruch Fischhoff, and Marcia Morgan*

---

Women are constantly faced with the threat of rape. To cope with it, they can choose from a wide variety of response strategies, each reflecting a somewhat different set of beliefs regarding what prevents assaults or deters rapists, each with somewhat different chances of success, and each entailing somewhat different side effects (e.g., how they affect a woman's self-image). How women choose response strategies is determined, in large part, by how they perceive these uncertain options. As a result, the quality of a woman's choice is bounded by the number and appropriateness of the options she considers. This chapter is based on a study examining in depth how women perceive the repertoire of possible strategies for preventing rape. In particular, it focuses on strategies for defending oneself during an assault.

Support for this work was provided by the NIMH Center for the Prevention and Control of Rape, under Grant No. MH40481-02. We thank Mark Layman, Nancy Collins, and Cecelia Hagen for their invaluable assistance.

## PROFILE OF THE WOMEN INTERVIEWED

The data collection and analysis procedures are described at length in Furby, Fischhoff, and Morgan (1990). Briefly, three groups of women (college students, lower-income young mothers, and higher-income middle-aged women), one group of men (college students), and one group of sexual assault experts completed an open-ended questionnaire asking them to list as many rape-prevention strategies as they could. Its first half dealt with strategies for preventing rape assaults from occurring, and the second half asked specifically about strategies for stopping an assault once it was under way. For the questionnaires given to the three groups of women, each half began with questions specific to the individual (i.e., "Imagine that you personally are the victim of a rape attempt. What kinds of things do you think you would do to try to keep from being raped and to stop the assault?") and then proceeded to more general questions (i.e., "We are also interested in things that you wouldn't do yourself but which might be appropriate for someone else when confronted with a rape attack"). Once respondents exhausted the store of strategies that came to mind spontaneously, they were presented with several situational prompts (e.g., "A woman living alone awakens to hear someone breaking into her bedroom") and asked whether the situation reminded them of any additional strategies a woman might use to thwart a rape attempt. For the male and expert groups, questions were reworded slightly to ask what they thought a woman typically does or could do if assaulted (rather than what they personally would do).

## RESULTS AND DISCUSSION

In interpreting the data, we identified three stages at which a strategy is designed to be effective: (1) preventing an assault from ever occurring, (2) preparing to react to an assault, and (3) defending yourself during an assault as well as two action levels (societal and individual). Table 17.1 presents the eight categories of intended effects for Stage 3 strategies, roughly in order of increasing assertiveness or forcefulness. Where a very large number of strategies had the same intended effect, we also developed suitable subcategories, which are also presented in Table 17.1.

Table 17.2 lists the strategies mentioned by at least 10% of any of the respondent groups in answer to the general questions regarding what women are likely to do if assaulted. The table lists first all 18 strategies mentioned by at least 10% of women, in order of citation frequency, then the four as-yet-unlisted strategies that were mentioned by at least 10% of the men, and finally the 14 as-yet-unlisted strategies that were cited by at least 10% of the experts. The lengths of these lists indicate that few strategies thought to be used by women are widely known to men that are not also widely known to female respondents, whereas

TABLE 17.1 Rape Self-defense Strategy Categories with Verbatim Examples[a]

Manage yourself in ways that maximize ability to implement self-defense measures successfully
    Control own thoughts/emotions/actions
        • Know/believe that you do not have to be a rape victim
        • Do not faint or pass out
    Assess the situation
        Evaluate rapist
            • Consider attacker's strength
            • Assess attacker's personality
        Evaluate surroundings
            • Mentally assess the situation for alternatives
    Wait/stall/use guile until good self-defense opportunity
        • Go along until you can safely react
        • Use something as a distraction, then react
Reduce/minimize assailant's propensity to rape
    Avoid antagonizing assailant
        • Do not fight back
        • Pretend you are asleep
    Don't miscommunicate intentions
        • State clearly you like him as a person but do not want a physical relationship
    Create bizarre/unattractive impression
        • Feign a seizure
        • Do crude, unfeminine things
    Appeal to assailant's sympathy, morals
        • Plead or beg
        • Make him see you as a human
    Reason with assailant
        • Tell attacker your friendship might be ruined
        • Talk your way out of the situation
Increase perceived ability to cope with assailant
    • Assume a karate stance
    • Make it known you have a weapon
    • Clear verbal resistance
Increase perceived chances of outside intervention
    • Fake arrival of others
Increase actual chances of outside intervention
    General appeal (to anyone who might be aware of it)
        • Yell "fire"
        • Use whistle
    Directed appeal (to specific individuals)
        • Call the police
        • Summon nearest male
Increase perceived chances of punishment
    • State you will press charges against attacker
Establish distance or barrier between self and assailant
    • Get out of house
    • Run away

(continued)

TABLE 17.1 (continued)

Physically impede or incapacitate assailant
  With nonforceful means
- Give him drugs
- Get him drunk

  With physical force
    Weapon
- Use Mace
- Call dog

    Physical struggle/fight
- Kick
- Use self-defense techniques

[a]Verbatim examples from open-ended questionnaire data. A given strategy might, of course, have more than one intended effect; strategy examples are categorized here according to our best judgment of their principal intended effect (described in more detail in Fischhoff, Furby, & Morgan, 1986).

many more are widely known to experts. This is not surprising, given experts' experience with a larger number of rape cases and a broader set of assault situations.

One notable feature of these results is that the two most frequently mentioned strategies were the same for all three groups: "scream or yell" and "run away." The third and fourth items in the females' list ("talk way out of situation/reasoning" and "fighting/physical self-defense techniques") also appeared prominently in the other two groups' lists. These items represent four different intended effects (nos. 2, 5, 7, 8 in Table 17.1), suggesting that all groups recognize some breadth in women's repertoire of strategies. At the other end of the spectrum, no strategies designed to increase the assailant's perceived chances of punishment or the perceived chances of outside intervention (intended effects nos. 4 and 6) were mentioned by even 10% of any respondent groups. Apparently, women see and are thought to see little value in these "psychological manipulations."[1] After this agreement, the groups tend to diverge.

## Female Respondents

For female respondents, the other frequently mentioned strategies fell into just two categories: those intended to physically impede or incapacitate the assailant (effect no. 8 in Table 17.1) and those designed to reduce or minimize his

1. Of course, many strategies that increase the *actual* chances of outside intervention (e.g., scream or yell) also increase the *perceived* chances of it (i.e., they increase the assailant's estimate of the chances that someone will intervene). Because we categorized each strategy according to its principal intended effect only, the extent to which women rely on increasing the perceived chances of outside intervention may be somewhat underestimated here.

TABLE 17.2 What People Think Women Are Likely to Do If Assaulted[a]

| | | % Who mentioned strategy[c] (rank order in parentheses) | | |
|---|---|---|---|---|
| Stage-level-intended effect[b] | Strategy | Females | Males | Experts |
| III-i-outside intervention[a] | Scream or yell | 66.7 | 56.8 (1) | 69.8 (1/2) |
| III-i-establish distance or barrier | Run away | 57.6 | 52.3 (2) | 69.8 (1/2) |
| III-i-reduce assailant's propensity to rape | Talk way out of situation, reasoning | 44.7 | 18.2 (8/10) | 41.9 (4) |
| III-i-physically impede assailant | Fighting/physical self-defense techniques (e.g., martial arts or specific blows/hits) | 43.9 | 38.6 (4) | 53.5 (3) |
| III-i-physically impede assailant | Knee/kick him in the groin | 42.4 | 47.7 (3) | 11.6 (28/32) |
| III-i-reduce assailant's propensity to rape | Make yourself seem less attractive; do crude, "unfeminine," gross, dirty things (e.g, vomit, urinate, defecate, pick nose, fake menstrual cramp, pass gas) | 30.3 | 11.4 (17/18) | 27.9 (8/9) |
| III-i-minimize assailant's propensity to rape | Cooperate with rapist/submit | 28.8 | 15.9 (11/13) | 34.9 (5) |
| III-i-physically impede assailant | Poke, jab, or claw rapist's eyes | 26.5 | 27.3 (5) | 20.9 (12/15) |
| III-i-physically impede assailant | Kick | 25.8 | 18.2 (8/10) | 25.6 (10) |
| III-i-reduce assailant's propensity to rape | State you have VD, are a virgin, menstruating, recovering from operation, diseased | 22.7 | 13.6 (14/16) | 32.6 (6) |
| III-i-physically impede assailant | Bite attacker; draw blood (e.g., bite his tongue or lips hard) | 21.2 | 20.5 (6/7) | 23.3 (11) |
| III-i-physically impede assailant | Use Mace, tear gas and chemical sprays | 16.7 | 15.9 (11/13) | 11.6 (28/32) |

| | | | | | |
|---|---|---|---|---|---|
| III-i-physically impede assailant | Make use of gun | 15.9 | 4.5 (28/42) | 2.3 (73/137) | |
| III-i-physically impede assailant | Stomp on rapist's feet (e.g., instep, shin, toes, etc.) | 11.4 | 4.5 (28/42) | 7.0 (40/54) | |
| III-i-physically impede assailant | Scratch attacker | 11.4 | 20.5 (6/7) | 9.3 (33/39) | |
| III-i-reduce assailant's propensity to rape | Feign illness, heart attack, seizure, fainting | 11.4 | 4.5 (28/42) | 18.6 (16/19) | |
| III-i-outside intervention[a] | Use whistle (police-type) | 10.6 | 15.9 (11/13) | 4.7 (56/72) | |
| III-i-physically impede assailant | Make use of "any" object as a weapon (i.e., nail file, hat pin, lamp, umbrella) | 10.6 | 4.5 (28/42) | 18.6 (16/19) | |
| III-i-increase ability to cope with assailant[p] | Clear verbal resistance (e.g., "Leave me alone," "No," "Stop," "Get out," ask him to leave, make him leave) | 5.3 (35/39) | 18.2 (8/10) | 30.2 (7) | [d] |
| III-i-physically impede assailant | Make use of weapons carried specifically for preventing assault | 9.8 (19) | 13.6 (14/16) | 11.6 (28/32) | |
| III-i-outside intervention[a] | Yell/scream for help | 3.8 (44/51) | 13.6 (14/16) | 20.9 (12/15) | |
| III-i-physically impede assailant | Hit | 7.6 (26/27) | 11.4 (17/18) | 16.3 (20/24) | [e] |
| III-i-reduce assailant's propensity to rape | Plead/beg | 3.8 (44/51) | 6.8 (22/27) | 27.9 (8/9) | |
| III-i-manage self | retain or regain your emotional stability (keep your cool, stay calm), think clearly | 9.1 (20/22) | 9.1 (19/21) | 20.9 (12/15) | |
| III-i-manage self | Go along until you can safely react | 8.3 (23/25) | 9.1 (19/21) | 20.9 (12/15) | |
| III-i-outside intervention | Yell "Fire" (rather than just "Help" or "Rape") | 8.3 (23/25) | 4.5 (28/42) | 18.6 (16/19) | |

(continued)

TABLE 17.2 (continued)

| Stage-level-intended effect[b] | Strategy | % Who mentioned strategy[c] (rank order in parentheses) | | |
|---|---|---|---|---|
| | | Females | Males | Experts |
| III-i-manage self | Stall for time/use small talk (get rapist relaxed and off guard) | 1.5 (70/92) | 0 | 18.6 (16/19) |
| III-i-increase ability to cope with assailant[p] | "Freeze," do nothing | 2.3 (60/69) | 2.3 (43/75) | 16.3 (20/24) |
| III-i-outside intervention[p] | Fake presence or arrival of others | 4.5 (40/43) | 4.5 (28/42) | 16.3 (20/24) |
| III-i-manage self | Mentally assess situation for alternatives | 3.8 (44/51) | 0 | 16.3 (20/24) |
| I-i-increase chances of punishment | Get description of assailant and preserve evidence for later identification | 6.1 (30/34) | 4.5 (28/42) | 16.3 (20/24) |
| III-i-manage self | Use something/someone as distraction then escape/react | 1.5 (70/92) | 0 | 14.0 (25/27) |
| III-i-outside intervention[p] | Make loud noises/attract attention (e.g., knocking over garbage) | 9.1 (20/22) | 0 | 14.0 (25/27) |
| III-i-manage self | Conning | 0 | 4.5 (28/42) | 14.0 (25/27) |
| III-i-physically impede assailant | Use physical force to vital/vulnerable parts of the body | .8 (94/147) | 0 | 11.6 (28/32) |
| III-i-increase ability to cope with assailant[p] | Verbal aggression (e.g., calling him names) | .8 (94/147) | 0 | 11.6 (28/32) |

[a] Strategies mentioned by at least 10% of respondents in one or more groups, in answer to questions R and S (females) or R (males and experts). See Furby, Fischoff & Morgan (1990) for verbatim questions. A difference of approximately 20% between females and either of the other groups is significant at $p < .01$.
[b] Stage codes: I = prevent assault from occurring; II = prepare for reacting to an assault; III = defend yourself during an assault. Action level codes: s = societal action; i = individual action. Intended effect subscripts: p = perceived; a = actual. See Fischhoff, Furby, and Morgan (1990).
[c] Tied ranks are indicated by giving the range of ranks that are tied (e.g., 8/10 means that there were three strategies all mentioned with the same frequency and thus tied for the 8th, 9th, and 10th slots).
[d] Ordering shifts to frequency of citation by men.
[e] Ordering shifts to frequency of citation by experts.

motivation to rape (no. 2) (no strategy from any other category appears until 17th place). The emphasis on these two intended effects can also be seen in the summary statistics of Table 17.3, where 43% of all strategies mentioned by women were aimed at physically impeding the assailant and 24% at reducing the assailant's motivation to rape. These are clearly the principal ways that women think they and other women would try to defend themselves if assaulted. Citations for the next two intended effects categories in Table 17.3 came predominantly from the popularity of "scream or yell" (intended to increase the chances of outside intervention) and "run away" (intended to establish distance or a barrier between self and assailant). The absence of subsidiary ways to achieve these two effects suggests that these categories are not well elaborated, and they may be more popular than these figures suggest. A practical implication is that women might have difficulty finding an alternative way of achieving either of these goals if a first attempt failed.

## Male Respondents

As seen in Table 17.3, the men mentioned on the average somewhat fewer strategies than did the women. This may mean that men know of fewer strategies or that men believe that women will do fewer things than women think they (and other women) will do. Like the women, these men placed greatest emphasis (relative to other intended effects) on physically impeding the assailant. On the other hand, relatively fewer of the strategies they attribute to women are intended to reduce or minimize the assailant's propensity to rape. In particular, considerably fewer men than women (18% vs. 45%) mentioned that a woman would try to talk her way out of the situation, make herself seem less attractive (11% vs. 30%), or cooperate with the assailant (16% vs. 29%). Perhaps men underestimate the sense of physical helplessness experienced by many women (Riger & Gordon, 1981) and thus the degree to which women would rely on such nonconfrontational strategies. Perhaps men are simply less aware of methods such as doing "unfeminine" things or claiming "unattractive" physical attributes; or perhaps men are aware of these nonforceful strategies but feel that they will not work with assailants (and believe that women feel the same way).

## Experts

The average expert mentioned almost 50% more strategies than did the average female respondent when asked what they thought a woman would do if assaulted (Table 17.3). This probably reflects experts' contact with a wider variety of rape cases (and victims), though it might also reflect, in part, a greater willingness to work hard at this task.

Although "physically impede the assailant" is the intended effect cited most often by experts (Table 17.3), its plurality is much smaller than with the other

TABLE 17.3 Number and Distribution of Strategies People Think Women Would Use If Assaulted—by Intended Effect Category[a]

| | | | | Distribution by category | | |
|---|---|---|---|---|---|---|
| | | | | | Females | |
| Intended effect[b] | Females | Males | Experts | They would do | Others would do, they would not |
|---|---|---|---|---|---|
| Physically impede assailant | 43% | 46% | 29% | 40% | 55% |
| Reduce assailant's motivation to rape | 24% | 14% | 25% | 23% | 27% |
| Increase actual chances of outside intervention | 14% | 17% | 14% | 17% | 6% |
| Establish distance or barrier between self and assailant | 8% | 9% | 8% | 10% | 2% |
| Manage yourself to better implement self-defense strategies | 6% | 5% | 13% | 6% | 5% |
| Increase perceived ability to cope | 4% | 8% | 9% | 4% | 2% |
| Increase perceived chances of outside intervention | 1% | 1% | 2% | 0% | 2% |
| Increase perceived chances of punishment | 0% | 0% | 0% | 0% | 0% |
| Means | 8.12 | 6.41* | 11.81** | 6.31 | 1.81 |

[a]Responses to question R & S (females) or R (males and experts). For the full text of these questions see Furby, Fischhoff, and Morgan (1990).
[b]A few Stage 1 (prevent assault from ever occurring) and Stage 2 (prepare for reacting to an assault) strategies were mentioned. They are omitted from this category analysis.
*Significantly different from females at $p < .05$.
**$p < .01$.

groups. Compared to the women, experts' shifts in emphasis are toward strategies designed to "manage oneself to better implement self-defense strategies" (from 6% to 13%) and to "increase one's perceived ability to cope with the assailant" (from 4% to 9%), that is, steps a woman can take toward taking control of herself and of the situation. Perhaps experts are slightly more cognizant than lay women of the importance of self-management to successful self-defense, and they may have an exaggerated perception of how widely women have adopted these strategies. Conversely, they may feel that this is a step that many women overlook, and they have mentioned it (inadvertently) here as something women *should* do (even though they were asked about what women actually do).

Given the experts' higher overall rate of strategy production, it is notable that fewer experts than women say that women might knee an assailant in the groin (12% vs. 42%). It may be that few women actually do this and that experts know that, whereas women may be led to view this as a commonly used strategy because of the frequency with which it is cited among lay people as something women can do. Since many experts recommend *against* this strategy (because assailants might become very angry or because it is a difficult move to execute given the usual height differential), it may also be that many did not mention it here because they think women *should* not do it (not because they think women *would* not).

## What Women Say They Themselves Would Do

Women provided strategies that they think they would use if assaulted and strategies that they believe at least some other women (but not themselves) might use. The fourth column of Table 17.3 shows the mean number of strategies that women report being likely to use themselves, along with the distribution across categories. Because these constitute over three-quarters of total strategies mentioned (a mean of 6.31 out of 8.12), it is not surprising that the two distributions, as well as the specific strategy lists, are quite similar.

With respect to specific strategies, it is noteworthy that the two most frequently mentioned things that all three respondent groups (women, men, and experts) think women would do if assaulted, "yelling or screaming" and "running away," are in fact the two most frequently mentioned things that women say they themselves would do. The only significant discrepancy is that fewer women say they would cooperate with the rapist (17%; Table 17.4) than experts think that women would (35%; Table 17.2).

In contrast to the above results, Furby, Fischhoff, and Morgan (1990) showed substantial differences in the behavior attributed to oneself and that attributed to women in general with regard to strategies designed to prevent assaults from ever being initiated. In that study, the average woman attributed 3.68 strategies to others (compared to 1.81 here). Moreover, those strategies were seldom mentioned by (other) women as things that they themselves do. For example, few

TABLE 17.4 What Women Think Others Would Do but They Would Not Do to Defend Themselves If Assaulted[a]

| Stage-level-intended effect[b] | Strategy | % who said they would not use this strategy but other women would | % who said they would use this strategy[c] |
|---|---|---|---|
| III-i-physically impede assailant | Fighting/physical self-defense techniques (e.g, martial arts or specific blows/hits) | 23.5 | 27.3 |
| III-i-physically impede assailant | Make use of gun | 15.2 | 2.3 |
| III-i-reduce assailant's propensity to rape | Make yourself seem less attractive; do crude, "unfeminine," gross, dirty things (e.g., vomit, urinate, defecate, pick nose, fake menstrual cramp, pass gas) | 13.6 | 18.9 |
| III-i-physically impede assailant | Use Mace, tear gas and chemical sprays | 12.1 | 6.1 |
| III-i-reduce assailant's propensity to rape | Cooperate with rapist/submit | 12.1 | 17.4 |

[a] Strategies mentioned by at least 10% of respondents in answer to question S.
[b] See Table 17.2, note 6.
[c] Strategies mentioned in response to question R.

women said that they learn self-defense or carry spray chemicals like Mace, but many women said that they think other women do those things.

Table 17.4 presents the comparable data for thwarting an assault. It lists specific self-defense strategies that at least 10% of the women said that other women would use if assaulted but that they would not use themselves. A substantial number of women say they would not use physical fighting, but an equally large number think that they themselves would use it (right-hand column). A similar dichotomy exists for the strategies of cooperating with the rapist and making yourself seem less attractive. Results for these three strategies provide the clearest evidence of disagreement among women regarding which strategies they themselves are willing to implement.

By contrast, the second and fourth most common attributions to other women but not oneself (use gun, use chemicals) were seldom cited by women for themselves. These two strategies, being more widely known than they are personally relevant, account for the greater emphasis attributed to others than to oneself on physically impeding the assailant (Table 17.3).

There were few differences among the three female groups with respect to specific strategies they say they would use if assaulted. The most notable (greater than 20%) were that the higher-income middle-aged women mentioned running away and fighting less frequently than did the other two groups (38% vs. 63% and 64% for running; 16% vs. 33% and 34% for fighting). Perhaps these women feel less confident about their ability to implement those particular physical strategies successfully. In contrast, they mentioned biting significantly more than did the college students (with the lower-income young mothers falling in between). Perhaps this physical strategy seems more readily implemented and fills the niche for strategies designed to impede the assailant physically.

The only other notable difference among the three female groups was that college students were least likely (7%) and the lower-income young mothers were most likely (27%) to say that they would cooperate with the rapist (with higher-income middle-aged women falling in between).

## Neglected Strategies

Both males and experts were asked what strategies women could but rarely do use to defend themselves when assaulted. Table 17.5 lists all of the strategies mentioned by at least 10% of respondents. The men had relatively few suggestions; moreover, all three of the listed strategies were mentioned by substantial numbers of women as something they would do (right-hand column). They are also mentioned by at least as large a number of men who believed that women would use these strategies (Table 17.2). Thus, it is hard to see any new insights being offered to women here.

Experts mentioned many more strategies that women could but rarely do undertake (Table 17.5, "Experts"). Three involve ways to impede the assailant

TABLE 17.5 What People Think Women Could but Rarely Do to Defend Themselves If Assaulted

| Stage-level-intended effect[a] | Strategy | % who said women could but rarely do use this strategy | % women who said they would use this strategy |
|---|---|---|---|
| Males[b] | | | |
| III-i-reduce assailant's propensity to rape | State you have VD, are a virgin, menstruating, recovering from operation, diseased | 13.6 | 18.2 |
| III-i-physically impede assailant | Poke, jab, or claw rapist's eyes | 11.4 | 20.5 |
| III-i-reduce assailant's propensity to rape | Make yourself seem less attractive; do crude, "unfeminine," gross, dirty things (e.g., vomit, urinate, defecate, pick nose, fake menstrual cramp, pass gas) | 11.4 | 18.9 |
| Experts[c] | | | |
| III-i-physically impede assailant | Fighting/physical self-defense techniques (e.g., martial arts or specific blows/hits) | 32.6 | 27.3 |
| III-i-physically impede assailant | Poke, jab, or claw rapist's eyes | 25.6 | 20.5 |
| III-i-physically impede assailant | Physically harm him | 20.9 | 6.8 |
| III-i-outside intervention[a] | Scream or yell | 20.9 | 62.9 |
| III-i-outside intervention[p] | Make loud noises, attract attention (e.g, knocking over garbage) | 14.0 | 9.1 |
| III-i-increase ability to cope with assailant[p] | Clear verbal resistance (e.g., "Leave me alone," "No!" "Stop" "Get out," ask him to leave) | 14.0 | 5.3 |
| III-i-establish distance or barrier | Run away | 11.6 | 54.5 |

[a]See Table 17.2, note b.
[b]Strategies mentioned by at least 10% of males in response to question S.
[c]Strategies mentioned by at least 10% of sexual assault experts in response to question S.

physically; two involve ways to obtain outside intervention. Of the seven listed strategies, four were cited by at least 20% of the women as things they would be likely to do. Thus, either experts underestimate the degree to which women use these strategies, or women misjudge how they would be likely to behave. Five of the seven strategies listed here as things women could but rarely do use were mentioned by larger numbers of experts as things that they believe women would be likely to do (Table 17.2). Thus, there is disagreement among experts regarding whether women are likely to use these five strategies (and Table 17.5 presents a minority opinion). In sum, there was little evidence here that women were seen as missing important options.

## Situational Prompts

After the two general questions regarding strategies for defending oneself during an assault, respondents were asked whether two specific situations reminded them of any additional self-defense strategies. One situation described a woman who hears someone breaking into her bedroom; the other described a woman being accosted on a sidewalk. The effect of these situational prompts was considerable. The women produced an additional 56 different strategies (i.e., beyond the 147 different strategies that they mentioned in response to the two general questions); the men produced an additional 37 (beyond their original 100); the experts produced an additional 39 (beyond their 170). Thus, people apparently know quite a few self-defense strategies that are recalled only when the cues of a specific situation are present. This suggests that the decision-making burden women face in an assault situation may be of greater magnitude than is indicated by considering even a relatively comprehensive list of strategies (e.g., Fischhoff, Furby, & Morgan, 1986). A specific situation inevitably evokes additional strategies from which to choose. This presents a problem for those attempting to help women prepare for reacting to an assault because it suggests that, without knowing the specific assault situation she will face, one cannot reasonably expect to specify all of the most appropriate strategies.

## CONCLUSION

Women who find themselves the target of a rape assault must decide how best to defend themselves. Even when not facing the imminent threat of an assault, many women attempt to prepare themselves for making that decision by engaging in contingency planning, trying to imagine assault situations and how they would respond to them. A significant plurality of the strategies that women say they would use in reacting to a rape assault are intended to physically impede the assailant. Sexual assault experts emphasize physical resistance strategies less than do women when asked how women are likely to react to an assault, but they recommend that women should use these strategies more. Perhaps both groups know that physically forceful resistance is relatively effective (Furby & Fischhoff, in press). However, when faced with an actual assailant, some women may find themselves choosing other strategies. If so, many experts may know that, whereas some women may not (although 27% of our sample consciously anticipate that they would not fight physically).

The other principal means women say they would use to thwart an incipient assault consists of strategies at the other end of the forcefulness continuum: those designed to reduce or minimize the assailant's propensity to rape. They are intended to lead the assailant noncoercively into deciding that he does not want to rape the woman. There is no empirical evidence that these strategies reduce the chance of being raped; if anything, they seem to increase it (Furby & Fischhoff, in press). Perhaps women do not know this. Or perhaps some women see no other viable options when faced with an actual assault. In addition, the threat of general physical injury may become more salient during an actual assault, so that some women may find themselves trying to minimize the assailant's anger by using nonforceful strategies. Again, however, there is no empirical evidence that these "psychological" strategies decrease the chances of other physical injury.

It is remarkable that the two most frequently mentioned specific strategies, "yelling or screaming" and "running away," were the sole representatives of their categories here. If their intended effects (increasing the chances of outside intervention, establishing distance or a barrier between self and assailant) are indeed effective methods of stopping an assault (as both their popularity here and the limited empirical evidence suggests; see Furby & Fischhoff, in press), women need alternative ways of achieving them (e.g., if you are in a car, yelling will not attract outside intervention; causing an accident might be a better strategy for achieving that effect).

More generally, women might benefit from a varied and articulated set of strategies for achieving a given effect, thereby permitting them to choose the most appropriate for a particular assault situation as well as for their own person (i.e., their beliefs, values, physical abilities, and prior preparation). This was highlighted by the substantial disagreement among women regarding the use of physical fighting. Approximately one-fourth of our sample said that they would fight with an assailant, whereas an equal number said that they would not. The latter's rejection of physical force was not necessarily categorical, however. For example, the middle-aged women in our sample were more likely to reject physical fighting than the other two groups, but they were also more likely to say that they would bite the assailant, a method of physically impeding him that they apparently find more acceptable.

Despite the above considerations, it is impossible for women to consider all potentially relevant strategies for all possible situations just as it is impossible for investigators to study them all. As a result, those providing advice to women might focus their attention at the level of intended effects. Women might be best served by knowing which effects are most likely to deter rape and then using their ingenuity to devise the best way to achieve those effects in a given situation. Serving that need would suggest that researchers reduce the myriad of situation-strategy combinations by focusing their studies of effectiveness on the impact of intended effects on the outcome of rape assaults.

## REFERENCES

Fischhoff, B., Furby, L., & Morgan, M. K. (1986). *Rape prevention: A typology and list of strategies* (ERI Technical Report 86-1). Eugene, OR: Eugene Research Institute.

Furby, L., & Fischhoff, B. (in press). Rape self-defense strategies: A review of their effectiveness. *Victimology*.

Furby, L., Fischhoff, B., & Morgan, M. K. (1990). Preventing rape: How people perceive the options: 1. Assault prevention. In E. Viano (Ed.), *The victimology handbook*. New York: Garland.

Riger, S., & Gordon, M. T. (1981). The fear of rape: A study in social control. *Journal of Social Issues, 37*, 71-92.

# 18

# The Adolescent Sexual Offender: Victim and Perpetrator

*Carol B. DiCenso*

In recent years, professionals in the field of offender and victim research and treatment have begun to recognize that juvenile sex offenders have a significant history of their own victimization(s). Left unreported and untreated, and with a coalescing of other variables, they then go on to victimize others. Their offenses usually mirror their own victimization and are not seen as isolated behavioral incidents. Their history points to an escalation of behavior, and an offender profile can be offered.

It is the intent of this chapter to address the issue of offender as victim whether the offender is a rapist, a child molester, or one who engages in a "nonvictim" pattern of behavior. Utilizing information collected from offenders involved with the Juvenile Sex Offender Program of the Rhode Island Training School for Youth, the relevant data will be presented as they relate to the victim/offender cycle. The results of the data will suggest that the early victimization of the offender is the most significant factor contributing to their offending.

## THE PATH OF OFFENDING: EARLY VICTIMIZATION

Sexual offenders, adult and juvenile, do not act out of lust nor out of a need for sexual gratification. In fact, the latter is the secondary gain as a result of the offense. Rather, the offending behavior comes from unreleased, unresolved anger and from a need for power, revenge, and control. The offender sexually assaults in an effort to discharge the anger and the contempt, to hurt, degrade, and humiliate. It is an effort to counteract feelings of vulnerability and inadequacy and to assert strength and power to control and exploit (Groth, 1979).

> My father committed suicide when I was young. Shortly after his death my older brother began to "hit on me." Over a period of years he sodomized me. I didn't like it at first, but I was too scared to tell, and who would believe me anyway. He threatened to hurt me if I did tell. The longer "it" went on, the more I realized that I liked it and as I got older, I began to wonder if I was a "queer." At fourteen, I raped my two younger brothers. I held a knife to one and a chain to the other. It felt good. I was in control. I was getting even. [Adolescent offender in treatment]

A review of the literature indicates that as early as 1941, professionals were concerned with the juvenile who engaged in unacceptable sexual behavior because it remained among the less well understood of the behavior patterns. More attention then and now is placed on the activities of adult offenders because they gain the attention of the media. Then as now, few in the field can definitively point to a single etiology that would explain the juvenile sexual offender. Waggoner and Boyd (1941) report that the etiology may be biological, behavioral, or psychological; fixated trauma, aberrant stages of development, insufficient or supersufficient nurturing, lack of appropriate role models, environmental stressors, or constitutional predisposition. Sexual experimentation cannot be excluded from the list of causative factors; neither can the impact of soft- and hard-core pornography be overlooked. Any of these factors, as well as others not mentioned, in any combination and in any degree, may contribute to the profile of the adolescent offender.

Groth (1979) reported in his study of 348 men convicted of sexual assault that 32% of the offenders convicted of sexually assaulting children and 29% of those convicted of sexually assaulting adults reported experiencing some form of sexual trauma during their formative years. In other words, they were victimized as well as sexualized at very early ages, well before the identified stage within the parameters of normal growth and development.

The child victim of the molestation or rape is an accessible target for the perpetrator. The ability to lure a child into a sexual relationship is based on the all-powerful and dominant position of the adult or older adolescent perpetrator (Sgroi, 1982). The child is victimized not only by the assault but by feelings of betrayal, hopelessness, and isolation. The offender is usually someone the child knows and trusts, a family member, a baby-sitter, or the parent of a friend. Some form of secrecy, coercion, and/or bribery is usually involved.

> One of my older sisters started having sex with me when I was seven. This continued for a few years. After we moved another sister got involved when the first one stopped. I was afraid to tell, but they also treated me nice and gave me things so I never told until now. [Adolescent offender in treatment]

When the rapist is a child, there is no bribery. The threat of harm is usually the way the perpetrator attempts to gain the victim's acquiescence to maintain silence. "My brother raped me when I was seven. He told me to be quiet or he would beat me real bad. I never told until now" (Adolescent offender in treatment). The child rapist also uses threats and physical force to gain access to his victim, unlike the child molester, who attempts to entice his victim into sexual activity.

The adolescent perpetrator does not always select younger victims. Peer-age assaults, sexual assault of an older person, and gang rape are also part of the behavior patterns. The premise that the offenses mirror the victimization appears to be borne out even in the more violent behaviors. Children who are sexually victimized and feel a loss of control may repeat that experience in a way that places them in control (Porter, 1986).

More recent literature points to the fact that a large proportion of sexual offenses are committed by adolescents (Fehrenback, Smith, Monastersby, & Deisher, 1986). The 1980 *Uniform Crime Report*, reflecting a period in the late 1970s, indicated that 30% or more of the individuals arrested for rape were in fact adolescents (U.S. Department of Justice, 1980). It should be noted, however, that the information reported by the Department of Justice is limited in scope because it does not include areas of "non-aggressive" behaviors, including voyeurism, obscene phone calls, and exhibitionism.

Why does the adolescent turn to aggressive sexual behaviors to express anger, lack of control, and the need for power? Maclay (cited in Deisher, Wenet, Paperny, Clark, & Fehrenback, 1982) concluded that the 29 boys studied who committed sexual offenses came from homes that failed to give them adequate emotional support. A later study concluded that the male adolescent offender, in this case a child molester, was a loner, had minimal peer involvement with either gender, and preferred playing with younger children. He was seen as naive, without suitable sex education; and along with this social and sexual immaturity, there appeared to be distorted family relations as well as personality patterns of maladjustment (Shoor, Speed, & Bartlet, 1966). Groth's study of male adolescent offenders presented a profile of a 16-year-old white youth of average cognitive ability. In about 33% of the incidents weapons were used; drugs and alcohol were relatively incidental, and about 75% had committed a previous offense (Groth, cited in Deisher et al., 1982).

## THE ADOLESCENT OFFENDER/VICTIM

Forty-three case histories of adjudicated male adolescent sex offenders sentenced to the Rhode Island Training School or having received suspended sentences with probation were selected for study. This represents all sex offenders referred since the time the treatment program was begun in January 1985. The Rhode Island Training School is a facility housing adolescents sentenced by the family court. The primary focus of the facility, in addition to custody and control, is habilitation. There are no adjudicated female offenders.

Data were obtained from a wide variety of sources. In addition to formal evaluations utilizing standardized instruments (Table 18.1), the Diagnostic Interview for Children and Adolescents, a structured psychiatric interview developed by the Washington University School of Medicine, was administered. The Structured Interview of Psycho-Sexual Experience, developed by the Forensic unit of Bradley Hospital, a psychiatric hospital for children, and by therapists from the Rhode Island Training School, was also given. Data sources included police and witness reports, court dispositions, probation findings, ongoing assessments while in treatment, and offender reporting.

The administration of the appropriate Wechsler Intelligence Scale yielded the following results: 9% scored below average, 9% as borderline (70-79), 28% as low average (80-89), and 28% as average (90-100); in 26% of the cases, data were not available.

**TABLE 18.1 Instruments Used in Evaluation of Adjudicated Offenders**

Bender Gestalt; Memory Bender
Diagnostic Interview for Children and Adolescents
House, Tree, Person Drawings
Kinetic Family Drawings
Peabody Individual Achievement Test
Peabody Picture Vocabulary Test
Rorschach
Rotter Sentence Completion
Structured Interview of Psycho-Sexual Experience
Thematic Apperception Test
Wechsler Adult Intelligence Scale—Revised
Wechsler Intelligence Scale for Children—Revised
Wide Range Achievement Test

Educational testing and placement in school programs showed that 15% were at the elementary school level; 9%, junior high school (grades 7-9); 2%, high school equivalency; 44% special education (including students in high school programs); and 61%, high school. Data that would further refine those in special education (learning-disabled or behavioral problems) were unavailable.

Ages at the time of conviction ranged from 13 to 18 years, with a mean age of 15 years, 6 months. Eighteen-year-olds are tried in the adult system, except in those cases where the offense occurred prior to the 18th birthday and the attorney general's office does not seek a waiver of jurisdiction from family court. Eighty-one percent of the adolescent offenders were white; 14%, black; and 5%, Hispanic.

The marital status of the offenders' parent(s) at the time of the offense was as follows: intact, natural parents, 26%; divorced, remarried, 21%; divorced, 31%; single parent, never married, 7%; widow, 7%; common-law, 2%; widower, 2%; unknown, 5%.

More definitive information about the offenders indicated that 88% had a history of fire setting. Incidents included setting fires to leaves and other trash, as well as setting fires in their own homes either when alone or with others present. The offenders uniformly reported that they started at an early age, approximately 6 years, and that they were motivated to engage in this behavior because they gained a sense of power and control. It should be recognized that their thinking was retrospective because the information was obtained from them as adolescents.

Enuresis was prevalent in 49% of the cases. In 10% of the population this problem continued until the preadolescent stage of development. Thirty-nine percent denied any difficulty in this area, and in 5% of the situations data were not known.

This population exhibits a degree of substance use and abuse: 79%, polysubstance abuse (marijuana, crack, cocaine); 2%, alcohol only; 7%, no substance abuse; 12%, unknown.

Eighty-seven percent of the offenders acknowledged substance abuse to varying degrees at the time of the offense, but this information could not be measured because of nebulous recall. Several (about 15%) thought they might have been drugging or drinking at the time *they* were victimized; but again, because of vagueness in recall, accuracy cannot be assured. It should also be noted that the adolescent, like his adult counterpart, seeks out mitigating circumstances to rationalize behavior. Substance abuse is one of the rationalizations most often used.

Prior hospitalization in a psychiatric facility accounted for 12% of the cases. Seventy-six percent were never hospitalized, and the status of 5% was unknown.

Five percent of the offenders admitted to engaging in animal abuse. One suspects that this figure is an underestimate. There is a reluctance to be honest about this behavior because it is generally met with criticism by peers. One offender did acknowledge torturing, mutilating, and killing more than 300 cats.

The most significant data obtained involved the prior victimization of the offender. Fully 95% were victimized as children. The forms of victimization ranged from molestation with no penetration to penetration with force (rape/sodomy). In addition, the offenders witnessed a variety of other forms of sexual behavior, such as adult heterosexual intercourse, adult homosexual relations, adult/child molestation (including intercourse), and pornographic videos depicting gang rape, bondage, and sadomasochistic behavior. All were sexualized very early in their development, some as young as 3 years of age.

In 100% of the situations studied, dysfunctional adult relationships were present. Physical and maternal boundaries were blurred or nonexistent. In retrospect, the offender viewed the adult as failing to protect him while the victimization was occurring. The relationship between the victim/offender and the parent lacked intimacy during this period, and it was not until the offender began therapy that he was able to disclose his victimization.

The data seen in Table 18.2 reflect the type of offenses engaged in by the population studied. Sexual assault as defined by the General Law of the State of Rhode Island was the basis for categorizing offenses.

Offenses occurring at the time of the sexual offense conviction included kidnapping, 7%; assault with a deadly weapon, 2%; robbery, 2%; and carrying a firearm, 2%. Prior detentions for nonsexual offenses were seen in 14% of the cases.

Of those adjudicated on a sexual offense, 77% revealed when relating their histories that they repeated the acts that were done to them. There is no substantiation of this information. The ages of their victims approximated the age at which they were victimized.

> When I was eight or nine, I was sitting on the edge of the pool while my mother was vacuuming it. I kept bothering her until finally she said, "You want to bother me? See

**TABLE 18.2 Types of Offenses Committed by Adjudicated Offenders**

| Offense | % |
| --- | --- |
| First-degree sexual assault | 44 |
|   Multiple counts | 65 |
| Gang rape | 14 |
| Second-degree sexual assault | 26 |
|   Multiple counts | 2 |
| First-degree child molestation | 19 |
| Second-degree child molestation | 3 |
| Exhibitionism, obscene phone calls | 4 |
| Assault with intent to commit sexual assault | 7 |
| Sexual assault amended to simple assault | 7 |
| Earlier sexual assault convictions | 5 |

how it feels to be bothered." She then shoved her fingers up my rectum. When I "stalked" my victim he was about the age I was when my mother did that to me. I did the same to him. [Offender in treatment]

I remember being touched by my baby-sitter when I was really little. When I baby-sat for my sister I gave the baby a bath. [The baby was a six-month-old female]. I wondered what little girls were like and I began to touch her. Something came over me and the next thing I saw blood all over her. I had penetrated her vagina. [Released offender]

The youths' status in treatment was as follows: 27%, in treatment and resident; 34%, outpatient as condition of probation with suspended time; 22%, resident, released to probation; 9%, treatment terminated; 8%, refused participation.

Further, 15% were seen in individual therapy prior to the program's inception, and 19% of those terminated are currently serving time at the adult correctional institution, none on sexual offense charges. A note of caution: when a resident or probationer has completed his sentence, there is nothing to compel him to remain in the therapeutic setting. Therefore aftercare, although offered, is generally not accepted. Long-term follow-up studies, although urgently needed, are not practical because of strict rules of confidentiality regarding juveniles.

## Commonalities and Background Variables

What conclusions can be drawn from these data? How can clinicians proceed as an attempt is made to break the victim/offender cycle?

First, although there is no specific demographic profile, there are commonalities. More than half had low to average cognitive functioning (functioning at a high school level). Seventy-five percent or more were white, and the average age was 15½ years. Twenty-five percent came from intact families; another 33% had experienced divorce. Within this group, 21% had remarried. Almost all (88%) had a history of fire setting, and 50% were enuretic. Polysubstance abuse was prevalent. Eighty percent acknowledged involvement with drugs and alcohol, but only 15% stated that they had used these substances at the time of the offense. More than 75% were never hospitalized in a psychiatric facility.

The most striking information is the overwhelming number (95%) who experienced prior victimization, some as early as age 3. In addition, all came from a dysfunctional family system. More than 75% of the offenders acknowledged that their offense paralleled their own victimization.

Let us pause at this point and postulate the possible ramifications of the sexual victimization perpetrated on the offender. At the core is the assault(s) itself. Whether a one-time occurrence or a series of acts over a long period of time, the male child victim is isolated, angry, robbed of self-esteem, betrayed, powerless, helpless, guilt-ridden, and, more often than not, questioning his sexual identity.

Doubts of masculinity and thoughts of homosexuality go largely unresolved because disclosure usually does not happen. The victim is intimidated.

On the basis of the data, one could conclude that all victims will go on to offend. This is certainly not the case because the number of convicted offenders is small compared with the number of victims reported. However, when viewing the offender within the framework of therapy and presenting history, it becomes obvious that there are dynamics impacting on the offender's personality and behavior. Key to these is the family constellation and the ability of the caregivers to provide the safety and boundaries needed by the child.

Second, victimization occurs at an early age, and an environment needs to be created in which the victim can come forward and report. Resources need to be brought to bear on all facets of the community at large having contact with children. Schools, churches, day care, camps, parent groups, and a multitude of other significant adults and organizations need to be educated about child victimization so that they can act appropriately.

Third, for those working with the adolescent offender, there is a need to recognize that the problem is never resolved but can only respond to lifelong management.

## Treatment at the Rhode Island Training School

The Rhode Island Training School initiated a treatment modality for the adjudicated offender in January 1985 after a period of rigorous training by Forensic Mental Health Associates.

The basic premise of the program is twofold. The first is that the most important initial aspect of offender treatment for the adolescent is to be held responsible for the offense. Prosecution and then treatment are viewed as the most appropriate intervention because treatment in lieu of criminal prosecution lessens the degree of responsibility an offender must acknowledge. It is the contention of the program that, until a viable alternative is found, it is the responsibility of the criminal justice system to provide the external controls necessary for preventing offenses until the offender has responsibly understood and accepted that responsibility. Mandatory specialized treatment is the only effective way to achieve that goal because the offenders have learned deviant and perverse use of their own authority, power, and control from others for many years, starting with their own victimization. Offender histories show that the perpetrators were parents, foster parents, grandparents, step-parents, brothers, sisters, bosses, close family friends, and baby-sitters—all significant adults or caretakers in their lives.

Second, treatment for the sexual aggression must employ an all-or-nothing model. Prevention is the primary goal of treatment, and the ultimate client is, and should be, the potential victim. Offenders need to learn to view their potential victim as their ultimate concern as well, an actual undoing of what they were taught. To accomplish such a task, the adolescent offender needs to learn to own and manage his behavior and gain awareness into his underlying motivations for sexual aggression. He needs to face his own victimization and all of the ramifications this confrontation implies.

Essential characteristics of the model being used are authoritative intervention and concrete therapeutic structure. Confrontation is used in an appropriate manner to counteract a firmly entrenched denial system, thus enabling the therapist and participant to begin the slow and painful task of disclosing the past personal history.

Weekly group treatment in a specialized offender group is the central focus of the program. Treatment is long-term because there is no cure for sexual assault, only problem management. The task of treatment, therefore, is to help the offenders manage lifelong issues of poor self-esteem, generalized helplessness, impaired relationships with others, their own sexual victimization, and any other issues significant to developing a life-style that precludes reoffending.

Over time the adolescent learns to address a variety of issues relevant to his developing new patterns of behavior. Role playing their own victimization as well as assuming the role of their victim(s) are dramatic events within the treatment modality and no doubt the first overt experience of expressing feelings or empathy for the victim. It is viewed by therapists as a major breakthrough in the offenders' ability to gain needed insight into behavior and the development of their own understanding of cause-and-effect relationships. All of the offenders to date have been unable to shed feelings of guilt about their own victimization, the myth that somehow, even at ages 3, 4, and 5, they were at fault. When their perception of reality takes on a new focus, the healing can begin. The aggressive behavior employed for power and control can now be replaced with socially accepted patterns. The rich, violent fantasy life that each offender acknowledges in the therapeutic milieu can now be understood and diverted in a variety of nonaggressive behaviors. The offender begins to learn the warning signals that put him at risk, whether exposure to sexually explicit material, newspaper advertisements of scantily clad males and females, school playgrounds, or offers to baby-sit.

## CONCLUSIONS

The profile of the adolescent offender as presented here clearly points to a significant childhood trauma, his own victimization. Though this does not lead to the postulation of a hypothesis that every victim will become an offender, it does give cause for concern. The methodology employed to break the victim/offender cycle is critical if clinicians are to effect change. Attention must focus on creating a safe climate that will empower the young victim to disclose. This notwithstanding, those in the field must be cognizant that offenders don't just happen; they are created from their own history. At the time of this writing, to our knowledge, no offender who has been in the program or who is currently involved has reoffended sexually.

> I do not know a time in my life when I was free from fear of being sexually assaulted. It began with a baby-sitter, and I soon was being victimized by older youths. I finally raped my sister and was sentenced to the Training School. When I left at the end of my sentence, I really had no roots except for the group home I was living in and my weekly group sessions. I was rearrested on a "breaking and entering" charge, but at least I am proud of the fact that I didn't sexually assault anyone while I was in the community. [Released offender]

There are important areas that need to be examined if clinicians are to have an effect on the victim/offender cycle. Longitudinal studies are needed to definitively identify those factors that preclude male victims from going on to become offenders. Why do some male victims choose sexual offending as an acting-out behavior, but others do not, or they turn on other unacceptable patterns? Is there any significance as to the gender of the person who victimized them as children? In addition to the victimization, is family dysfunction a corollary that increases the probability that the victim will go on to offend? Long-term follow-up of adolescent victim/offenders who have been in treatment is critical. Does the intervention have a positive impact? Does the adolescent continue to reoffend despite treatment? This chapter deals with the male offender. Little if any research is available about female offenders. This disparity seems to convey the message that females may only be victims but do not go on to offend. This is a specious argument that requires attention.

## ACKNOWLEDGMENT

I would like to thank the therapist team members, Mark Weston, Susan McKenna, Joseph Clifford, Martha Ames, and William Votto for their efforts in obtaining data from their clients. Rob Dufresne served as an able research assistant in the preparation of this chapter.

## REFERENCES

Deisher, R. W., Wenet, G. A., Paperny, D. M., Clark, T. F., & Fehrenback, P. A. (1982). Adolescent sex offense behavior: The role of the physician. *Journal of Adolescent Health Care, 2*, 279–286.

Fehrenback, P. A., Smith, W., Monastersby, C., & Deisher, R. W. (1986). Adolescent sexual offenders: Offenders and offense characteristics. *American Journal of Orthopsychiatry, 56*(2), 225–233.

Groth, A. N. with Birnbaum, H. J. (1979). *Men who rape*. New York: Plenum Press.

Porter, E. (1986). *Treating the young male victim of sexual assault: Issues and intervention strategies.* New York: Safer Society Press.

Sgroi, S. M. (1983). *Handbook of clinical intervention in child sexual abuse.* Lexington, MA: D. C. Heath.

Shoor, M., Speed, M. H., & Bartlet, C. (1966). Syndrome of the adolescent child molester. *American Journal of Psychiatry, 122*(7), 783-789.

U.S. Department of Justice. (1980). *Uniform crime reports, Federal Bureau of Investigation.* Washington, DC: U.S. Government Printing Office.

Waggoner, R. W., & Boyd, D. A. (1941). Juvenile aberrant sexual behavior. *American Journal of Orthopsychiatry, 11,* 275-291.

# PART V
# Society's Reaction to Victimization

Victimization and the involvement of the victim with the justice system create many problems and difficulties for victims for which they generally have little or no remedy. The consequences of the crime can be psychological, medical, financial, or practical and can affect personal relations, family life, productivity and ability to function at work, and general outlook on society. Trauma, fear, lost income, medical expenditures, and short- and long-term medical problems and disabilities also affect many victims.

When victims become involved with the justice, medical, and social assistance systems, they do so with certain expectations that are often not met. Other problems develop as well. Victims frequently are or feel exploited, inconvenienced, shabbily treated, at times even threatened, at a minimum ignored, and faced with considerable financial expenditures. Involvement with the justice system for them means a considerable commitment of time and resources and having to absorb substantial losses. There are transportation expenses, child care expenses, lost income, the threat or real possibility of losing one's job, missed opportunities, and added burdens to one's daily schedule because of the considerable amount of time that must be allocated to dealing with any bureaucracy.

Victims expect at least some information on the progress of the case, protection in situations when it is dangerous to cooperate with the system, some active role in the conduct of the case, and a satisfactory resolution of the matter, all of this within a reasonable amount of time. Most of all, victims want to prevent a recurrence of their victimization. Unfortunately, they are often disappointed on one or more counts.

Many programs with different goals, philosophies, allegiances, and approaches have been established during the past two decades in various countries and most notably in the United States to help victims deal with the many problems they encounter in the aftermath of their victimization. Assessments of their usefulness, effectiveness, and legitimacy vary. Certainly, there are considerable disparities among victim programs and even controversy, at times, as to who the true client may be.

Although the different types of victim assistance programs perform, by and large, a useful and needed function, comparable to medical intervention to repair the damage inflicted by an injury or illness, there is no question that they also represent a certain defeat of society. After all, the crime has been committed—the criminal has been able to carry out his plan, exert his dominance, and impose his will—and now society, impotent to stop the criminal from prevailing, is helping the victim pick up the pieces and rebuild his or her life. In most cases, the victimizer goes undetected and unpunished.

In many ways, victim assistance programs face some of the same troubling questions and ethical dilemmas that confront other help organizations. There are indeed reasons to question, for example, international assistance and relief efforts when no steps are taken to correct the underlying reasons that famine, civil strife, religious or ethnic conflicts, man-made disasters, and other calamities take place. Not only is it worthwhile, but is it correct to mobilize the community to alleviate the suffering of people, whatever the cause, particularly when it is chronic and recurrent, without questioning the causes of what one is trying to correct? One could argue that this way one may even become a conspirator and collaborator of a repressive, exploitative, or warmongering regime or of various oppressive ideologies by softening the impact of their actions and making it bearable, while at the same time not challenging the causes and the roots of the evil.

Gloria Steinem, a foremost femininist in the United States, is often quoted as saying: "We are swimming through a river of change. . . . We have spent the last decade standing over the river bank, rescuing women who are drowning. In the next decade, some of us have to go to the head of the river to keep women from falling in." This statement aptly summarizes the need to think not only of helping the victim but also, and foremost, of stopping the victimization.

The importance of prevention is finally being recognized. Just as in the medical field it has been learned that preventing instead of just curing illness should be the foremost goal of medicine and is the only way to improve a population's health on a more permanent basis, so we are learning that preventing victimization must at least go hand in hand with treatment.

Preventing victimization also reminds us of the role of the state as protector of the safety and well-being of its population. This role is basic to responsible government and constitutes the foundation for the introduction of policies and concrete measures to lessen the likelihood of victimization. Some legal experts in the United States even argue that there is a still unrecognized right to be free of victimization based on the guarantee of the pursuit of happiness affirmed in the Declaration of Independence. This argument is further reinforced, proponents say, by the overall social contract theory that is at the foundation of the American state. It is also supported by the clear vision of the state as an organization providing public services that has characterized the American republic, as opposed to European thought, from the very beginning. There is no doubt that the present constitutional government is clearly based on the concept of the state as a public service-rendering organization.

This section of the book addresses several issues related to the interaction between the victim and the justice system.

In chapter 19, J. van den Bogaard and O. Wiegman present the preliminary results of a field experiment in which police officers provided information in three different ways to victims of burglary. The results raise some doubts about the police officers' sensitivity to the needs of burglary victims. They also indicate the possibility that information on further procedures under certain conditions can lessen the victims' "illusion of controllability," thus heightening fear reactions. Specific results on the reactions and needs of women and the elderly are discussed with respect to the concepts of vulnerability and coping.

Paola Violante, in chapter 20, analyzes crime victims' discretionary reporting of crime in Italy and examines the reasons victims there gave for not reporting the crime to the police. The results of her study indicate that selective criteria operate along the dimension of "seriousness of crime." As far as "personal crimes" are concerned, data suggest that the gravity of the injury or the intolerance of standing the harassment influence the victim's decision making.

Chapter 21, prepared by Mario Gaboury, summarizes the 1982 federal Victim and Witness Protection Act and the 1984 Victims of Crime Act, two laws that constitute the centerpiece of the federal response to criminal activity in the United States. The first seeks to provide certain protections and services to victims of federal crimes. The second subsidizes state and local crime victim assistance and compensation programs and certain federal initiatives through funds collected from convicted federal criminals.

Thomas Castellano, in chapter 22, reviews evaluative research assessing restitution's impact on recidivism. He concludes that there are relatively few solid studies using experimental and quasi-experimental designs and that we still know relatively little about the specific linkages between restitutive sanctions, contexts, and individuals. This leaves restitution vulnerable to being utilized more for the benefit of the community at large than for the individual victim and to being bypassed when other forms of controlling the offender and protecting the community become available, as in the case of electronic monitoring of offenders.

# 19

# Police Reactions to Victims of Burglary

*Joop W. van den Bogaard and Oene Wiegman*

---

### THE PROBLEM AND ITS RELEVANCE

Though crime rates in the Netherlands have risen sharply in the past two decades, the government has begun only recently to pay systematic attention to fear of crime among the public and to the effects of crime on the victims. In cooperation with the police and the state attorney's office, we conducted a field experiment that tested the effects of three different ways in which the police provided information to victims of burglary.

Burglary is unquestionably one of the most frequently committed crimes in the Western world (Waller, 1984). Victims of burglary often suffer a loss of privacy or grieve about the loss of certain possessions that have an emotional value for them. The first more thorough studies (e.g., Maguire, 1980) showed that this emotional impact is often more important for the victim than is the material or financial loss. Waller even estimated that serious psychological trauma could occur in approximately 1 in 20 cases, a huge group of people given the high incidence of burglary. Thus, from a social point of view it is very important that more research attention be directed toward victims of burglary. From both a practical and a theoretical point of view one could ask if there are differences in reactions, needs, and coping styles between different groups of burglary victims (e.g., men and women or different age groups) (see also Burt & Katz, 1985).

Another question is if the coping of different victim groups can be made more effective by providing them with certain kinds of information.

## Role of the Police

For several reasons the police are often the first and only officials to talk to victims of burglary. They are the agency best situated to initiate crisis support to victims. Research (e.g., Maguire, 1982; Maguire & Corbett, 1987; Shapland, Willmore, & Duff, 1985) shows, however, that victims of burglary are not always satisfied with the way they are treated by the police. According to Shapland et al. (1985), the police underestimate victims' needs for consideration, respect, and help. Common reasons for victims' dissatisfaction with the police are failure to inform the victims of the outcome of the investigation and showing an uncaring attitude or devaluing the incident. Such dissatisfaction could have several negative effects both for society as a whole and for the individual victim (e.g., Yantzi & Brown, 1983). Given the above observations, it is very relevant to conduct systematic research on attitudes and behaviors of police officers toward victims and to compare these with the expectations, needs, and satisfaction or dissatisfaction of the victims.

## Background of the Studies

In April 1987, the Ministry of Justice of the Netherlands issued new policy guidelines for the police and the criminal justice system, to provide better advice and information to victims of petty crime. Implementation of these guidelines was meant to have a broad positive effect on victims. However, apart from the possibility that police services for victims could have unwanted side effects (e.g., Skogan & Wycoff, 1987; Winkel, 1987), we doubted that positive effects would be generated if these guidelines were followed out literally. There had not been a pilot study, and in our view it was likely that a busy police officer, not used to being "victim-oriented," would not do more than the required minimum. Therefore, in our study we wanted to compare the effects of the "minimum approach" with the effects of more extensive approaches. We were especially interested in the effects on victims' satisfaction with the police, their reactions to and coping with victimization, and their behavior and intentions toward burglary prevention. The practical goal was the improvement of police services for victims. A field experiment in cooperation with the police seemed to be the most appropriate method to evaluate these approaches in day-to-day practice. This approach is consistent with the recommendations of the American Psychological Association's Task Force on victims of crime and violence (APA, 1985). To combine an experimental with a policy-oriented approach, our design had to fulfill three criteria. First, our intervention methods should not depart too far from routine police activities in order to increase the possibilities of implementation after the experimental stage. Second, we should cooperate with existing police teams and experienced police officers, without training them extensively in advance of the project. Third, we should stress the importance of the first face-to-face contact between victim and police officer. The management of the police teams took part in a permanent working group in order to tune the project to everyday practice and supervise the introduction, organization, and execution of the project.

In this chapter, some preliminary results of two complementary studies are presented. The data stem from both sides of the victim–police system. In Study 1 some results on police officers' attitudes and behaviors toward victims are presented. In Study 2, we present preliminary results on differences between our experimental groups and on reactions, needs, and satisfaction with the police of the victim group as a whole. At this point, we cannot present a complete account of our results nor of our final conclusions on the consequences for theory and practice. The long-term effects of the burglary and of the police interventions on these victims will be examined in a follow-up study.

## STUDY 1:
## POLICE OFFICERS' ATTITUDES AND BEHAVIOR TOWARD VICTIMS

### Method

Five police teams, about 140 police officers, from three cities took part in the experiment. Before and after the project we measured their attitudes toward police services for victims. During the project they completed 385 checklists on their contacts with victims of burglary. Our scale to measure attitudes of police officers toward police services for victims was adapted from an existing questionnaire (Voskuil, 1987) and consisted of 15 items. The items had to be scored on a 5-point scale. About half of the items were formulated negatively and recoded afterward. Reliability analysis showed that one item did not fit well into the scale. Internal consistency of the remaining 14 items was high (Cronbach's $\alpha = .86$).

By means of the 385 checklists completed by the police officers after their face-to-face contact with a victim, we got extra data on some contact variables. These included place (i.e., victim's home or police station), duration of contact, presence of other people during the contact, and level of emotionality attributed to the victim. Level of emotionality was measured on a 5-point scale with extremes ranging from "quiet and in control" to "very emotional." For reasons of further analyses we recoded this variable in two categories: controlled (a score of 1) and emotional (a score of 2 through 5). On the basis of our experience with officers, we assumed a willingness to provide some support to a victim when they noticed that the victim needed it. A further assumption was that giving support would cost some extra time during the contact with a victim. So we hypothesized a positive relation between the victim's need for support as observed by the officer and the duration of the contact. To operationalize "need for support" we used two available indicators: first, the absence of other people, such as relatives or neighbors who could provide support during the contact between victim and officer, and second, the level of emotionality attributed to the victim.

## Results

In general, attitudes toward police services for victims were very positive. Both before and after the project, scale means were above 3.0 for the five police teams. Though officers did not disclaim their individual responsibility for victims, inspection of single items revealed, on the whole, more acceptance of responsibilities of the police as an organization. Police officers doubted the availability of time for better victim support, and many agreed it should not be developed at the cost of other police tasks. Answers to an open question attached to the attitude scale showed that many police officers think that follow-up services to victims should be given by specialized police officials or victim support schemes. Interestingly, the item that was dropped from the scale showed that most officers strongly agree that a victim is served best by the police solving the victim's case.

Analysis of the checklists revealed that sex and age of victims were not related to the absence or presence of other people or to duration of the contact. In general, more emotionality was attributed to women than to men ($p < .01$). Our analysis showed that contact duration was somewhat shorter when the victim was, according to the police officer, "controlled" than when he or she was seen as "emotional." However, this difference was not significant. Contrary to our expectations, we found a tendency for contact duration to be shorter when the victim was alone (ANOVA, $F[1, 326] = 3.59, p < .10$). Interestingly, our results showed an interaction between the victim's sex and the level of emotionality in determining contact duration (ANOVA, $F[1, 303] = 5.68, p < .05$). Contact duration became longer when male victims were classified as emotional and shorter when female victims were seen as emotional. The effect of the interaction between victim's age and level of emotionality on contact duration was not significant.

## Discussion

The police officers in our project showed a positive attitude toward police services for victims. This is an important finding for at least two reasons. First, it shows that police officers are basically motivated to assist victims of crime. Second, it shows the existence of a sound motivational basis for our experimental project. However, officers view their own tasks and responsibilities as predominantly restricted to rendering "first aid" for victims. On the basis of our findings we suspect that the majority of police officers in our project still believe that victims are most worried about the outcome of the investigation. This was also the conclusion of Shapland et al. (1985).

Duration of the first face-to-face contact between police officer and victim is undoubtedly a product of many influences and is not primarily a function of victim's need for support. With our results in mind we can raise some doubts about police officers' sensitivity to the needs of burglary victims.

It must be noted that about 90% of the officers in our experiment were men. Our finding that contact duration is slightly longer with some "emotional" victims could mean that there is some sensitivity to victims' needs, but the significantly shorter contact duration when the victim is alone could plead against this interpretation. Perhaps the effect of an increasing number of questions and communications when others are present offsets the possible effect of a greater need for support when the victim is alone.

Finally, there is a possibility that police officers are selectively sensitive to victims' needs. Policemen in our study spent less time with female victims when they thought the victim was emotional. This could mean that the needs of these victims are not sufficiently met by the police. One possible explanation is that men and women express emotions differently. For example, men express more anger; women, more fear. Perhaps it is easier for a male police officer to deal with feelings and needs that he would express himself if he was the victim.

# STUDY 2:
# VICTIMS' REACTIONS, NEEDS, AND SATISFACTION

## Method

### Experimental Design

If a citizen reported a burglary, he or she received one of three "treatments" during the first face-to-face contact with a police officer. During the 12 weeks between January and April 1988, each police team worked with all three treatments in different sequences to control for possible disturbing influences. Treatments were cumulative. Treatment 1 was restricted to the minimum required by the new policy guidelines. This meant that, besides the customary procedure of making a report, the victims would be told they would be advised on further procedures if a suspect was apprehended and they should be asked if they wanted financial restitution. The rationale behind Treatment 2 and Treatment 3 was to provide the victim with information in order to lessen the emotional impact of the crime on the victim. Therefore, in Treatment 2, victims received extra information on the police investigation and on possibilities for coping with the practical, financial, and emotional consequences of their victimization. In

Treatment 3 they received extra information on burglary prevention and were visited in their homes by a crime prevention officer. Note that the information in Treatment 1 was given only orally. In Treatments 2 and 3, both oral and written information was used. We expected that the victims would show better coping and weaker secondary emotional reactions in the groups receiving treatments 2 and 3. Likewise, we expected more awareness of and utilization of burglary prevention techniques in the Treatment 3 group.

## Variables and Operationalizations

The items in the questionnaire related to a wide range of topics. In this chapter we will give special attention to differences in results between men and women and between different age groups because it is generally assumed that women and the elderly have more problems with the threat and consequences of victimization. Little is known about their recovery processes (Burt & Katz, 1985).

We distinguished between the victims' primary reactions in the first hour after detecting or hearing about the burglary and the victims' secondary emotional and cognitive reactions in the period between reporting the crime and the interview. We developed two scales to measure primary reactions: a primary Fear-Upset scale (6 items, Cronbach's $\alpha = .88$) and an Anger scale (3 items, Cronbach's $\alpha = .77$). To measure secondary reactions we asked victims to rate the present impact of the burglary, and we used a secondary Fear-Upset scale (4 items, Cronbach's $\alpha = .82$).

The concept of self-efficacy (Bandura, 1977) was central to our operationalization of coping and burglary prevention. A self-efficacy expectation denotes the conviction that one can successfully execute the behaviors required to produce certain outcomes. According to Bandura, self-efficacy expectations can affect both initiation and persistence of coping behavior. Types of coping behavior in our questionnaire included problem-focused behaviors (e.g., try to get financial restitution), emotion-focused behaviors (e.g., try to distance yourself from the event), and seeking social support (see also Lazarus & Folkman, 1984).

All victims in this project received information from the police on one or more topics. We asked victims who maintained they received no information on a topic if they had wanted it. Finally, we asked them to rate their satisfaction with the police investigation and with the way the police officer behaved toward them. To measure the individual's evaluation of the police officer we used an Empathy scale (5 items, Cronbach's $\alpha = .85$), a general-evaluation item, and a business-like item.

## Data Collection and Subjects

About 13% of the 385 victims refused to cooperate in the study; another 15% was excluded for other reasons (e.g., they had no personal contact with the police). A standardized questionnaire was used to interview 276 victims within a few weeks after the crime. Of these victims, 45.5% were men, and 54.5% were women. Ages varied from 18 to 92 years, and the victims also varied on other relevant demographic factors, for example, education and income. Nearly all victims interviewed were willing to cooperate in our planned follow-up study.

Our evaluation revealed that, on the whole, treatments were successful; that is, the intended information was given to the proper experimental groups. However, treatments were executed better with written information (brochures, leaflets) than with oral information and explanations that officers should have given face-to-face. The analysis also revealed some small but undesirable differences on some crime-related and victim-related variables between the experimental groups.

## Results

First we present some preliminary experimental results, followed by general results and then differences between sex and age groups within the victim group as a whole. First, univariate analyses of variance revealed that people who got the least information (Treatment 1) showed weakest secondary Fear-Upset reactions ($p < .05$), least fear about another burglary ($p < .01$), and strongest intentions to try to get financial restitution from the perpetrator ($p < .05$). The group who received information on the investigation and on coping possibilities but not on burglary prevention (Treatment 2) showed the most severe reactions. Note that these results are against expectations and show a possible occurrence of side effects. Table 19.1 presents an overview of the strength of differences in results between men and women and among the five age groups.

Strongest *primary* reactions, immediately after detecting the burglary, were "being angry" and "being frightened." In general, women scored much higher on the Fear-Upset scale. On the Anger scale we found an interaction between sex and age. The youngest and the oldest groups of males reacted least angrily of all men; for women the reverse was true. Present impact at the time of the interview (an average of 18 days after reporting the crime) was still high: 50.9% of the victims said the burglary still had a high or very high impact on them. Strongest *secondary* reactions were: "feeling angry," "feeling powerless," "feeling afraid," and "feeling sad." Women showed stronger secondary reactions than men.

We were also interested in the role of anger in the coping process. Therefore, we analyzed the relation between primary anger reaction and experiencing secondary symptoms such as having a headache and feeling angry. Multivariate analysis of variance showed a strong positive relation between primary anger and these secondary symptoms. People who were angrier at first complained more of headaches ($p < .05$) and of feeling angry ($p < .001$) in the weeks after the crime. People who said they got information from the police on one or more topics were satisfied with it. Of those who maintained they did not get information, a

TABLE 19.1 Strength of Some Differences in Victims' Reactions, Wish for Information, and Satisfaction with the Police

| Victims' Reactions | Sex | Age | Sex × Age |
|---|---|---|---|
| Primary reactions | | | |
| Fear-Upset scale 1 | <.001 | n.s. | <.10 |
| Anger scale | n.s. | n.s. | <.05 |
| Secondary reactions | | | |
| Present impact | <.001 | n.s. | n.s. |
| Fear-Upset scale 2 | <.001 | n.s. | n.s. |
| Feeling angry | n.s. | <.10 | n.s. |
| Headache | <.001 | n.s. | <.10 |
| Wish for information | | | |
| On investigation | *<.01* | n.s. | |
| On insurance | *<.05* | n.s. | |
| On emotions | *<.05* | *.01* | |
| On burglary prevention | n.s. | *<.01* | |
| Satisfaction with police | | | |
| Investigation | n.s. | <.05 | <.10 |
| Evaluation of officer | | | |
| General evaluation | n.s. | <.01 | n.s. |
| Empathy scale | n.s. | <.001 | <.05 |
| Businesslike | .001 | <.001 | n.s. |

Chi-square tests in *italic*; others are F tests (univariate).
n.s., nonsignificant difference.

majority would have liked to have information on further procedures. Women wanted more information than men did on aspects of the investigation, on insurance matters, and on emotional aspects. Especially people between 30 and 50 years of age wanted more information on emotional aspects, and older people showed less need for information on burglary prevention. Our data showed that our respondents were, on the whole, satisfied with police activities and evaluated the officer's behavior positively, though their expectations of an active and successful police investigation proved to be low. In general, older people were more satisfied with the police than were younger people.

## Discussion

### Unexpected Results

Contrary to our expectations, victims in treatment groups 2 and 3 did not show fewer secondary symptoms and more interest in burglary prevention than did victims in the minimum-treatment group. Though we were aware of the possibility of negative side effects of police services for victims, we did not expect these effects in our study. In comparison with the Skogan and Wycoff (1987) study, we had many fewer victims from cultural miniorities or with language problems. In comparison with Winkel's study (1987), we not only provided victims with information on prevention but also on coping with the consequences of the burglary. We offer two possible explanations for these surprising results. First, there is a possibility that these effects will be smaller when we correct for some small differences between treatment groups on some subject variables. For example, slightly more people in Group 2 lived in rented houses and alone. Second, it is possible that information about coping took away from victims an "illusion of controllability." It is quite probable that officers, given the present statutory regulations in the Netherlands, told victims in groups 2 and 3 the difficulties involved in trying to get financial restitution from the perpetrator. This information could have lowered victims' self-efficacy expectations. We indeed found that Group 2 showed lower self-efficacy expectations with respect to getting financial restitution ($p < .05$). Besides, Group 2 also showed lower trust in the benefit of inquiring about their stolen property at the police station ($p < .05$). Such perceived loss of problem-focused control could lead to more emotion-focused coping. Victims in Group 2 indeed tried more "distancing" ($p < .10$) and showed stronger behaviors ($p < .10$) and intentions ($p < .05$) toward seeking social support in their own environments. Victims in our third treatment group showed fewer side effects than those in Group 2. We think this is because they received extra information on burglary prevention. A study by Winkel (1987), in which the controllability of burglary was stressed in the information on burglary prevention given to victims, also showed a decrease of side effects such as fear of crime.

### Anger as a Common Reaction

As in other studies, the prevailing reaction to burglary proved to be anger. Our analysis suggests that a primary anger reaction is a strong predictor of some psychosomatic and emotional symptoms at the time of the first interview, irrespective of demographic factors such as sex and age. Sales, Baum, and Shore (1984) found the same relationship with victims of sexual assault. Future analyses should clarify the predictive value of primary and secondary anger reactions, relative to characteristics of the crime and other victim variables with respect to long-term coping and adaptation. It is our opinion that anger can be a strong motivating force, not only with respect to the need for revenge but in the more general sense of coping and the need for controllability of future events (see also Frijda, 1986).

### Explaining Age and Sex Differences

Our finding that most victims would have liked to have information on further procedures is consistent with the results of other studies (Maguire, 1982; Waller,

1984). Women wanted more information from the police on topics related to coping with the consequences of the burglary than did men. This could be explained by the finding that they showed more severe reactions to the burglary. An alternative explanation could be found in the concept of social vulnerability: women, on the whole, held weaker social positions (educationally, professionally, financially) than did men. Yantzi and Brown (1983) found that people who had less education and lower incomes knew less how to cope with their victimization than did other groups.

Interestingly, women did not want more information on the topic of burglary prevention than men did, but in general women were much more afraid of a new burglary (MANOVA, $p < .001$) and expected more severe emotional ($p < .001$) and material ($p < .01$) consequences of a new victimization. A comparable paradox is our finding that older people who did not get information on burglary prevention showed less need for this information than did younger people, but on the whole, older people expected the material consequences of a new burglary to be more severe ($p < .05$). One can speculate on some explanations, which have to be tested in future analyses.

First, a possible sex-specific explanation is that victims primarily equate burglary prevention with "target hardening" of a technical kind. We indeed found indications of this in our data on preventive behaviors and intentions. Furthermore, it is part of our Western sex role expectations that technology is men's business. Thus, women can delegate more far-reaching preventive measures to the males in their social environment. Second, a possible age-specific explanation is that older people did not want to be a nuisance to the police. Some older victims said that this was the reason for not asking further help from neighbors or relatives. This "nuisance hypothesis" could also partly explain why older people were more satisfied with the police. Third, a possible general explanation is the "control hypothesis," which needs some elaboration. In the area of health research, Woodward and Wallston (1987) found a lower desire for control and information among individuals over 60 years of age, which was mediated by lower self-efficacy expectations with regard to health-related behaviors. In their study on fear of crime among elderly women, Normoyle and Lavrakas (1984) found that the better educated expressed greater perceived control, which was related to less fear of crime. In our study both older people and women were much less educated than younger victims and men. Apart from that, both groups show other characteristics that make them more vulnerable.

Lazarus and Folkman (1984) also point to the possibility that people who are socially or physically more vulnerable could show more emotion-focused coping and less problem-focused coping. So we hypothesize that a greater vulnerability, whether subjective or objective, physical, mental, or social, could be related to lower self-efficacy expectations with respect to burglary prevention. Lower self-efficacy could in turn mean less problem-focused coping (i.e., searching for information on burglary prevention) and more emotion-focused coping (e.g. distancing).

Older people were more satisfied with the police. To test our assumption that this could be explained by our findings that older people had fewer contacts with the police in the past 5 years and had less education than younger people, we performed a MANOVA. We could not find any significant effect of the precontact and educational variables on the dependent satisfaction variables. In our first discussion we suspected that police officers still think that victims are most worried about outcome. Given our findings that victims were satisfied with the police but at the same time showed low expectations of an active and successful investigation, one can question the validity of this police attitude. Perhaps police officers mix up their own role expectations with victims' needs and expectations.

## CONCLUSIONS

It is relevant to study the coping processes of burglary victims. This means not only the 5% of victims estimated to suffer serious emotional trauma (Waller, 1984) but also the other 95%, who have to cope with the burglary in their daily lives. Attempts to develop general models of coping processes (e.g., Casarez-Levinson, this volume; Janoff-Bulman & Frieze, 1983) can provide us with important insights into the factors common to all kinds of victimization. But we believe, with Burt and Katz (1985), that it is equally important to study the crime-specific reactions and the coping processes of different sex and age groups to provide theoretical refinements and more specific and applicable policy recommendations.

Our results showed the importance of police interventions for victims of burglary. Victims are in need of information and reassurance from the police, and most of the time they get what they need. However, our two complementary studies point to the possibility that police officers are not always aware of victims' needs and expectations and of their own biases in their contacts with victims.

The kind of information victims most want from the police is information on further procedures. However, there seems to exist a paradox here because our research shows the possibility that this kind of information can actually lessen the victims' trust in their own coping potentials. This could mean that existing policy guidelines with respect to informing victims must be reassessed and refined. We have already mentioned some directions for further analyses. Relations between victims' characteristics (e.g., sex and age), primary and secondary reactions, coping processes, and the information victims receive should be given special attention.

## ACKNOWLEDGMENTS

The authors wish to thank Eric Taal and Jan Gutteling for helpful suggestions on earlier drafts of this chapter.

## REFERENCES

APA Task Force on the Victims of Crime and Violence. (1985). Executive summary of the final report of the task force on the victims of crime and violence. *American Psychologist, 40,* 107-112.
Bandura, A. (1977). Self-efficacy: Toward a unifying theory of behavioral change. *Psychological Review, 84,* 191-215.
Burt, M. R., & Katz, B. L. (1985). Rape, robbery, and burglary: Responses to actual and feared criminal victimization, with special focus on women and the elderly. *Victimology, 10,* 325-358.
Frijda, N. H. (1986). *The emotions.* Cambridge: Cambridge University Press.
Janoff-Bulman, R., & Frieze, I. H. (1983). A theoretical perspective for understanding reactions to victimization. *Journal of Social Issues, 39,* 1-17.
Lazarus, R. S., & Folkman, S. (1984). *Stress, appraisal, and coping.* New York: Springer Publishing Co.
Maguire, M. (1980). The impact of burglary upon victims. *British Journal of Criminology, 20,* 261-276.
Maguire, M. (1982). *Burglary in a dwelling.* London: Heinemann.
Maguire, M., & Corbett, C. (1987). *The effects of crime and the work of victims support schemes.* Aldershot, UK: Gower.
Normoyle, J., & Lavrakas, P. J. (1984). Fear of crime in elderly women: Perceptions of control, predictability, and territoriality. *Personality and Social Psychology Bulletin, 10,* 191-202.
Sales, E., Baum, M., & Shore, B. (1984). Victim readjustment following assault. *Journal of Social Issues, 40,* 117-136.
Shapland, J., Willmore, J., & Duff, P. (1985). *Victims in the criminal justice system.* Aldershot, UK: Gower.
Skogan, W. G. & Wycoff, M. A. (1987). Some unexpected effects of a police service for victims. *Crime and Delinquency, 33,* 490-501.
Waller, I. (1984). Assistance to victims of burglary. In R. Clarke & T. Hope (Eds.), *Coping with burglary* (pp. 233-249). Hingham, MA: Kluwer-Nijhof.
Winkel, F. W. (1987). *Politie en Voorkoming Misdrijven: Effecten en neveneffecten van voorlichting.* Amsterdam: Mens en Recht.
Woodward, N. J., & Wallston, B. S. (1987). Age and health care beliefs: Self efficacy as a mediator of a low desire for control. *Psychology and Aging, 2,* 3-8.
Voskuil, E. (1987). *Interimverslag Effektmeting; betreffende de vierde periode van het trainingsproject omgaan met slachtoffers en benadeelden.* Unpublished manuscript.
Yantzi, M., & Brown, S. D. (1983). Behoeften van slachtoffers van misdrijven. *Justitiële Verkenningen, 6,* 86-92.

# 20

# The Victim and the Failure to Report the Crime in Italy

*Paola Violante*

Starting from an initial typology of unreported crimes, further analysis is seen as relevant to the victim's decision making. This chapter examines the reasons victims in Italy gave for not reporting the crime to the police.

Reference is made to victims of collective violence and of acquaintance and "intrafamily" abuse, in which most potential and protected victims of the "dark figure of crime" are minors.

## THE VICTIM AND THE DECISION TO REPORT THE CRIME

In his distinction between validity and efficiency of the norm, Kelsen (1945) emphasized not only hypothesis A, the rule is obeyed, and hypothesis B, the rule is not obeyed and the offender is condemned, but also hypothesis C, the law is ineffective and the offender escapes punishment.

The rapist who escapes and avoids trial is a particular case, but the problem becomes more complex when, as it happens in Italy, 80% of crimes are attributed to an "unknown offender," 50% of perpetrators of collective assault escape punishment, 95% of crimes against the person are reported only by the citizen victim, 50% of rapes are not reported, and official statistics (Istat, 1987, 1988a, 1988b) show a decrease in rape and say nothing about domestic assault, in open disagreement with data collected by the press and by mechanisms outside the courts.

At this point attention turns to the citizen victim who is the principal "gatekeeper" of the entire criminal justice process. The victim's decision whether or not to report a crime is the main determinant of the input into the criminal justice system. Rather than being discovered by the police, the vast majority of crimes are reported to them; this suggests that urban policing is a much more reactive than a proactive process. Its role in the definition of "notitia criminis" is limited to cases in which the police are on the scene or the crime is reported by the citizen, especially crimes of petty theft and assault.

Supposing that victims serve as a preliminary filter for crimes and that official statistics remain silent about some crimes, one could say that victims control the phenomenon of decriminalization and thus have considerable impact on the goals of reduction in the number of trials, recently identified as a key issue in criminal justice. Therefore, it is difficult to overestimate the influence that these victim decision makers have on traditional concepts of equality and certainty that are the central aim of every justice system.

In the analysis of the victim's discretionary reporting of crime, it appears that selective criteria operate along a dimension of "seriousness of crime" as interpreted by each victim. For example, many victims decide to report a crime for personal utilitarian reasons. Thus, a high rate of reported crimes could suggest a personal gain motive. In this case, "seriousness" is defined by monetary loss or physical harm.

As far as personal financial loss is concerned, some studies reveal that protection of property and personal gain, more than any other cause, lead the victim to report crimes in which damages may be immediately or easily paid. As far as "personal crimes" (assault, rape) are concerned, some data suggest that the gravity of the injury or intolerance of continuing harassment influences the victim's decision making.

Thus, regardless of the victim, crimes categorized as of "low seriousness" include "victimless crimes" characterized by victim consent (abortion, homosexuality, drug addiction, prostitution, gambling), crimes with no direct victims (pollution, consumer fraud), and crimes with collective victims (terrorism, attempted political crime) or with the organization as victim (shoplifting). If one accepts this initial typology of unreported crimes, one can easily answer the question of whether the goals of victim decision making are compatible or in conflict with those of the criminal justice system in striving to be efficient, equitable, and certain.

Studies of victims' discretion have essentially used two methods. The first involves asking victims directly why they did or did not report their victimization to the police. The second method studies various aspects of victimization, for example, the characteristics of the victim, the offender, and the victim-offender relationship. This method is more traditional and generally used more frequently than the first, especially in Italy, but has recently been shown to be less efficient and accurate, especially in "personal crimes" (rape, assault, harassment).

For example, Istat statistics from 1980 to 1986 show that northern Italians report more than do southern Italians, without correlations to which area has more victimization, more women than men, more married than unmarried women, more older than younger persons, more low-income than high-income brackets, more strangers than nonstrangers, more inhabitants of urban areas than of rural areas or suburbs. These limited data and demographic variables contribute only slightly to the enucleation of constant factors operating in the process of victims' decision making.

## REASONS GIVEN BY VICTIMS FOR NONREPORTING

Victimization surveys have undergone a good deal of development, especially in the United States (Drapkin & Viano, 1975a). Relevant data analyze the reasons victims gave for not reporting the crime to the police. These surveys are limited in their scope of coverage to personal crimes (rape, assault, harassment) and provide data gained through interviews, the press, researchers' studies, and unofficial or informal mechanisms in the years 1980-1988.

"Nothing could be done": 42% of victims believe that nothing could be done. One-third of those surveyed stated that rapes were not reported to the police for this reason. Generally, these are cases of collective rapes by two or three strangers (51% of assaults). In these cases the victim is reluctant to file suit because the unknown assailants, whom the victim may not be able to identify, may not be apprehended or recognized.

However, in domestic assault as well—for example, in the case of incest—the victim gives the same reason for not reporting the event. It is extremely difficult to provide evidence in a closed place, such as the family, because of the relationship among guilty parties, victims, and witnesses. In the Italian penal code the charge is conditioned by the "public scandal." Data reveal only 20 reports with 10 sentences in a year.

"A private matter": This reason is invoked by 38% of victims. It is the main reason for unreported domestic violence and incest. In assaults involving a married couple, serious injury is reported as "an accident" when the prognosis exceeds 20 days and filing suit would be mandatory. Many cases of victimization were reported to someone else: 30% of "notitia criminis" are contained in medical reports. Violence against the elderly by family members is not reported because the elderly are afraid of abandonment or hope to achieve a peaceful solution.

In cases of acquaintance rape, the victim, especially if she is a southerner, is less likely to report it because of feelings of isolation compared to the strong unity among the families of the accused or among offenders and their fellow townspeople, who frequently see them as only "overly exuberant boys."

"Police wouldn't be bothered": 50% of the victims saw the police as not being interested in their complaints. This perception added to psychological (shame) or social reasons (reputation with neighbors) leads to procrastination. In 50% of cases, rape reports are delayed. This is then used against the victim at the trial, with the defense lawyer arguing that the delay is evidence that she consented to sex. Data show that, when the complaints were made within 24 hours, nearly 80% resulted in convictions. In 10 cases reported after 24 hours, no one was convicted, one was acquitted, and nine were not prosecuted.

Because of lack of trust in the police, a sizable number of attempted rapes and assaults were not reported by the victims. Moreover, Italians generally consider the police to be more involved in fighting organized economic or domestic crime than in incidents affecting the victims' private lives. Thus, Italian official statistics (Istat, 1988b) cover economic crimes well, sexual crimes poorly, and sexual abuse of children not at all.

Another reason these data are not informative is that the Istat survey includes the general category "maltreatment," which in the Italian penal code (art. 572) generally covers family or extrafamily abuse between older and younger persons.

"Did not want to take time": This is the reason given for not reporting by 10% of victims. This reason is based on the mistrust of the legal system, which is definitely strong in Italy.

For many victims, seeking judicial relief means the beginning of an involvement with the various agencies of the criminal justice system that may make substantial demands on the victim's time and resources that will not be compensated by the outcome of the trial. This explains the large number of acquittals (50%) because of "lack of evidence."

On the whole, in the Italian system, sexual freedom comes second when compared to property interests. This is quite clear when one examines the penalties. For example, kidnapping for the purpose of extortion is punishable with 5 years, whereas the penalty for sexual harassment or abuse or for rape is from 2 to 8 years in prison.

If the offender causes the victim's death through kidnapping for purposes of extortion, the sentence is 30 years; but if the victim's death is caused by kidnapping for sexual abuse, the law is silent. The applicable punishment is for manslaughter (10-15 years). Penalties envisioned in the penal code are further weakened by the use of every extenuating circumstance. As an example, perpetrators of collective rapes carried out during one month against inhibited and unprotected young women were sentenced to 2 years, 1 month of imprisonment. A father who had raped his daughter for 10 years was fined only 10 million lire (approximately $9,000). Meanwhile, the victim feels further victimized by the publicity of the trial.

"Did not want to get involved": This is the reason given by 11% of victims. These statistics suggest that for many victims the decision to report a crime to the police may be influenced by a sort of personal cost-benefit analysis.

Some victims fear the publicity of their illegal activity (prostitution, homosexuality, drug addiction) or are afraid to lose their reputation in their neighborhood, where rape is generally seen to be provoked or consented to by the woman. For example, in 1988 slanderous statements were written on the walls of a school in Monza by classmates of a girl who had had the courage to report her sexual victimization.

Very interesting cases are represented by "whistle-blowers" who report crimes in which they themselves are involved; for example, doctors involved in organized medical fraud and the "customers" of illegal gambling and drug operations.

"Fear of reprisal": Only 20% of victims give this reason for not reporting, which is cited in organized crime figures. It is noteworthy that recently statistics show an overall decrease in extortion, whereas it is actually increasing in southern Italy. As far as rape is concerned, the increase in collective violence (70%) is also worth noting, although it is not mentioned in the official statistics but rather reported in the press.

Minors keep quiet about abuse and sexual abuse within the family. Unofficial statistics are alarming: 36,000 assaults described by children in a year, of which 25% involved sexual abuse.

## ALTERNATIVE REMEDIES AVAILABLE TO VICTIMS

Although alternative decisions available to victims of crime are quite limited, their importance should not be underestimated. The power vested in victims is fundamental: their major choice is either to report the crime to the police or to do nothing. However, decision making by the victims is not analogous to that of the police.

Actually, there is a norm in the Italian code that commands that crimes be reported (art. 2 c.p.p.) and establishes a punishment for its violation (art 361 2 c. c.p.). However, the duty to report is applicable only to persons who become aware of the crime because of their professional responsibilities, such as medical doctors (art 361 1c., 362, 363, 364 c.p.). In reality medical reports are rare. There were only seven in 1987.

In crimes of "abuse and maltreatment" of minors, the lack of reporting is motivated by the fear of exposing the minor to further victimization by members of family, once the victim returns. Thus, there is a great deal of complaint about the lack of social services or refuges for the victims, especially in the case of minors. In child abuse, reporting is necessary in order to change the situation, but it is not enough. What is needed is a number of legal provisions and social mechanisms able to protect minors during and after trial.

The area of remedies for victims of rape is also controversial. Recently, bills have been introduced to require the prosecution of rape. The Italian legal system limits the prosecution of rape by giving the victim the power to decide whether the suspect should be prosecuted or not. The reasons for this are to protect the reputation of the victim and, most of all, of her family, which could be damaged by the publicity and stigma of the trial. Actually, this provision strongly discourages prosecution and contributes enormously to the "dark figure" of rapes in Italy. The victim who wants to prosecute is often alone, going against the wishes of her own family and of the family of the accused.

Thus, at the end of this analysis we may be left with one overall feeling: the solitary position of the citizen-victim. It has been said that the first reform should be this: how to make the citizen-victim feel less neglected and defenseless when faced with the abuse, deafness, and absence of others, especially of the state.

## ACKNOWLEDGMENTS

The author would like to thank Mr. John Credico and Dr. Emilio Viano for reviewing and editing the final English version.

## REFERENCES

Delogu, T., & Giannini, M. C. (1982). *L'Indice di Criminalità di Selling e Wolfgang nella Teoria Generale della Misurazione di Gravità dei Reati*. Milan: Giuffre.

Drapkin, I., & Viano, E. (1974a). *Society's reaction to victimization*. Lexington, MA: D. C. Heath.

Drapkin, I., & Viano, E. (1974b). *Theoretical issues in victimology*. Lexington, MA: D. C. Heath.

Drapkin, I., & Viano, E. (1974c). *Victimology*. Lexington, MA: D. C. Heath.

Drapkin, I., & Viano, E. (1975a). *Crimes, victims and justice*. Lexington, MA: D. C. Heath.

Drapkin, I., & Viano, E. (1975b). *Exploiters and exploited*. Lexington, MA: D. C. Heath.

Drapkin, I., & Viano, E. (1975c). *Violence and its victims*. Lexington, MA: D. C. Heath.

Ferracuti, F. (1988). *Alcoolismo e Violenza Intrafamiliare in Alcoolismo, Tossicodipendenza e Criminalità*. Milan: Giuffre.

Gottfredson, M., & Gottfredson, D. M. (1980). *Decision making in criminal justice: Toward the rational exercise of discretion*. Cambridge, MA: Ballinger.

Gulotta, G. (1976). *La Vittima*. Milan: Giuffre.

Hindelang, M. (1976). *Criminal victimization in eight American cities: A descriptive analysis of common theft and assault*. Cambridge, MA: Ballinger.

Hindelang, M. (1975). *National crime survey: National sample survey documentation.* Washington, DC: U.S. Government Printing Office.
Hindelang, M., Gottfredson, M. R., & Garofalo, J. (1978). *Victims of personal crime: An empirical foundation for a theory of personal victimization.* Cambridge, MA: Ballinger.
Istat. (1987). *La criminalità attraverso le Statistiche: anni 1981, 1982, 1983 (note e relazioni).* Tivoli (Roma): Italian Government Printing Office.
Istat. (1987). *La criminalità attraverso le Statistiche: Anni 1981-1982-1983 (note e relazioni).*
Istat. (1988a). *La criminalità attraverso le Statistiche: anni 1984, 1985, 1986.* Tivoli (Roma): Italian Government Printing Office.
Istat. (1988b). *Statistiche giudiziarie, vol. 33.* Tivoli (Roma): Italian Government Printing Office.
Kelsen, H. (1945). *General theory of law and state.* Cambridge: Harvard University Press.
Merzagora, I. (1986). *Incesto.* Milan: Giuffre.
Reiss, A. (1971). *The police and the public.* New Haven, CT: Yale University Press.

# 21

# Implementation of Federal Legislation to Aid Victims of Crime in the United States

*Mario Thomas Gaboury*

## INTRODUCTION

Recognition of larger *societal* responsibilities to redress the wounds of innocent victims is a paramount factor in designing programs to aid them. Much progress has been made with regard to fair treatment of crime victims in the United States during the past 20 years, particularly the past decade. The purpose of this chapter is to focus on the implementation of two pieces of federal legislation aimed at providing aid to victims of crime. These two laws are (1) the 1982 federal Victim and Witness Protection Act and (2) the 1984 Victims of Crime Act, as amended.

## REVIEW OF PROGRESS

On April 23, 1982, President Ronald Reagan appointed the Task Force on Victims of Crime. The nine-member task force held public hearings in six cities across the country, receiving testimony from nearly 200 witnesses, about one-third of whom were themselves victims of crime. This task force effort was most successful as it was able to draw from the great community-based support for victims that had been developing since the mid-1960s. Its report, issued in December 1982, marked a significant step in the victims movement and signaled the emergence of victims' concerns on the federal level. Most important, the findings engendered a tremendous, bipartisan effort to improve the treatment of victims in the United States. This has resulted in a sustained cooperation among very divergent political groups.

The task force's 68 recommendations addressed the legislative and executive arms of government at the local, state, and federal levels; the criminal justice system; the medical, legal, educational, mental health, and religious communities; and the private sector. The recommendations comprise perhaps the most comprehensive set of proposals articulating the scope of victims' needs. Most important, the task force pointed out that coordination and cooperation among these entities was imperative to succeeding in this vital endeavor.

In 1982, the first major piece of federal victim rights legislation was enacted. It was the federal Victim and Witness Protection Act (VWPA), an omnibus measure intended to enhance and protect the necessary role of crime victims and witnesses in the federal criminal justice process. This act functions in much the same way as "Fair Treatment" laws or "Bills of Rights" for victims established by many state jurisdictions in the United States and elsewhere. One of the recommendations of the Crime Victims Task Force was that a Crime Victims Fund be established at the national level to encourage state governments to assume and expand their role in aiding victims. This desire became a reality when President Reagan signed the Victims of Crime Act of 1984 (VOCA). In a remarkably short time, VOCA's encouragement of state and local crime victim compensation and victim assistance programs has been established as a critically important component of this movement. VOCA is making a difference for the millions of innocent people victimized by crime in our country by expanding program availability and improving program quality.

## LEGISLATIVE IMPLEMENTATION

What follows is a detailed discussion of each bill and its respective accomplishments.

## Federal Victim and Witness Protection Act of 1982

The VWPA recognizes the important role of crime victims and witnesses in the criminal justice process and seeks to ensure that the federal government provides them with assistance ("without infringing on the constitutional right of defendants") and to provide model legislation for state and local governments.

The Act provides rights for victims of federal crimes, including the following:

- Fair treatment of victims and witnesses.
- Victim impact statements in presentence reports.
- Protecting victims and witnesses from intimidation or retaliation, including provisions for civil restraining orders.
- Restitution to victims, in addition to other criminal penalties.
- Consideration of victims' situation in bail determinations.
- Prohibiting federal felons from deriving profit from the sale of literary or other related rights.
- Provision of waiting areas for victims and other prosecution witnesses separate from all other witnesses.
- Prompt return of property held as evidence.
- Employer intervention services.
- Victim assistance education and training offered to persons at federal law enforcement training facilities and to government attorneys.

The VWPA was amended to make U.S. attorneys the federal prosecutors, responsible for informing victims of parole hearing dates, and to permit an oral or written statement at the hearing.

## Federal Fair Treatment Guidelines

The U.S. Attorney General issued guidelines for the implementation of the VWPA that, in fact, provided further protections and services. The guidelines include consideration of such necessary victim services as emergency social and medical services, information regarding crime victim compensation and community-based victim treatment programs, orientation to the criminal justice system and judicial proceedings, information about the availability of protection services to guard against intimidation, and when possible, notification about court appearances and scheduling changes relating to their case.

In addition to the specific services outlined in the VWPA itself, the guidelines added the following provisions:

- Department officials avoid, to the extent possible, disclosure of victims' and witnesses' addresses.
- Creditors of victims and witnesses are notified if cooperation affects the ability to make timely payments.
- The appropriate U.S. Probation Officer is fully advised of the victim impact statement requirements of VWPA.
- Within 30 days, all related Justice Department components provide training to existing and new employees concerning their responsibilities.

It should be noted that in a recent survey of U.S. attorneys' offices, widespread compliance with the VWPA and guidelines was found. Victims and witnesses were accorded these rights, as needed, in 17,019 of the criminal cases accepted for prosecution. That meant that a total of 23,579 victims and 60,265 witnesses were afforded protection and service throughout the 94 federal districts.

## THE VICTIMS OF CRIME ACT

The second piece of legislation is the 1984 Victims of Crime Act. VOCA established a federal Crime Victims Fund, which consists entirely of revenues from convicted federal criminals—fines, penalty assessments, and appearance bond forfeitures. It must be emphasized that the centerpiece of VOCA is the creation of this Crime Victims Fund, which provides the money for crime victim compensation and victim assistance grants to states, for services to victims of federal offenses, for much needed training and technical assistance provided to victim programs, and for other related projects.

The principal sources of revenue are (1) federal criminal fines collected from individuals and corporations convicted of federal offenses; (2) special penalty assessments on criminal convictions; (3) the proceeds of forfeited appearance bonds, bail bonds, and collateral; and (4) profits from the sale of literary or other rights arising out of the criminal act by a federal defendant, or the so-called notoriety-for-profit prohibitions.

Due to the variability inherent in assessment and collection methods, the amounts deposited into the fund have fluctuated over the first three years. Overall, however, the fund appears to be on the rise. In fiscal year 1985, $68.3 million was deposited into the fund; in 1986, the total deposits decreased to $62.5 million; in 1987, the amount increased to $77.4 million. In 1988 a record $93.5 million was collected in the Crime Victims Fund. The Department of Justice expects fiscal year 1989 collections to reach the cap on the fund, currently set at $125 million. President Reagan signed a bill into law on November 18, 1988, that reauthorized the VOCA programs for 6 more years.

The importance of a criminal-based revenue-generating fund cannot be overstated. Philosophically speaking, it affords the individual, and society at large, some sense that justice has been done, that perhaps even a small bit of restitution has been made, that criminals are forced to aid victims. Practically speaking, these revenues, which are directly linked to the magnitude of the problem sought to be addressed, are specifically set aside for victim programs. This alleviates, to some extent, uncertainty in program funding and therefore in program planning. It is a sensible notion that the basic needs of victims should not be completely relegated to annual battles for general governmental tax revenues but afforded consistent special funds. In fact, this idea has proliferated in the United States—

currently about 36 of the 50 states now collect criminal fees and forfeitures to support all or part of their victim services and compensation. Another 10 states supply general revenues only. Therefore, federal Crime Victims Fund monies represent only a fraction of funds available for victims nationwide.

The federal fund augments state and local funding for both compensation (49.5% of the fund) and assistance (45% of the fund). The program relies heavily on the states to determine the precise nature and the level of services to be supported by VOCA. It is a reflection of the rightful role of local governments to determine the sort of programming that best suits their particular needs. This philosophy has resulted in great variations in the specific services that have been developed in each community, reflecting the diversity that exists among the various states. This sort of flexibility is most important in a country like the United States, where regional, cultural, geographic, and other such concerns render the imposition of a uniform, nationwide program ill-advised.

Also, it is clearly intended that the federal fund be used to the maximum extent possible to provide direct assistance to victims. Currently, neither the crime victim compensation nor the victim assistance funds may be used for state administrative expenses. Victim assistance programs may use VOCA funds for direct services and only those administrative costs attributable to direct services.

## OVERVIEW OF COMPENSATION AND ASSISTANCE
### Victim Compensation

The 1982 President's Task Force on Victims of Crime paid particular attention to the needs of victims for at least minimal financial relief from the most immediate costs of crime and was concerned about the status of crime victim compensation programs then in existence.

It is clear that during even the brief period VOCA has been in operation it has had a significant influence in expanding and improving the level of assistance afforded by crime victim compensation programs. Prior to VOCA, not all states had crime victim compensation programs, and many that did were facing serious funding shortages.

Seventeen of 33 compensation programs surveyed in 1982 reported having experienced insufficient funding. Victims would typically have to wait for many months before claims were paid. Benefits offered by programs were usually limited, and there were often severe restrictions on who could apply for coverage. Many of these limitations were attempts to contain program costs; victim advocates felt the restrictions reflected a cynical attitude by state legislators.

VOCA has helped alleviate these impediments to providing victims with financial assistance. States are now reimbursed for 40% of their respective previous awards, up to the 49.5% compensation fund ceiling. Among the purposes of the crime victim compensation portion of VOCA are (1) encouraging at least a minimal level of crime victim compensation coverage nationwide; (2) seeking to increase the use of programs, in large measure through referrals from victim assistance agencies; (3) enhancing the range and level of benefits available; and (4) utilizing state programs for victims of federal offenses rather than creating a separate, overlapping federal crime victim compensation program.

In line with the philosophy of VOCA, few eligibility criteria are imposed on states in order to qualify for funds. These eligibility requirements are as follows:

1. The program is operated by a state and offers compensation to victims of crime and survivors of crime victims for medical expenses attributable to a physical injury, including mental health counseling, loss of wages attributable to physical injury, and funeral expenses.
2. The program promotes victim cooperation with the reasonable requests of law enforcement authorities.
3. The state certifies that grants will not be used to supplant or replace state funds otherwise available for crime victim compensation.
4. The program compensates victims who are nonresidents of the state on the same basis used to make awards to victims who are residents.
5. The program compensates victims of crimes subject to federal jurisdiction occurring within the state on the same basis as victims of state crimes.
6. The program must consider victims of drunk driving or domestic violence applying for compensation in the same way other types of victims are considered, that is, no categorical exclusions of these victims are allowed.
7. States must compensate their residents who are injured by crime in another state if that state does not cover them.

The precise impact that VOCA funds have had in each state has varied depending on the states' needs. For some, VOCA comes as a life raft, keeping their programs afloat. One state reported that their program "almost ran out of money," and another program "would have gone broke without VOCA." For others, VOCA enabled them to keep pace with the accelerating rate of compensation claims. For example, one state used VOCA to reduce its 3- to 4-month backlog. For many, VOCA was the opportunity to improve their programs, to offer broader coverage and better benefits. It is evident that the caseload for state crime victim compensation programs is, indeed, increasing. As might be expected, the number and amount of crime victim compensation awards is also climbing dramatically. This national increase reflects the fact that several states had remarkable increases in the amounts their crime victim compensation programs paid out.

Recently, the Department of Justice analyzed specifically how the state programs were working. The 34 programs reporting for fiscal year 86 indicated that 60% of the awards went to pay for medical expenses. More than one-fourth of the payouts went for lost wages, loss of support, or disability. Although the amount spent for mental health counseling costs remains quite small, the indications are that this category will increase in spending because of wider recognition of the importance of psychological intervention with victims. Finally, funeral benefits amounted to 5% of total payments, and attorney fees were less than 1%.

The most prevalent type of crime for which a crime victim compensation award was made was assault, followed by the general category "other" (which obviously comprises various personal crimes) and then, in descending order, murder, sexual offenses, child sexual abuse, other violent offenses, drunk driving, other motor vehicle offenses, child physical abuse, and spouse abuse. Nationally, the average financial award was $1,836, ranging from an average of $4,087 for drunk driving to $322 for "other" offenses.

Referrals are an important program component. Police are the most commonly cited source of referrals to crime victim compensation programs. Thirteen of 33 compensation program directors ranked police as the top referral source, followed by hospitals and then victim assistance programs. All but six listed police as among the top three sources.

In addition to the fact that federal funds have augmented state efforts, significant progress in the state/federal partnership to assist victims of crime can be seen in several areas:

- Compensation for mental health services is almost universal.
- The range and level of benefits have increased; this is particularly important for the poor who are victimized.
- Improved information sharing and communication among victim service providers has increased victim access to compensation and other services.
- Cooperation between law enforcement agencies and victims has been improved considerably now that victims know that the "system" is not going to expect them to carry the financial burden of victimization all alone.

## Victim Assistance

The second major area of Crime Victims Fund usage is providing financial incentives for victim service programs. This recognizes that crime can touch all aspects of a victim's life: emotional, legal, physical, and social. It also often affects those close to the victim: survivors, friends, relatives, neighbors, and sometimes the larger community. Some of these effects may last for a relatively brief period of time—a few hours or days; others may last for years or for a lifetime. There are now many thousands of programs throughout the United States providing a wide variety of services to help victims. They are rape crisis centers, domestic violence shelters, victim/witness assistance units, child abuse treatment programs, and others. They are located in law enforcement agencies, prosecutors' offices, churches, independent community-based groups, hospitals, mental health associations, and social service agencies. They provide crisis intervention, counseling, emotional support, emergency assistance, court notification, case information, and an array of other services.

The principal goals of the victim assistance grants are to provide services directly to victims of crime by assisting local units of government and private nonprofit organizations to enhance or expand direct services to victims of crime, to encourage the states to improve their assistance to crime victims, and to promote the development of comprehensive, coordinated services to all victims of crime across the nation. To be eligible to receive a victim assistance grant under VOCA, states must certify that priority will be given to programs assisting victims of sexual assault, spousal abuse, or child abuse and that funding will be made available for "previously underserved" victim populations as designated by each state. The funds must not supplant or replace state or local funds otherwise available for crime victim assistance.

Further, individual programs are required to

- Be operated by a public agency or nonprofit organization, or both, and provide services to victims of crime.
- Demonstrate financial support from sources other than VOCA.
- Use volunteers, unless the governor has compelling reasons to waive this requirement.
- Promote coordinated public and private efforts to aid victims within the community.
- Assist victims in seeking crime victim compensation benefits.

The Act describes the types of services to crime victims as including crisis intervention; emergency services, such as temporary housing and security measures; assistance in participating in the criminal justice system, including transportation to court and child care; and payment for unreimbursed costs of forensic medical examinations.

Approximately 1,500 victim assistance programs receive VOCA funds. Almost 80% of the subgrantees are private nonprofit organizations. Of the 13% that are criminal justice agencies, two-thirds are located in prosecutors' offices. The remaining 7% of the subgrantees are non-criminal justice governmental agencies, mainly social services agencies. For 85% of the programs, VOCA funds represented less than half of their budgets. Thirty percent of the awards amounted to less than 10% of the recipient's budget, and a similar percentage fell within the 11% to 25% category. One-quarter of all subgrants accounted for between 26% and 50% of program budgets. Only 15% report depending on VOCA for more than half of their budget, with 3% indicating that VOCA represents more than three-quarters of their budget. This means that VOCA's intent to supplement local funding widely throughout the United States is being fulfilled.

As mentioned previously, states had to choose among three options to meet the requirement that programs serving victims of sexual assault, spouse abuse, or child abuse be given priority for funding. The overwhelming amount of VOCA funds for fiscal 1986 went to programs whose principal mission was serving one or more of these priority categories. In fact, over three-quarters of the funds (and, in terms of the actual number of programs, over 80%) went to these programs. Most such programs serve only one priority area, but others served two, and a few served all three. In order of service, most resources went to spouse abuse services, then sexual assault, followed by child abuse. By comparison, less than 20% of the funds went to programs whose principal mission was to serve all victims of crime. Unlike other programs, these tended to be based on prosecutor's offices. Less than 4% was awarded to programs that aimed at serving specific victim groups other than the priority categories.

By far, the most frequently reported use of VOCA funds was to increase capacity to provide services. This typically meant hiring additional staff with which to increase service volume. Over 200 of the subgrantees used some or all of the funds to begin offering new services to their clients. Many started telephone hotlines or established support groups to work with victims. Some began offering legal advocacy services or other forms of assistance. More than 100 new victim service programs were started with VOCA funds. Many of these (31) were newly established victim/witness assistance programs within prosecutor's offices.

## CONCLUSION

This chapter presents an overview of current federal initiatives on behalf of all crime victims in the United States. The U.S. Department of Justice's position is that these programs have truly advanced the victims movement in our country. Their offender-revenue-based approach affords a wide variety of services and encourages maximum local autonomy. It cannot be said, however, that the United States' federal program is *the* model program. Certain aspects of VWPA and VOCA implementation are continuing to be developed and improved as we gain more experience. Moreover, tradition, as well as legal and cultural differences between the United States and other countries, may require that much different programs be designed elsewhere. Overall, the principles of protecting victims and serving their needs are transferrable to any country and must be considered a central part of any efficient, effective, and just system of government.

## REFERENCES

Office for Victims of Crime. (1988). *Report to Congress on VOCA*. Washington, DC: U.S. Government Printing Office.
President's Task Force on Victims of Crime. (1982). *Final report*. Washington, DC: U.S. Government Printing Office.

# 22

# Assessing Restitution's Impact on Recidivism: A Review of the Evaluative Research

*Thomas C. Castellano*

---

The basic concept of restitution—that offenders repay their victims for the harm they have wrought—is one of the few concepts in any justice system that receives almost universal support. Despite the widespread appeal of restitutive sanctioning, it has been well documented that many restitution efforts have suffered notable problems of design, implementation, and impact (Austin & Krisberg, 1982; McCarthy & McCarthy, 1984; McGillis, 1986). This chapter's focus is a relatively neglected aspect of restitutive sanctioning: Has restitution as a criminal sanction resulted in the reduced recidivism of offenders so punished?

Although much of restitution's early promise was based on its potential rehabilitative and specific deterrent function, empirical studies linking restitution with recidivism have been sporadic, plagued with methodological problems, and not very well disseminated. Consequently, there appears to be a lack of conventional wisdom as to whether restitution reduces recidivism, and if so, under what conditions as applied to what offenders (for differing assessments, see, e.g., Lab, 1988; McCarthy & McCarthy, 1984; McGillis, 1986, Schneider & Schneider, 1985). A major reason there appears to be so much variation in assessments of the effects of restitution on recidivism is that no recent single study has systematically compiled and evaluated the available literature.

## THE IMPORTANCE OF RECIDIVISM FOR RESTITUTION

The current popularity of restitutive sanctioning is premised on a wide panoply of values and concerns, many of which appear unrelated to the rehabilitative or specific deterrent effects of such sanctions. These include victim reparation, offender desert, cost, humaneness, and needed alternatives to incarceration. Although the future of restitution should not and will not be based solely on the consequences of such sanctions for subsequent offender behavior, an analysis of the effects of restitution on recidivism is important because the success of restitution as a sanctioning alternative will be determined to a significant degree by its compatibility with traditional criminal justice goals and procedures.

This point can be amplified by reference to the trichotomy of concerns underlying correctional policy. The first two are more widely recognized and have a stronger, more modern historical basis within correctional policy. They are concern for the offender and concern for the community (O'Leary & Duffee, 1971). Concern for the offender is most commonly associated with rehabilitative policy, whereas concern for the community is most commonly associated with a punitive crime control policy. It is easy to recognize that the traditional aims of the criminal law and sanction, including deterrence, incapacitation, retribution, rehabilitation, and the symbolic revival of unity, primarily reflect concern for the community and secondarily concern for the offender.

In recent years, concern for the victim has received an increasingly important role in the correctional process. Concern for the victim is not simply a proxy for nor a displaced symbolic concern for community; it should be viewed as a separate, if unequal, partner among those concerns giving shape and form to correctional policies and practices. For instance, there can be little doubt that the current popularity of restitution is largely premised on this sanction's serving *both* victim (e.g., financial reparation) and community-based needs (e.g., reduced recidivism).

The actual success of translating concern for the victim into practice generally and the degree to which restitutive sentencing is embraced in particular depend largely, then, on the compatibility of the consequences of concern for the victim with concern for the community. Restitution may conflict with existing organizational frameworks and value structures in criminal justice and cannot be simply assumed to be easily integrated into current operations. An obvious example lies in restitution ordered as a condition of probation. Increased accounting and supervisory demands on probation personnel are often pronounced and may result in probation departments minimally enforcing restitution orders or actively discouraging sentencing judges from ordering such sanctions. This is especially the case when probation views restitution as being quite secondary to its organizational mandate, be it therapeutic intervention or law enforcement or some combination thereof.

In fact, in a number of legal structures the victim's claim to reparation is explicitly ancillary to the more traditional purposes of sentencing. It is not uncommon for criminal codes to state that restitution can be applied only when other purposes of sentencing can be appropriately served (e.g., Maine Revised Statutes, Title 17-A, 1978) and for court cases to place secondary importance on the victim-reparative aspects of restitution as opposed to the potential rehabilitative impact of restitution on the offender (Harland, 1983). The practical consequences of offender rehabilitation (or crime control) being given primacy over victim reparation as a rationale for restitutive sanctioning belies the importance of the effects of restitution on offender behavior for the ideological justifications, policy, and practice of restitutive sanctioning.

## DATA AND METHODS
## Selection and Retrieval of Studies

The forms of restitution included in this evaluative review varied from restitution as a condition of pretrial diversion to restitution as a condition of release from imprisonment. Studies examining community service sanctioning were originally excluded from the analysis, but because many of the reviewed studies involved restitution programs administering both monetary restitution to victims and community service, with differing treatment effects not being separated in the analysis, to some degree there is a confounding of the effects of these distinct treatment types. Similar to the broad range of restitution programming, measures of recidivism varied greatly and were restricted only to the extent that some measure of recontact with the justice system by the restitution subjects was provided within the study. All studies included in the present review utilized *somewhat* meaningful and "liberally" defined comparison groups in their analysis.

The present study identified target documents through an extensive search of *Criminal Justice Abstracts, Abstracts on Criminology and Penology, Sociological Abstracts, Dissertation Abstracts, Social Science Index*, the National Criminal Justice Reference Service Index, and references contained in prior literature reviews and papers. The review covered sources from 1975 to the present. Eleven studies that met the inclusion criteria were identified and available for review. Six studies involved adult populations, and five examined juvenile restitution subjects.

## Assessing Intervention Effectiveness

The small sample of studies under review and their uneven quality necessitated a qualitative/descriptive integration of the evaluative research rather than a quantitative one. Although a quantitative approach to the integration of research results is generally preferred to more literary and descriptive approaches, the wide diversity of treatment and outcome measures and the uneven reporting of even basic descriptive statistics within the reviewed studies indicated that a quantitative integrative approach (e.g., meta-analysis) would be premature.

# FINDINGS
## Adult Offenders

A review of Table 22.1, which presents summary information on evaluative studies that have examined the impact of adult restitution programs, indicates a number of important findings. Only six studies meeting the inclusion criteria have been identified and are available. They are relatively old pieces, all appearing before 1984. Two evaluate the same program, and only two involve an evaluation of restitution as a condition of probation, by far the most common form of restitutive sanction applied to adults. Obviously, more research in this area would be useful.

Closer inspection of Table 22.1 suggests a number of themes. The first two studies examined restitution applied to a postincarcerated population and suffer from extremely small sample sizes, rendering statistically significant differences difficult to achieve. The Heinz, Galaway, and Hudson (1976) study on the Minnesota Restitution Center is further limited by nonequivalent comparison groups and by the possibility that restitution itself was not the key factor associated with the apparently reduced recidivism of restitution clients. It could easily be related to the residential setting and intensive supervision under which the restitution occurred (multiple treatment contamination).

Hudson and Chesney's (1978) subsequent follow-up study of the Minnesota Restitution Center benefits from larger sample sizes, random assignment, a longer follow-up period, and stronger recidivism measures. It also suggests much more mixed results. Twenty-four-month postprison follow-up data reveal similar proportions of randomly assigned experimentals and controls still on parole (27%). The study also showed that 54% of the experimentals and 50% of the controls remained free of any legal sanctions and that 24% of the controls but only 6% of experimentals were returned to prison because of new court commitments. The experimentals were much more likely to be returned to prison for technical violations (40% of the returnees) than were the controls (10%). In general, experimentals had a higher rate of return to prison than did the controls (46% vs. 34%) and also returned more quickly—50% of the experimental returnees failed within 6 months, whereas only 9% of the controls did.

Noteworthy implications of this study include the high rate of in-program failures and early returns to prison among the experimentals. This is probably associated with more intensive parole supervision—a common confounding factor in recidivism research. There is also the possible confounding of multiple treatment effects associated with the restitution center, which included group therapy or individual counseling, continued parole supervision among the experimentals even after restitution payments had been completed, and a residential placement. Thus, both the dependent and independent variables witness significant measurement and interpretational difficulties (see also Austin & Krisberg, 1982). Although one may argue that this study suggests that community safety may have been improved by this program (i.e., the lower experimental recidivism rate for new crimes), the costs of such success are arguably very high for both clients and the state.

Bonta and colleagues (1983) have reported on a residential program in Ontario that shares many similarities with the Minnesota Restitution Center. Partially aimed at a male incarcerated population willing to serve the remainder of their terms in a halfway house type of setting on the condition that restitution be part of the placement, this community resource center also housed residents serving their sentences in the community so that they could maintain their employment. These residents had no restitution agreements and thus served as a comparison group in this assessment of restitution's impact on recidivism. Bonta et al. discovered that the restitution clients had a much higher in-program failure rate than the nonrestitution group (43% vs. 19%, $p = .001$) and that at both a 12- and 24-month follow-up period the restitution group exhibited higher rates of reincarceration than did the comparison group. The authors report that the differences in reincarceration rates are not statistically significant, but a reanalysis of the data indicates a significant difference at 24 months ($p = .03$). However, because the restitution group was younger and had more extensive criminal histories than did the nonrestitution group and because these predictors of recidivism (as well as others such as employment status) were not controlled in the recidivism analysis, little can be said about the effects of this restitution program on recidivism.

The only adult studies that have examined the impact of restitution as a condition of probation also suggest little reason for optimism. Analyzing the effects of restitution orders as a condition of probation among a relatively large sample of probationers who were well matched to a control group of probationers not ordered to pay restitution, Miller (1981) found little indication of any positive effects on recidivism. Rather, Miller found that probationers ordered to pay restitution were significantly more likely to face a filing of a revocation (the differences across the groups appearing primarily attributable to work- and payment-related problems) and slightly more likely to be sent to prison on an actual revocation than were probationers not ordered to pay restitution. As was the case with the Ontario halfway house residents, the strongest predictor of

TABLE 22.1 Evaluative Studies of Restitution with Adult Offenders

| Author/program | Significant treatment components | Research design/sample size[a] | Recidivism figure/significance level[b] | | |
|---|---|---|---|---|---|
| | | | | E | C |
| Heinz et al. (1976), Minnesota Restitution Center | Residential center receiving parolees (male property offenders) after average of 4 months incarceration; restitution contacts with victims; intensive supervision; staff to facilitate restitution payments | Matched control group; 16-month follow-up period; E = 18, C = 18 | Reconvictions: Felony reconvictions: Parole violations reports: Parole violations for new crimes: Glaser Index successes: | 28% 11% 39% 16% 61% | 67% 39% 61% 50% 39% |
| | | | | | na .025(1-tail) ns .05(1-tail) ns |
| Brewer (1977, 1979), California Restitution Project | Parolees found in technical violation returned to prison; if eligible can volunteer for parole release with restitution as a condition | Random assignment; 12-month follow-up period; E = 23, C = 10 | Rearrests: | 74% | 50% |
| | | | | | ns |
| Hudson and Chesney (1978), Minnesota Restitution Center | See Heinz et al. | Random assignment; 24-month follow-up period; slightly lower average risk period for controls; E = 63, C = 69 | Free of any legal sanctions: Court commitment/prison return: Technical violation/prison return: | | |

| Study | Description | Design | Outcome measure | E% | C% | p |
|---|---|---|---|---|---|---|
| Bonta et al. (1983), Rideau-Carleton Restitution Program, Ontario, Canada | Eligible incarcerates willing to pay restitution to victims served remainder of sentence in a community resource center (CRC). Only 4% had contact with victims in the restitution process | Availability comparison group; 12-month and 24-month follow-up period; E = 67, C = 177 | % returned to prison within 6 months | 50% | 54% | ns |
| | | | | 6% | 24% | na |
| | | | | 40% | 10% | na |
| | | | | 23% | 9% | na |
| | | | Within CRC failure rate: (unsuccessful completion): | 43% (N = 67) | 19% (N = 177) | .001 |
| | | | 12-month reincarceration rate: | 51% (N = 65) | 38% (N = 176) | ns |
| | | | 24-month reincarceration rate: | 68% (N = 59) | 51% (N = 131) | .03 |
| Miller (1981), Colorado, normal probation supervision | Restitution ordered as a condition of probation; no offender/victim contact; policy of probation to generate full payments | Matched control group; E = 635 days average and C = 540 days average follow-up period; E = 419, C = 179 | Revocations filed: | 36% | 26% | .05 |
| | | | Revocation to prison (if filed): | 27% | 33% | ns |
| | | | Arrests: | 18% | 22% | ns |
| | | | Convictions: | na | na | ns |
| Brown (1983), Project Repay, Multnomah County, OR | Restitution ordered as a condition of probation or as part of a split sentence | Nonequivalent availability-based comparison groups; 12-month follow-up period; E = 403, C = 119 | Probation failure: | 30.0% | 34.5% | ns |
| | | | New crime violations: | 7.9% | 7.6% | ns |
| | | | Revocations: | 6.0% | 5.9% | ns |
| | | | Incarcerations: | 12.7% | 11.8% | ns |
| | | | Arrests: | 25.3% | 32.8% | ns |
| | | | Convictions: | 8.2% | 12.6% | ns |

[a]E = no. of experimentals; C = no. of controls.
[b]na = not reported; ns = not significant.

failure among restitution clients was the actual degree to which restitution orders were paid. Thus, it does appear that concern for the victim in these cases generated notable consequences for offenders. This is perhaps acceptable, yet it must be emphasized that concern for the community benefits (e.g., reduced recidivism) does not appear to have been realized from either program. For instance, on the only measure independent of probation officer supervision in the Miller study (new arrests), the experimentals fared no better than the controls. Thus, as Miller suggests, the differences in failure rates across groups probably reflect differing social control mechanisms rather than differences in offender behavior.

The final adult study also examined restitution as a condition of probation and further suggests that the actual payment of restitution, if it is ordered, may contribute more to reduced recidivism than the imposition of restitution orders. Brown (1983) employed a relatively sophisticated statistical analysis (logit regression) on data derived from a sample of 522 probationers screened for restitution eligibility in Oregon in the late 1970s. Of these, 403 were ordered to pay restitution. The remaining probationers served as an availability comparison sample. Factors predictive of recidivism outcomes were controlled in the analysis, allowing for relatively strong inferences about restitution effectiveness.

Brown (1983) found that the mere imposition of a restitution order as a condition of probation was not related to a number of recidivism measures (all of which excluded failure based solely on noncompliance with the restitution order) at a 12-month follow-up period. In contrast, the actual payment of restitution among those ordered to pay was strongly and positively related to probation success. Probationers not ordered to pay restitution and those ordered to who didn't fully comply were about equally likely to fail on probation and at considerably higher rates than those who completely paid their orders.

Obviously, firm conclusions on the effectiveness of restitution imposed an adult offenders as a recidivism-reducing device must await more research. Nevertheless, the extant studies indicate room for concern and very little suggestion that adult restitution, particularly the mere imposition of a restitution order, achieves its desired effect on offender behavior.

## Juvenile Offenders

Table 22.2, which presents summary findings from studies on the impact of restitution on juvenile offenders, indicates that although fewer studies exist on juvenile populations than on adult populations, more juvenile programs affecting a greater proportion of juveniles under restitution orders (than the comparable percentage of adults) have been evaluated and that the general quality of the research is much stronger. As is the case with many of the adult studies, conclusions from the early juvenile studies must be quite tentative because of small sample sizes, nonexperimental designs, and relatively weak outcome data.

TABLE 22.2 Evaluative Studies of Restitution with Juvenile Offenders

| Author/program | Significant treatment components | Research design/sample size[a] | Recidivism figure significance level[b] | | | | |
|---|---|---|---|---|---|---|---|
| Wax (1977), Rural Washington state county | Juvenile shoplifters assigned informal court supervision with treatment varied by community service orders and victim presence at restitution agreement, counseling services provided | Random assignment; 6-month follow-up period $E_1 = 10$; community service, victim present $E_2 = 10$; community service, victim not present $C = 10$; straight supervision, no victim presence | Police contact Court contact | $E_1$ 20% | $E_2$ 20% | $C$ 30% | ns |
| Rhodes (1980), Minneapolis Restitution Project | Program administers restitution and community service sanctions; loss assessments, order recommendations, and monitoring of orders are part of probation | Random selection of available comparison subjects; no analysis of equivalence; 8 month follow-up period; $E = 102$; $C_1 = 123$ concurrent court dispositions; $C_2 = 104$ juveniles ordered restitution prior to project | Probation revoked: Guilty of new petition | E 4% 11% | $C_1$ 3% 22% | $C_2$ 2% 33% | ns na |

(continued)

TABLE 22.2 (continued)

| Author/program | Significant treatment components | Research design/sample size[a] | Recidivism figure significance level[b] | | | | |
|---|---|---|---|---|---|---|---|
| Shichor and Binder (1982), Orange County, CA | Diversion project with police referrals, voluntary participation, restitution specialists, active victim parent participation, community board establishing either financial or community service restitution | Assignment based on police referral agency; nonequivalent groups on instant offense and number of priors; E = 6-month follow-up period after restitution completed C = 9 months from arrest; E = 94; C = 63; subsequent randomized selection by sex resulted in E = 59; C = 59 | Arrests | E 6% | C 15% | | ns |
| Schneider and Schneider (1985); see also Schneider, 1986; Clayton County, GA | Restitution case workers to ensure compliance; 60% service, 40% monetary restitution; average probation supervision period, 3.5 months; confined to property offenders without violent crime, drug/alcohol, or mental health histories | Random assignment; 36-month follow-up period: $E_1$ = 73 (restitution), $E_2$ = 74 (restitution and counseling); $C_1$ = 55 (counseling); $C_2$ = 56 (any court disposition, 78% probation), $E_1$ had a significantly higher preintervention offense rate | Court recontact: Group offense rate per 100: Change in pre/post group offense rates: | $E_1$ 49% 64% −26 | $E_2$ 46% 47% −8 | $C_1$ 60% 84% +20 | $C_2$ 52% 75% 0 | .05 .05 .05 |

| Study | Description | Method | Measure | E | C₁ | C₂ | | |
|---|---|---|---|---|---|---|---|---|
| Schneider (1986) Boise, ID | Either monetary restitution or community service; exclude youth who experienced pretrial detention; average 2-month restitution supervision, 9 months total on probation | Random assignment; 22-month follow-up period; E = 86, C = 95; (sentenced to several successive weekend detention placements), E = had lower repeat offender rate, higher felony conviction history | Court recontact: Group offense rate per 100: Change in pre/post group offense rates: | E 53% 86 −17 | | C 59% 100 −37 | | ns ns ns |
| Washington, DC | Youth with at least one felony conviction recommended for probation could voluntarily enter this victim-offender mediation program | Random assignment; E₁ = 143 (restitution), C₁ = 131 (referred to restitution but refused) C₂ = 137 (probation). 31-32-month follow-up period. | Court recontact Group offense rate per 100: Change in pre/post group offense rate: | E 53% 54 −7 | C₁ 46% 52 −10 | C₂ 60% 65 +4 | | .05 .05 .05 |
| Oklahoma County, OK | Any youth for whom a monetary value could be placed on victim losses, excluding rape and murder offenders, eligible for restitution. 50% monetary and 50% community service restitution | Random assignment, 10% lack of judicial compliance; 23–24-month follow-up period; E₁ = 104 (restitution only), E₂ = 116 (restitution & probation), C = 78 (probation only) | Court recontact: Group offense: Rate per 100; change in pre/post group offense rates: | E 49% 72 +6 | E₂ 46% 64 +10 | C 60% 74 −1 | | ns ns ns |

[a] E = no. of experimentals; C = no. of controls.
[b] na = not reported; ns = not significant.

Wax's (1977) small-scale experimental study of the effects of community service restitution, coupled with and without the presence of the victim during the restitution process, is a model for larger-scale experimental field research. Unfortunately, Wax's small sample sizes (10 youths per group) and short follow-up period (6 months) rendered it virtually impossible that any significant differences in recidivism would be found.

Rhodes's 1980 study of a probation based-restitution program in Minneapolis is quite suggestive of the possibility that a well-staffed and coordinated restitution program that views restitution as a potentially therapeutic experience may be successful in reducing juvenile recidivism. This program witnessed significantly lower recidivism among its clients than among juveniles concurrently receiving dispositions not including restitution, but much more telling, lower than among a group of juveniles ordered to pay restitution shortly before the program was initiated. Although the comparison groups were not originally equivalent (less likely for the latter comparison) and the follow-up period was only 8 months, the apparently reduced recidivism was not associated with increased technical violations, as had been the case in the adult studies. Further, the findings are consistent with a later and more thorough study conducted by Anne and Peter Schneider (1984), which found that "programmatic" restitution is more effective in both generating offender completion of restitution and reducing recidivism than is ad hoc restitution. The former type of program is characterized by trained restitution counselors who oversee the entire restitution process, view it as a worthy method of achieving victim reparation and offender accountability, and both closely monitor and facilitate payments. Because payment completion appears to be such a strong correlate of reduced recidivism (Brown, 1983; Miller, 1981; Schneider and Schneider, 1984), programmatic restitution may have positive indirect effects on offender recidivism.

Despite assertions by its authors that the Orange County, California, diversion project, which features prominently a juvenile restitution component, has been effective in reducing recidivism, the associated evaluative design and the outcome measures are so weak that little can be said about the effectiveness of this project (Shichor & Binder, 1982). In particular this study suffered from the initial nonequivalence of youths on the basis of their current offense and prior delinquent histories, differing follow-up periods, and the potential confounding of monetary and community service restitution effects.

The strongest studies, by far, are experimental studies conducted by Schneider and Schneider as part of a national evaluation study (Schneider, 1986; Schneider & Schneider, 1985). A total of four programs utilizing randomly assigned nonrestitution control groups as well as the "programmatic versus ad hoc" comparative study mentioned earlier have been examined. Together, they give strong preliminary support to the notion that juvenile restitution under certain conditions is at least as effective and perhaps more effective in reducing recidivism than many other common sanctions.

In the Clayton County, Georgia, program, which applied both service and monetary restitution as a condition of probation to generally nonserious juvenile offenders not exhibiting complicating social handicaps, restitution was associated with statistically significant reductions in recidivism. Restitution alone or with counseling was associated with lower recidivism than counseling alone or other dispositions, typically probation. Recidivism was measured more thoroughly than in any other reviewed study through the inclusion of an "at risk" time factor, both incidence and seriousness indices, and a longer follow-up period. It is noteworthy that the restitution effect was found to be independent of the counseling (without counseling as an add-on) and offender characteristics (not spurious because of any possible group nonequivalence). Although the restitution effect was relatively small, this is the first study that unambiguously suggests positive effects of restitution on recidivism without any apparent negative implications (e.g., high in-program failure rate).

The second study site, a restitution program in Boise, Idaho, in which restitution was a condition of probation, involved the comparison of restitution effects on recidivism to those of successive weekend detention placements coupled with similar levels of probation supervision. Restitution was found to be no more and no less related to recidivism than short-term detention. Rather than being viewed as a program failure, however, this suggests reason for optimism. Given that detention is one of the harshest sanctions in the juvenile system, whereas restitution is generally much less intrusive and punishing, the lack of a differential effectiveness indicates that at least for offenders in Boise, restitution should be preferred over detention.

The Washington, DC, restitution program witnessed its clients exhibiting significantly lower recidivism rates than a comparable sample of probationers. This program, featuring a voluntary victim–offender mediation process, served a more serious offending population than the other juvenile programs examined. It is noteworthy that the restitution group exhibited similar levels of recidivism for youth who were referred to the program but who refused participation. Although the authors of the study suggest that a "participation" factor in the sanctioning process may account for this pattern of findings, any conclusions on the actual dynamics involved are purely speculative.

The last program, in Oklahoma City, Oklahoma, did not witness significant differences in recidivism across a restitution-only population, a probation-only population, and a combined restitution/probation population. The sanctioned groups all had high percentages of repeat offenders and youth with felony convictions. The experiment also suffered from a significant amount of contamination because of judges refusing to comply with the random assignment schedule. This further illustrates the difficulties of field research in this area and the strong likelihood that not all programs will be effective in all places for all types of youth.

## CONCLUSIONS

This evaluative review of studies examining the relationship between restitutive sanctioning and recidivism has yielded a number of important findings. There are relatively few solid studies using experimental and quasi-experimental designs. The better studies have been conducted with juvenile populations, indicating reasons for a sanguine view of restitution as a sanction that achieves measurable utilitarian goals. However, we still do not know whether financial restitution to the victim or service to the community—two very distinct types of sanctions along many important dimensions—are differentially successful in affecting recidivism among juveniles.

Among adult populations, one cannot assert with any degree of confidence that restitution achieves either a specific deterrent or rehabilitative effect. The literature does suggest, however, that restitutive sanctioning coupled with other sanctions may generate adverse social control effects from both the community and the offender's perspective.

What appears to be most important in determining restitution success among both groups is the degree to which the offender actually completes his restitution agreement. Simply increasing completion rates may not necessarily promote decreased recidivism rates, however. Causal relationships remain quite unclear. Does successful completion of restitution orders reflect relatively unmalleable preintervention levels of commitment to conventional values and/or the successful ability to compete in the workplace, and is the preselection of restitution clients thus the crucial factor in determining rates of recidivism? Or are factors that can actually be manipulated by restitution personnel once a person is ordered to pay restitution determinative? Is simply taking restitution seriously and providing programs with therapeutic integrity the key to reduced recidivism, as is suggested by some of the juvenile studies? Or is such an approach merely more likely to result in high in-program failure rates without clear benefits to the community, as some of the adult studies suggest? The answers to these and related questions are crucial to the development of efficacious restitution programs, yet they are currently unknown. Unfortunately, we still know relatively little about specific linkages between restitutive sanctions, contexts, and individuals.

Until evaluative research efforts that examine these linkages are undertaken, restitutive sanctioning premised as a method of showing concern for the victim will remain vulnerable to demands that concern for the community (i.e., public safety) dominate the correctional enterprise. An alternative sanction with promise of community protection (e.g., home confinement) can easily displace restitution as a preferred sanction given our current state of knowledge and trends in correctional philosophy. Because the public safety benefits of restitution are currently unclear, it is much easier for victims once again to be forgotten.

# REFERENCES

Austin, J., & Krisberg, B. (1982). The unmet problems of alternatives of incarceration. *Crime and Delinquency, 28*(3), 374-409.
Bonta, J. L., Boyle, J., Motiuk, L., & Sonnichsen, P. (1983). Correctional halfway houses: Victim satisfaction, attitudes, and recidivism. *Canadian Journal of Corrections, 20*, 140-152.
Brewer, D. L. (1977, November). *The California Restitution Project.* Paper presented at the American Society of Criminology Annual Conference, Atlanta.
Brewer, D. L. (1979). *Update of the California Restitution Project.* Unpublished manuscript.
Brown, E. J. (1983). Correlates and consequences of the payment of restitution. Unpublished doctoral dissertation. State University of New York at Albany.
Harland, A. (1983). One hundred years of restitution: An international review and prospectus for research. *Victimology, 8*(1-2), 190-203.
Heinz, J., Galaway, B., & Hudson, J. (1976). Restitution or parole: A follow-up study of adult offenders. *Social Service Review, 50*, 148-156.
Hudson, J., & Chesney, S. (1978). Research on restitution: A review and assessment. In B. Galaway and J. Hudson (Eds.), *Offender Restitution in Theory and Action* (pp. 131-148). Lexington, MA: Lexington Books.
Lab, S. P. (1988). *Crime prevention: Approaches, practices and evaluations.* Cincinnati, OH: Anderson.
McCarthy, B., & McCarthy, B. (1984). *Community-based corrections.* Monterey, CA: Brooks/Cole.
McGillis, D. (1986). *Crime victim restitution: An analysis of approaches.* Washington, DC: National Institute of Justice.
Miller, T. (1981). Consequences of restitution. *Law and Human Behavior, 5*(1), 1-17.
O'Leary, V., & Duffee, D. (1971). Correctional policy: A classification of goals designed for change. *Crime and Delinquency, 17*(4), 373-386.
Rhodes, C. (1980). An analysis of the relative effectiveness of the juvenile restitution project. Unpublished report. Minneapolis, MN: Walker and Associates.
Schneider, A. (1986). Restitution and recidivism rates of juvenile offenders: Results from four experimental studies. *Criminology, 24*(3), 533-552.
Schneider, A., & Schneider, P. (1984). A comparison of programmatic and "ad hoc" restitution in juvenile courts. *Justice Quarterly, 1*(4), 529-547.
Schneider, A., & Schneider, P. (1985). The impact of restitution on recidivism of juvenile offenders: An experiment in Clayton County, Georgia. *Criminal Justice Review, 10*(1), 1-10.
Shichor, D., & Binder, A. (1982). Community restitution for juveniles: An approach and preliminary examination. *Criminal Justice Review, 7*, 46-50.
Wax, M. L. (1977). *Effects of symbolic restitution and presence of the victim on delinquent shoplifters.* Unpublished doctoral dissertation, Washington State University.

# Author Index

Aborisade, B., 34
Abrahamson, D., 46, 56
Adams, J., 153, 155, 156, 163
Ahearn, F., 51, 56
Ahuja, R., 81, 86
Ajaya, S., 121, 129
Alexander, C., 131, 132, 133, 137, 138
Altheide, D., 28, 33
Amick, E., 152
Amick-McMullen, A., 152
Anderson, L., 118, 128
Ankara, 99, 102
Appley, M., 66
Ari, M., 101, 109
Ashkins, C., 25, 34
Atik, B., 101
Austin, J., 233, 237, 247

Bailey, N., 153, 156, 163, 164
Balbo, L., 70, 79
Ballentine, R., 121, 129
Balloni, A., 14, 17, 23, 77, 79
Bandura, A., 210, 216
Barbieri, M., 141, 147
Bard, M., 46, 47, 48, 49, 51, 56, 59, 60, 66
Barickman, R., 151, 153
Barkas, J., 48, 56
Bartlet, C., 192, 200
Bartoli, G., 70, 79
Bastiaans, J., 66
Baum, M., 213, 216
Bauschard, L., 43, 44
Beardsworth, A., 27, 34

Becker, H., 132, 133, 138
Benedek, E., 142, 145, 147
Bennett-Alexander, D., 155, 163
Berliner, L., 37, 44, 141, 147
Besharov, D., 140, 146, 147
Best, C., 152
Best, L., 152
Best, R., 48, 55, 57
Bettelheim, B., 20, 21, 23
Betz, N., 153, 163
Biaggio, M., 161, 163
Bienen, L., 151, 152
Bilir, S., 101, 109
Bimbi, F., 70, 79
Binder, A., 242, 244, 247
Birnbaum, H., 199
Blake, P., 33
Block, C., 88
Block, R., 88
Bok, S., 142, 147
Bond, M., 153, 156, 163
Bonta, J., 237, 239, 247
Bourque, L., 151, 152
Boyd, D., 191, 200
Boyle, J., 247
Brewer, D., 238, 247
Brooks, B., 111, 117
Brooks, L., 160, 164
Brown, E., 239, 240, 244, 247
Brown, J., 28, 34, 40
Brown, L., 44
Brown, S., 206, 214, 216
Browne, A., 37, 44, 128, 130
Brownell, A., 161, 163

Brownmiller, S., 76, 79
Bryant, C., 99, 124
Burgard, R., 62, 66
Burgess, A., 48, 51, 56, 66, 67
Burke, K., 143, 147
Burt, M., 158, 164, 205, 210, 216

Carmen, E., 37, 44, 112, 117
Casarez-Levison, R., 36, 46, 215
Castellano, G., 70, 79
Castellano, T., 203, 249
Chapel, J., 111, 117
Chesney, S., 236, 238, 247
Clark, T., 192, 199
Cofer, C., 66
Cohen, R., 51, 56
Cohen, S., 33
Cohn, D., 57
Colantuono, A., 40, 44
Colorado, 239
Conte, J., 37, 44
Coons, R., 120, 128
Corbett, C., 206, 216
Corson, J., 138, 139
Courtois, C., 130, 138
Cox, C., 33
Craig, M., 100, 130, 131, 132, 137, 138, 139
Cronin, L., 29, 33
Cumberbatch, G., 27, 34
Cummings, E., 42, 44
Cuyahoga County (Cleveland), 88, 90, 91, 92

Dannotti, R., 42, 44
Daro, D., 140, 147
Dave, L., 46, 56
Dederick, J., 157
Deisher, R., 192, 193, 199
De Jong, A., 130, 138
Deutsch, H., 72, 79
deYoung, M., 142, 147
DiCenso, C., 152, 190
Doughty, D., 131, 138
Douglas, (Dutton) M., 40, 44
Dovan, J., 159, 163

Drapkin, I., 219, 222
Drechsel, R., 34
Duff, P., 206, 216
Duffee, D., 234, 247
Dzeich, B., 153, 164

Eagleston, J., 49, 57
Edelman, M., 143, 147
Elkwork, A., 137, 139
Ellsworth, P., 139
Emmitt, G., 130, 138
Emslie, G., 111, 117
Epstein, E., 25, 34
Erikson, E., 60, 66, 100, 121, 128

Faccioli, P., 36, 73
Faller, K., 128, 140, 141, 144, 148
Faulkner, R., 25, 34
Fehrenback, P., 192, 199
Feinberg, G., 88, 95
Fields, R., 48, 56
Figley, C., 40, 44, 48, 56
Finkelhor, D., 37, 44, 130, 138, 144, 148
Fischhoff, B., 151, 174, 175, 177, 180, 182, 183, 187, 188, 189
Fitzgerald, L., 153, 154, 157-160, 163, 164
Folkman, S., 60, 61, 67, 210, 214, 216
Follingstad, D., 100, 130
Ford, D., 47, 49, 50, 51, 54, 56
Ford, M., 47, 50, 55, 56
Frankl, V., 20, 21, 23, 124, 128
Freud, S., 37, 69, 79, 114, 177
Frieze, H., 54, 56, 215, 216
Frijda, H., 213, 216
Fuchs, W., 62, 66
Furby, L., 151, 174, 175, 177, 180, 182, 183, 187, 188, 189

Gaboury, M., 203, 224
Galaway, B., 236, 247
Galdston, R., 113, 117
Gaquin, D., 28, 34
Garcia, L., 131, 139
Gardner, R., 148
Garfinkel, B., 145, 148

# Author Index

Garfinkel, H., 143, 148
Garofalo, J., 34, 223
Gelinas, D., 130, 138
Gelles, R., 25, 34, 45, 89, 95, 97, 100
Gerbner, G., 27, 34
Gerwitz, M., 89, 95
Gewerth, K., 89, 95
Gidycz, C., 149, 152
Gilsinan, J., 27, 34
Girelli, S., 149, 152
Goffman, E., 143, 144, 148
Gold, Y., 153, 160, 164
Golding, J., 149, 152
Goldstein, J., 27, 34
Goodman, G., 142, 148
Gordon, M., 181, 189
Gottfredson, M., 223
Gramsci, A., 28, 34
Green, A., 142, 148
Grof, S., 119, 128
Gross, L., 27, 34
Grossman, M., 159, 163
Groth, A., 191, 192, 193, 199
Günçe, G., 101, 108, 109
Gunn, R., 151, 166, 173

Hagemann, O., 36, 58, 66, 67
Hall, S., 28, 29, 34
Harel, Z., 51, 57
Haring-Hidore, M., 160, 164
Harland, A., 235, 247
Hastorf, A., 137, 139
Hauggard, J., 130, 138
Heinz, J., 236, 238, 247
Herman, J., 113, 117
Hervada, A., 130, 138
Hindelang, M., 223
Holmstrom, L., 48, 51, 56, 66, 67
Horowitz, M., 51, 55, 56
Howard, D., 153, 164
Hudson, J., 236, 238, 247
Humphrey, H., 145, 148
Husain, A., 111, 117
Hutter, C., 149, 152

Istat, 218, 220, 223

Jackson-Beeck, M., 34
Jacobsen, J., 98, 100
Jain, R., 36, 80
Jaipur, Rajasthan, 81
James, J., 131, 136, 139
Janoff-Bulman, R., 54, 56, 60, 67, 215, 216
Jaspers, J., 59, 66
Jensen, J., 145, 148
Jerry, M., 113, 117
Johnson, L., 158, 164
Jones, D., 142, 148
Jordan, Minnesota, 144
Jordan, C., 149, 152

Kağitçibaşi, C., 104, 109
Kahana, B., 51, 57
Kahn, A., 47, 56
Kalf, D., 120, 128
Kalichman, S., 100, 130, 131, 132, 136, 137, 138, 139
Katz, B., 205, 210, 216
Kaufman, I., 99, 110, 111, 112, 113, 117
Kelly, W., 51, 56
Kelsen, H., 217, 223
Kenig, S., 157, 158, 164
Khosla, D., 88, 95
Kilpatrick, D., 149, 152
Kimmons, C., 131, 136, 139
Kindermann, J., 159, 163
King, M., 141, 148
Kleining, G., 62, 67
Kneupfel, G., 89, 95
Konanç-Onur, E., 99, 101, 102, 108, 109
König, R., 70, 79
Koss, M., 149, 152, 155, 160, 164
Kottke, J., 153, 155, 163
Kozcu, S., 99, 101, 104, 109
Kratcoski, P., 36, 87
Krauss, L., 156, 164
Krisberg, B., 237, 247
Kritsberg, W., 127, 128, 233
Krupnick, J., 51, 56
Kübler-Ross, E., 51, 54, 56, 127, 128
Kumari, R., 81, 86

Lab, S., 234, 247
Lavrakas, P., 214, 216
Lazarus, R., 59, 60, 61, 67, 210, 214, 216
Lerman, H., 37, 44
Levine, D., 139
Lewin, K., 22, 23, 28
Lewis, D., 28, 34
Licht, M., 66, 67
Lloyd, D., 117
Lorber, R., 45
Lott, B., 153, 164
Lukianowicz, N., 110, 117

Maclay, D., 192
Maguire, M., 59, 67, 205, 206, 213, 216
Marhoefer-Dvorak, S., 149, 152
Martin, H., 118, 128
Masson, J., 37, 44
Mathias, U., 66, 67
Matula, S., 159, 163
Mawby, R., 28, 34
Maxfield, M., 58, 67
May, R., 159, 164
McCann, L., 46, 48, 56
McCarthy, B., 233, 234, 247
McGillis, D., 233, 234, 247
McGraw, J., 142, 148
McPherson, M., 28, 34, 131, 139
Mead, G., 60, 67
Mead, M., 163, 164
Melody, W., 27, 34
Melton, G., 138, 139
Merton, R., 70, 79
Merzagora, I., 223
Miller, A., 118, 121, 128
Miller, T., 237, 239, 240, 244, 247
Mills, T., 37, 44, 112, 117
Minch, C., 151, 166, 173
Mitchell, V., 89, 95
Mohr, J., 113, 117
Monastersby, C., 192, 199
Moos, R., 47, 48, 56
Morgan, M., 34, 151, 174, 175, 177, 180, 182, 183, 187, 189
Motiuk, L., 247

Mrazek, D., 127, 128
Mrazek, P., 127, 128
Muehleman, T., 131, 136, 139
Musty, T., 142, 148

Nadelson, C., 49, 56
Nader, K., 127, 129
Netteburg, K., 34
Newman, D., 89, 95
Newman, E., 89, 95
Nightingale, N., 132, 136, 138, 139
Normoyle, J., 214, 216
Notman, M., 49, 56

Ochberg, F., 20, 23, 46, 47, 49, 54, 57
O'Leary, V., 234, 247
O'Malley, H., 89, 95
Ormerod, M., 153, 160, 164
Osborne, Y., 131, 139

Padgitt, J., 153, 155, 163
Paludi, M., 151, 153, 157, 159, 160, 163, 164, 165
Paperny, D., 192, 199
Patterson, G., 42, 44
Peck, A., 112, 117
Perez, B., 89, 95
Peters, J., 130, 139
Petzold, H., 66, 67
Piaget, J., 116, 117, 120, 128, 129
Pierce, L., 132, 136, 139
Pierce, R., 132, 136, 139
Pinar, N., 101, 109
Piquet, D., 48, 55, 57
Pogrebin, L., 143, 148
Porter, E., 192, 200
Putman, F., 120, 129
Pynoos, R., 127, 129

R. v. A., 172, 173
Rabinowitz, V., 151, 153, 156, 164
Rama, S., 121, 129
Rappaport, N., 131, 139
Reagan, R., 224
Reid, J., 42, 45
Reiker, P., 37, 44, 112, 117

# Author Index

Reilly, M., 153, 164
Reiss, A., 223
Resick, P., 149, 152
Rhodes, C., 241, 244, 247
Rich, R., 57
Richards, M., 153, 156, 163
Riger, S., 181, 189
Robin, M., 100, 140
Rorschach, 193
Rose, V., 150, 152
Rosenfeld, A., 111, 117
Rosewater, L., 40, 45
Rosnow, R., 27, 34
Rothenberg, M., 143, 148
Rotter, J., 60, 67
Ruff, G., 152
Ryan, J., 157, 158, 164

Sakheim, D., 46, 56
Salasin, S., 57
Saldana, T., 57
Sales, B., 139
Sales, E., 213, 216
Saltzman, K., 27, 34, 46
Sandler, B., 157, 161, 164
Sanford, L., 121, 124, 128, 129
Sangrey, D., 46, 47, 48, 49, 51, 56, 59, 60, 66
Saraceno, C., 72, 74, 79
Saunders, B., 152
Schaefer, J., 48, 56
Scheingold, S., 26, 29, 34
Scheper-Hughes, N., 143, 148
Schetky, D., 142, 145, 147
Schlesinger, P., 25, 34
Schneider, A., 234, 242, 243, 244, 247
Schneider, D., 139
Schneider, H., 46, 57, 129, 131, 137
Schneider, P., 234, 242, 244, 247
Schultz, L., 144, 148
Schuman, D., 141, 148
Scott, C., 159, 163
Sedney, M., 111, 117
Segars, H., 89, 95
Selye, H., 51, 57
Sessar, K., 58, 66, 67

Sgroi, S., 118, 129, 191, 200
Shapland, J., 206, 209, 216
Sheley, J., 25, 34
Sherizen, S., 30, 34
Shichor, D., 242, 244, 247
Shoor, M., 192, 200
Shore, B., 213, 216
Shullman, S., 153, 154, 157, 158, 159, 160, 164
Siegel, J., 149, 152
Signorielli, S., 34
Skogan, W., 58, 67, 206, 212, 216
Smelser, N., 71, 79
Smith, W., 192, 199
Sonnichsen, P., 247
Soskis, D., 46, 57
Spates, R., 57
Speed, M., 192, 200
Spiegal, D., 55, 57
Stahley, G., 42
Stauss, F., 131, 139
Steele, B., 110, 112, 113, 117, 120, 129
Stein, H., 143, 148
Stein, J., 149, 152
Steinem, G., 202
Steinmetz, C., 60, 67
Steinmetz, S., 45, 61, 67
Stephens, M., 34
Stimpson, C., 163, 164
Straus, M., 45, 61, 67, 97, 100
Summit, R., 118, 121, 127, 129, 141, 148
Swoboba, J., 131, 136, 139
Symonds, M., 21, 23, 57

Tagiuri, C., 112, 117
Tangri, S., 158, 164
Taplin, P., 45
Tatschmurat, C., 60, 67
ten Bensel, R., 146
Terr, L., 141, 148
Thoresen, C., 49, 57
Toscano, M., 22, 23
Truax, A., 160
Turkey, 99, 102
Turner, R., 113, 117

Van den Berg, J., 59, 66
Van den Berg-Schaap, T., 59, 66
Van den Bogaard, J., 203, 205
Van der Ploeg, H., 59, 66
Vaughan, F., 119, 129
Ventimiglia, C., 69, 79
Veronen, L., 152
Viano, E., 1, 14, 15, 24, 29, 34, 38, 45, 219, 222
Villeponteaux, L., 152
Violante, P., 203, 217
Voskuil, E., 207, 216

Waggoner, R., 191, 200
Walker, D., 88
Walker, E., 132, 136, 138, 139
Walker, L., 35, 37, 38, 40, 43, 45
Waller, I., 66, 67, 205, 213, 215, 216
Wallston, B., 214, 216
Walsh, R., 119, 129
Watts, D., 161, 163
Wax, M., 241, 244, 247
Weiner, L., 153, 164
Weis, K., 59, 66, 67
Weitzman, L., 153, 160, 164

Wenet, G., 193, 199
Whitmore, R., 154, 160, 164
Whiskin, F., 89, 95
Wiegman, O., 203, 205
Wilber, K., 120, 126, 129
Williams, H., 131, 139
Willmore, J., 206, 216
Wilson, J., 51, 57
Wilson, K., 156, 164
Winkel, F., 203, 213, 216
Wisniewski, N., 149, 152
Womack, W., 131, 139
Woodward, N., 214, 216
Wycoff, M., 203, 212, 216

Yantzi, M., 206, 214, 216
Yates, A., 142, 148
Young, M., 62, 67
Yuille, J., 141, 148

Zacker, M., 157, 165
Zahn-Wexler, C., 42, 44
Zalk, S., 156, 157, 165
Zeytinoğlu, S., 99, 101, 102, 104, 109
Zimring, F., 88

# Subject Index

Abortion, 6
Abstract on Criminology and Penology, 235
Aid to Families with Dependent Children, 143
Alcohol, 6
  and homicide, 91
Alzheimer's disease, 94
American Psychiatric Association, 41, 44
American Psychological Association, 47, 48, 49, 56, 206, 216
Amnesty International, 5
Andren v. Knight Ridder Newspapers, 30
Animal abuse
  and sex offending, 194
Ann Arbor, Michigan, 150
APA Task Force on the Victims of Crime and Violence, 216
Arson
  and sex offending, 194

Battered women
  and childhood abuse, 42
  in India, 80
  in Italy, 68-79
  needs of, 43
  and their perception of violence, 70
Boise, Idaho, 243, 245
Bologna, City of, 70
Booth v. Maryland (1987), 2
Burglary
  coping processes of its victims, 205-215
  police reactions to victims of, 205-215

California Restitution Project, 238
Canada, 166, 168
  sexual assault in, 166-173
Canadian Criminal Code, 168
Chakra centers
  and child abuse, 121-126
  levels of treatment, 122-127
Chicago, 88, 90, 91, 92
Child abuse, 2, 6, 8, 9
  and bulimia, 115
  assignment of stigma, 143
  attribution of responsibility, 131-132
  and chakra centers, 121
  delayed consequences, 99
  denial of false allegations, 142
  false accusations of, 100, 144-146
  growing awareness of, 141
  in Italy, 221
  in Turkey, 99, 101-109
  investigation, 98, 140-147
  mandatory reporting, 130-131
  overwhelming impact of, 119-120
  power issues, 113, 116
  professionals' reactions, 132-136
  psychological effects, 130
  psychological maltreatment, 98, 99
  reasons why clinicians may not report, 136-138
  reporting as result of victim's reactions, 134, 135
  reporting laws, 140
  responsibility attributed to parents, 137
  terror and anxiety, 114
Child labor, 6

Child neglect: see Child abuse
Child sexual abuse: see Child abuse, Incest
Clayton County, Georgia, 242, 245
Colorado, 239
Community service, 43
Compensation
  in the U.S., 228-230
Compulsive behavior, 8, 9
Convention to Protect Man's Rights and the Basic Freedoms (Treaty of Rome, 1950), 17
Coping
  as central problem of victims, 59
  functions and strategies, 61
  models of, 51-55
  reactions of significant others, 65
  the process, 60-61
  research methodology, 61, 62
  variety of coping activities, 64
  by victims, 24, 32, 47, 48
Council of Europe, 4
Cox Broadcasting v. Cohn, 30
Crime
  reporting, 14, 15
  as trauma, 48
Crime Victim Fund, 227, 228, 230
Criminal Justice Abstract, 235
Criminal justice system, 2, 10
  and sexual assault in Canada, 167
Criminals
  and childhood abuse, 42
Criminology, 12, 23
Cronbach's Test, 207, 210

Date rape, 2
Declaration of Basic Principles of Justice for Victims of Crime and Abuse of Power, 4
Declaration of Independence, 203
Diagnostic and Statistical Manual of Mental Disorders (DSM-III), 48
Diagnostic Interview for Children and Adolescents, 193
Dissertation Abstract, 235
Dissociative disorders, 41

Domestic violence, 2, 4, 9, 38
  in Italy, 219
Drugs, 6
  addiction, 8
  trafficking, 5

Education Department's Office of Civil Rights, 155
Ego boundaries and trauma, 119
Eighth Amendment, 2
Eighth United Congress on the Prevention of Crime and the Treatment of Offenders (Cuba, 1990), 4
Elderly victims, 2, 36
  and satisfaction with police, 215
  and violent crimes, 87-94
Equal Employment Opportunity Commission, 155
European Convention on Compensation of Victims of Crime, 4

Family
  types of, 71, 72
Family violence
  as a complex phenomenon, 69
  definition of, 97
  in India, 80
  in Italy, 68-79
Family Violence Task Force (1984), 2
Fathers
  characteristics of abusing fathers, 112-113
Fear of crime, 28
Federal Bureau of Investigation (FBI), 87, 95
Federal Victim and Witness Protection Act, 203, 224, 225
Feminism
  political gender analysis, 38
  and victims, 150-151
Firearms, and violence by the elderly, 91
Forensic Mental Health Associates, 197
Forensic Unit of Bradley Hospital, 193
Foster Grandparents, 94
Funding of victim assistance programs in the U.S., 231-232

# Subject Index

Gender issues, 38
Germany
   research on victims in Hamburg, 58, 62-63
Glasgow University Media Group, 29, 34
Government intervention, 47
Guilt, felt by victims, 39

Hamburg, West Germany, 58
Harm, psychological harm to victims, 40
Harvard University, 155, 157
Helplessness, 64
Homicide, 36
   and alcohol, 91
   by the elderly, 88-94
   patterns of, 93
Human rights, 5, 17
Hunter College of the City University of New York, 161, 162
Hyde v. City of Columbia, 30

Impact statements, 2
Incest, 99
   attribution of responsibility, 131-132, 135-136
   and college women, 111
   as an international problem, 110, 111
   false allegations, 144-146
India
   battered women in, 80
   family violence, 36
   women in, 6
Inequality, 6
Istanbul, 99
Italy, 203, 217, 219, 220
   acquaintance rape in, 220
   child abuse in, 221
   crime in, 217-218
   domestic violence in, 219
   rape in, 217-218
   regional differences in crime reporting, 219
   victim reporting, 203
   violence against women, 36
Izmir, 99, 102

Justice Assistance Act of 1984, 2
Juvenile Court Act, Turkey, 102
Juvenile sex offender program, 190
Juvenile sex offenders
   commonalities and background variables, 196-197
   and dysfunctional relationships with adults, 195
   review of the literature, 191-193
   study of, 193-197
   and their own victimization, 190
   treatment, 197-198

Kinetic Family Drawings, 193
Kidnapping, 18, 19

Labor Act, Turkey, 102
Law reform
   evaluation of new laws in Canada, 172-173
   federal laws in the U.S., 203, 224-228
   new sexual assault laws in Canada, 168
   and rape, 151
   the Victims of Crime Act in the U.S., 227-228
   the Victim/Witness Protection Act in the U.S., 232
Los Angeles, California, 150

Maine Revised Statutes, 235
Marital rape
   marital rape exemption in Canada, 172
Media and victims, 25-32
Mental health, problems of victims, 42
Meritor Savings Bank v. Vinson, 155
Ministry of Justice of the Netherlands, 206
Minneapolis Restitution Project, 241
Minnesota Restitution Center, 237, 238
Mothers Against Drunk Drivers (MADD), 1
Multnomah County, Oregon, 239
Murder, 18

National Center for the Prevention and Control of Rape, 150
National Center on Child Abuse and Neglect, 98, 100

National Criminal Justice Reference Service Index, 235
National Organization for Victim Assistance, 48, 56
Netherlands, 205
New Brunswick Court of Appeal, 169
New Delhi, 81

Office for Victims of Crime, 232
Oklahoma County, Oklahoma, 243, 245
Ontario, Canada, 169, 237, 239
Ontario Court of Appeal, 169
Orange County, California, 242, 244
Oregon, 239, 240
Organized crime, 21

Peabody Individual Achievement Test, 193
Peabody Picture Vocabulary Test, 193
Penal Code, Turkey, 102
Pervis Tyrone Payne v. Tennessee (1991), 2
Police
    expectations of the victims, 213-214
    importance of police intervention, 215
    lack of trust in, 220
    reactions to victims of burglary, 205-215
    sensitivity to victims, 203
    services for victims, 212-215
Posttraumatic Stress Disorder (PTSD), 40-42
President's Task Force on Victims of Crime, 232
Presidential Commission on Victims of Crime, 2
Prison
    as a victimizing experience, 43
Project on the Status and Education of Women, 154, 164
Project Repay, 239
Psychiatric patients, and previous abuse, 112
Psychological perspectives on victims, 38

R. v. A., 172, 173
R. v. Chase, 169, 173
R. v. Cook, 169, 173
R. v. Cormier, 171, 173
R. v. Daychief, 169, 173
R. v. Gardynik, 169, 173
R. v. Guiboche, 172, 173
R. v. J. A., 171, 173
R. v. McDonald, 172, 173
R. v. Page, 170, 173
R. v. Ryan, 172, 173
R. v. Thorne, 169, 173
Racism, 6, 29, 30
Rape
    see Sexual assault
Rape crisis center
    in Winnipeg, 167
Recidivism
    and restitution, 234-235, 246
Reporting
    cost-benefit analysis about reporting, 221
    false allegations, 144-146
    as a function of a victim's reactions, 134, 135
    mandatory r. of child abuse, 130, 131
    reasons why clinicians may not report, 136-138
    reporting laws, 140
Research on victims
    current issues, 47
Restitution, 43, 203, 233-246
    adult programs, 236-240
    as a condition of probation, 237, 240
    empirical studies of, 233-245
    evaluative review, 235-245
    juvenile programs, 240, 244-245
    and recidivism, 234-235, 246
Rhode Island, 98, 195
Rhode Island Training School for Youth, 152, 190, 193, 197
Rideau-Carleton Restitution Program, 239
Rotter Sentence Completion, 193

Self-help groups, 43
Sex offenses
    see Sexual assault

# Subject Index

Sex offenders
  in Rhode Island, 152
  see also Juvenile sex offenders
Sexism, 6
Sexual abuse, 9
Sexual assault, 7, 9, 10
  in Canada, 151, 166-173
  court cases in Canada, 169-172
  corroboration and recent complaint requirement, 170
  cross-examination of the victim, 171
  and feminist analysis, 149-151
  gender-specific offenses in Canada, 168
  and impact on victim, 149-151
  in Italy, 217-218
  patriarchal context, 166
  penalties in Italy, 220-221
  prevention, 174-189
  reasons for as provided by offenders, 191-192
  results of study of preventive measures, 175-189
  sexual background and reputation of the victim, 170-171
  visibility of, 149
  women's response to threat of, 174-189
Sexual harassment, 2
  consensual relationships, 157-159
  definitions, 154-155
  different perceptions, 159-160
  explanatory models and institutional structure, 156-159
  Hunter college program and procedures, 161-163
  and impact on studies, 154
  legal prohibitions, 154-155
  male attitudes, 160
  policies and programs against it, 161-163
  in U.S. colleges and universities, 153-163
Shelters for battered women, 43
Social Science Index, 235
Social Welfare and Child Protection Act, Turkey, 102

Society's responsibility to the victim, 224-232
Sociological Abstracts, 235
South Carolina v. Gathers (1989), 2
Stockholm syndrome, 19, 20
Stress and violence, 89
Structure Interview of Psycho-Sexual Experience, 193
Supreme Court of Canada, 169
Survivors of victims of homicide, 2

Task Force on Victims of Crime, 224, 228
Tennessee, 98
Terrorism, 5, 19, 21
Thematic Apperception Test, 193
Therapists' abuse of patients, 2
Transpersonal perspective
  treatment model, 120-127
  and victimization, 119
Trauma of victimization, 35-37
Treatment
  and chakra centers, 120-127
Turkey
  child abuse in, 99, 101-109
  offenders' characteristics, 106
  penal code of Turkey and child abuse, 103
  sanctions for child abuse, 106-108
  sexual abuse in, 104
Turkish Penal Court, 108

United States, 47, 55, 97, 98, 110, 150, 202, 203, 224, 225, 230, 231, 232
  adolescent sex offenders, 192-193
  child abuse in, 98, 130-132
  compensation to victims, 228-230
  elderly homicide victims and offenders, 87-94
  false allegations of child abuse, 140-147
  federal fair treatment guidelines, 226-227
  federal initiatives for victims, 47, 224-232
  growth of victimology in, 1-2
  mandatory reporting of child abuse, 136-138

United States (continued)
  media coverage of victims, 24-33
  sexual assault in, 149-150
  the Victims of Crime Act, 227-228
  the Victim/Witness Protection Act, 232
Universal Declaration of Human Rights (UN), 17
U.S. Department of Justice, 47, 87, 95, 192, 200, 229, 232
U.S. Department of Justice, Law Enforcement Administration, 57
U.S. Supreme Court, 155
U.S. Victim Compensation Act (1986), 43
University of Iowa, 157

Victims
  anger as a common reaction, 213
  definition of, 38, 48
  discretion of, 218-221
  fear of reprisals, 221
  as a gatekeeper of the justice system, 218-221
  history of, 38
  and the justice system, 201-203
  latent victim, 77-79
  reactions, needs, and satisfaction, 209-212
  reasons given for non-reporting, 219-221
  their expectations of various systems, 201-203, 213-214
  typology of, 48
  as a whole person, 47
Victim assistance, 4, 11, 14-23
  programs, 202-203
  in the U.S., 224-232
Victim compensation, 4
Victimization, 5, 7, 8, 10, 17-22
  as a crisis, 64
  definition of, 54
  media coverage of, 25-33
  prevention of, 202-203
  as trauma, 49-51

Victimology, 3, 4, 10, 22, 23
  child victimology, 118
Victim's Bill of Rights (Proposition 8), 2
Victim's movement, 1, 2, 3, 12, 33
  in the U.S., 150
Victims' rights, 24, 31, 32
Victim's role, 17, 18
Victims of Crime Task Force, 2
Victims Right Movement, 2
Victims of Crime Act, 2, 203, 224, 225, 227, 229, 231, 232
Victim-Witness Programs, 2
Violence, 7, 9, 13, 14, 21, 27, 69
  experience of violence by women, 74-79
  in India, 82-86
  and mental deterioration, 93
  mistaken for love, 76-77
  and physical illness, 93
  sexual: see Sexual assault
Vulnerability, 39, 65

Washington, D.C., 150, 243, 245
Washington State County, 241
Washington University School of Medicine, 193
Wechsler Adult Intelligence Scale-Revised, 193
Wechsler Intelligence Scale, 193
Wechsler Intelligence Scale for Children-Revised, 193
Wide Range Achievement Test, 193
Winnipeg, Canada, 167
Women
  and body image, 72
  and incest, 111
  and relationship to men, 72-74
  and threat of rape, 174-189
Womens' movement, 1
  and victims, 150-151
World Health Organization, 7

Yogic chakra centers, 121-126